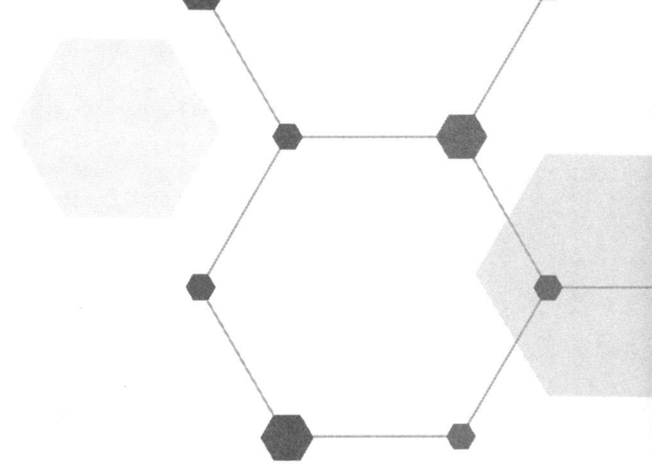

EXPERIMENTING WITH AI

Activities, Discussions, and Prompts for the Classroom and Beyond

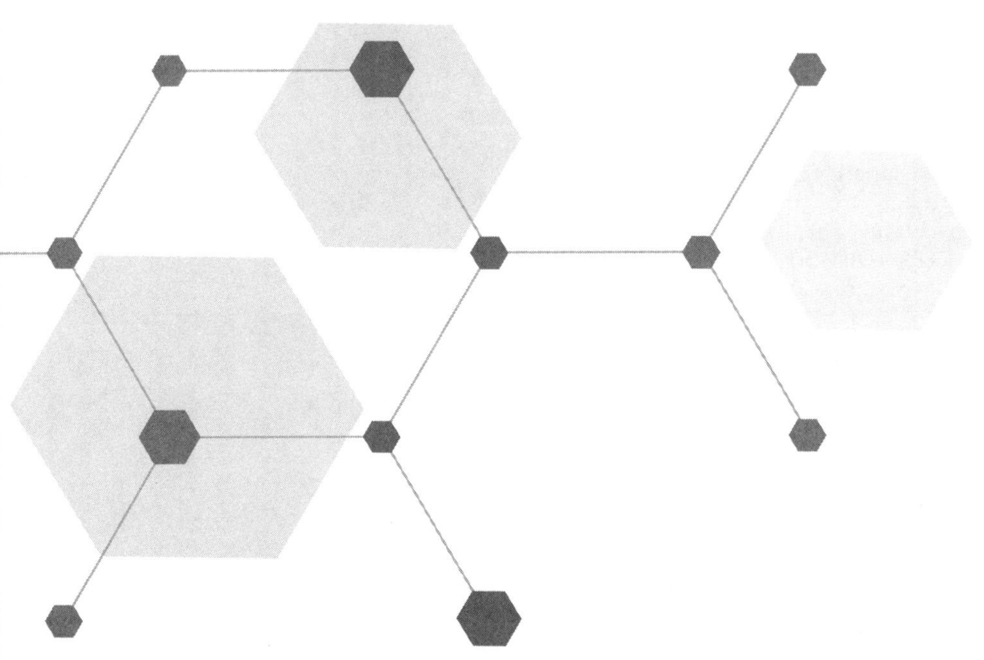

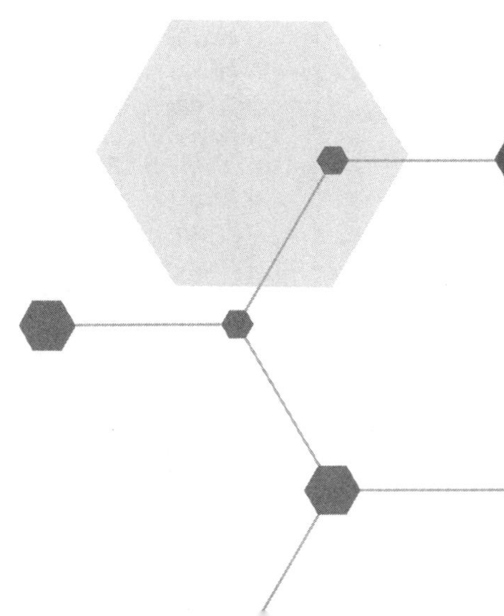

STACIE CHANA

Solution Tree | Press

Generative AI was used to create curricular integration examples throughout the book.

555 North Morton Street
Bloomington, IN 47404
800.733.6786 (toll free) / 812.336.7700
FAX: 812.336.7790

email: info@SolutionTree.com
SolutionTree.com

Visit **go.SolutionTree.com/technology** to download the free reproducibles in this book.

Printed in the United States of America

Library of Congress Cataloging-in-Publication Data

Names: Chana, Stacie, author.
Title: Experimenting with AI : activities, discussions, and prompts for the classroom and beyond / Stacie Chana.
Description: Bloomington, IN : Solution Tree Press, [2026] | Includes bibliographical references and index.
Identifiers: LCCN 2025019479 (print) | LCCN 2025019480 (ebook) | ISBN 9798893740639 (paperback) | ISBN 9798893740646 (ebook)
Subjects: LCSH: Artificial intelligence--Educational applications.
Classification: LCC LB1028.43 .C435 2026 (print) | LCC LB1028.43 (ebook) | DDC 371.33/463--dc23/eng/20250616
LC record available at https://lccn.loc.gov/2025019479
LC ebook record available at https://lccn.loc.gov/2025019480

ACKNOWLEDGMENTS

This book is more than words on pages—it is evidence of purpose, calling, and grace.

First, I give honor to God. In seasons of uncertainty, when the path was unclear, divine guidance provided clarity and direction. What began as a quiet prompting while tending my garden has grown into this work, written to serve educators at the intersection of artificial intelligence and human purpose.

To my father, John Chana, an educator of over forty years, who planted my earliest love for STEM, education, and inquiry: Thank you for showing me how to think, build, and create with intention.

To my mother, Dorothy Chana, who taught me to move fearlessly, to stand my ground, and to remain anchored in wisdom: Your strength has been my steady covering.

To the team at Solution Tree: Thank you for recognizing the value of this work and creating space for this vision to unfold. I am honored to stand alongside educators who lead with both integrity and impact.

To my former students, whom I was charged to teach but who, in truth, have taught me so much more: You are the reason for this work. Every child deserves opportunity. Your resilience, brilliance, and promise fuel my commitment to create spaces where equity, innovation, and possibility intersect.

To my readers: May this book be a tool that empowers you to embrace experimentation, innovate boldly, and lead with both wisdom and courage in a rapidly evolving world.

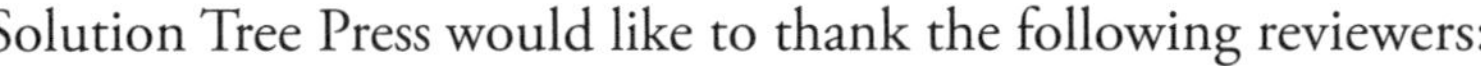

Solution Tree Press would like to thank the following reviewers:

Drew Bowman
Mental Health Education Specialist
Headwater Learning Foundation
Calgary, Alberta, Canada

Kimberly Freiley
Eighth Grade English Language Arts Teacher
Ingersoll Middle School
Canton, Illinois

Janet Gilbert
Principal
Deer Valley Unified School District
Phoenix, Arizona

Shauna Koopmans
Instructor, School of Arts and Education
Red Deer Polytechnic
Red Deer, Alberta, Canada

Erin Kruckenberg
Fifth Grade Teacher
Jefferson Elementary School
Harvard, Illinois

Ian Landy
Regional Principal
qathet School District No. 47
Powell River, British Columbia, Canada

Lana Powers
Department Chair for Business, FACS, Fine Arts and Technology
Evansville Central High School
Evansville, Indiana

Lauren Smith
Assistant Director of Elementary Learning
Noblesville Schools
Noblesville, Indiana

Sarah Svendsen
Pre-Kindergarten Teacher
Pine Crest School
Boca Raton, Florida

Allison Zamarripa
Reading and Language Arts Specialist
Pasadena Independent School District
Pasadena, Texas

TABLE OF CONTENTS

CHAPTER 2

PART 2

CHAPTER 3

CHAPTER 4

CHAPTER 5

Visit **go.SolutionTree.com/technology** to download the free reproducibles in this book.

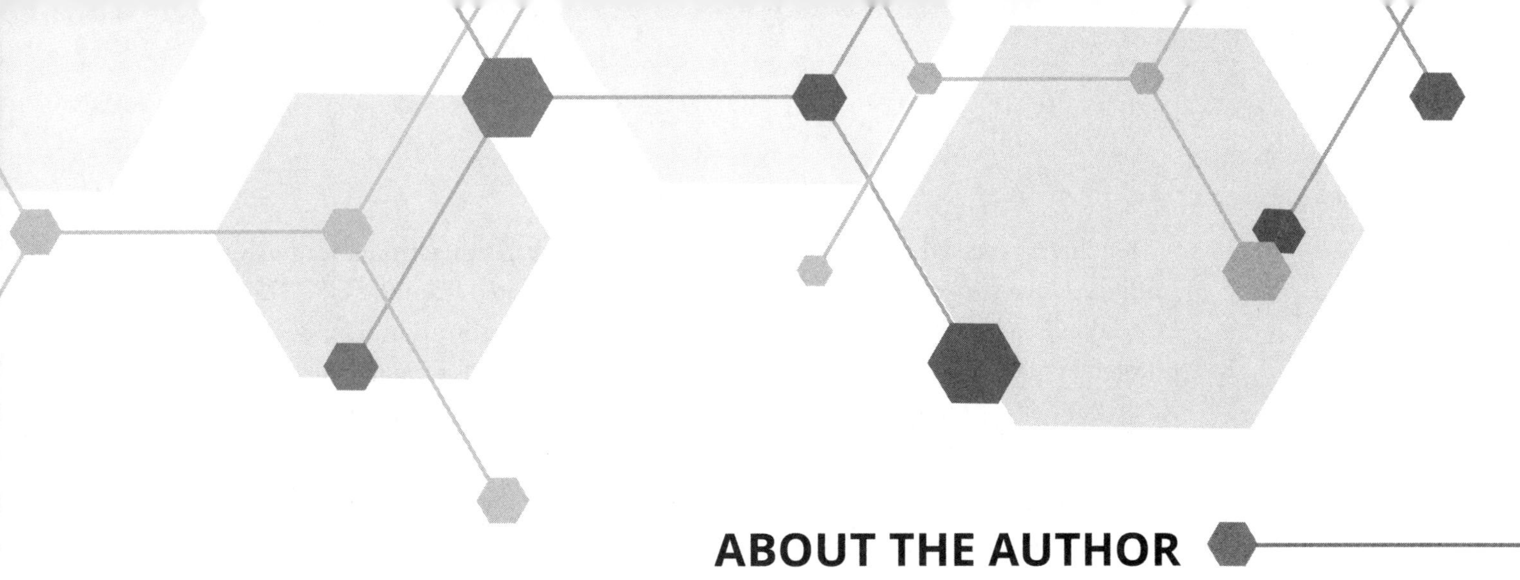

ABOUT THE AUTHOR

Stacie J. Chana, EdD, is an educational leader, consultant, and professor who is committed to empowering educators, schools, districts, and organizations to navigate and integrate emerging technologies in transformative ways. As the founder and principal consultant of TechEd Maven Consulting, she supports organizations in leveraging artificial intelligence, instructional innovation, and strategic planning to drive meaningful change.

With over two decades of experience in education, Dr. Chana began her career as a high school science teacher before moving into school and district leadership, STEM innovation, and large-scale school transformation efforts. She played a key role in designing a public STEM high school in Chicago and has focused on instructional improvement, professional learning, and AI-enhanced education. Her work is deeply rooted in a commitment to equity, especially for students historically underrepresented in STEM, and reflects a lifelong dedication to optimizing teaching, learning, and student outcomes.

Dr. Chana's mission is to empower educators so they can empower students to engage with emerging technologies not just as users but as critical thinkers, problem solvers, and creators. Her work continues to champion experimentation, ethical leadership, and the transformative power of technology to advance educational equity and innovation.

Dr. Chana has been recognized by the AI Show @ ASU+GSV as a 2024 AI Classroom Innovator, one of the 2025 Leading Women in AI and Education, and an EDSAFE AI Ally. She is an active contributor to global conversations on the ethical integration of AI in education.

Dr. Chana received a doctorate of education in urban educational leadership from the University of Illinois Chicago (UIC) and graduated from the UIC Urban Education Leadership program with a superintendency certification. Her doctoral research in mathematics leadership, teacher collaboration, and student achievement reinforces her expertise in strategic school improvement, leadership development, and equity-driven education.

To learn more about Dr. Chana's work, follow her at www.linkedin.com/in/drstaciechana (LinkedIn), www.facebook.com/DrStacieChana (Facebook), www.youtube.com/@TechEdMaven (YouTube), https://x.com/TechEdMaven (X), www.instagram.com/TechEd_Maven (Instagram), www.pinterest.com/TechEdMaven (Pinterest), and www.tiktok.com/@TechEdMaven (Tik Tok).

To book Dr. Stacie Chana for professional development, contact **pd@SolutionTree.com**.

INTRODUCTION

Imagine stepping outside of conventional norms into a space where the boundaries of possibility are continually being pushed and redefined. The walls pulse with interactive displays showcasing the latest breakthroughs in science, literature, and art. Clusters of dynamically engaged learners fill the air with conversations rich in curiosity and intellectual rigor. This is a realm where learning transforms into an exhilarating adventure, each moment a chance to explore, innovate, and grow through the boundless power of imagination and experimentation.

In one corner, a group harnesses generative artificial intelligence (AI) to brainstorm ideas for revitalizing local parks, seamlessly integrating suggestions, visualizations, and data analyses. The group members' collective imagination transforms potential into tangible outcomes that benefit their community. Across the room, others delve into history with AI's assistance, uncovering intricate patterns and connections across different eras. Engaging in dynamic dialogues, they deepen their understanding and sharpen their critical thinking skills. This collaborative environment, fueled by AI, sparks endless possibilities and innovations. This isn't a fantasy. It is a very possible reality—one this book aims to help you create.

Welcome to *Experimenting With AI*, your interactive resource designed to support you to integrate generative AI into your daily practice as an educator and to enhance the tool kit of the learners you serve.

We are embarking on a transformative journey into the era of AI—one that resonates deeply with the archetypal hero's quest. In *The Hero With a Thousand Faces*, Joseph Campbell (1949) describes the hero as someone who accomplishes the following:

> [The hero] ventures forth from the world of common day into a region of supernatural wonder: fabulous forces are there encountered and a decisive victory is won. The hero comes back from this mysterious adventure with the power to bestow boons on his fellow man.

Like the hero in Campbell's narrative, you—whether an educator, a professional, or a lifelong learner—are stepping into the unknown, prepared to revolutionize how you understand and apply AI. This journey demands courage: leaving behind the familiar, embracing cutting-edge tools and technologies, and navigating challenges that drive growth and innovation.

Fortunately, you are not alone. Along the way, professional development and collaborative communities will provide support, helping you gain the insights and skills you need to thrive. *Experimenting With AI* is your trusted guide, equipping you with the resources to navigate this evolving landscape with resilience and confidence.

As you grow, your transformation will ripple outward. You will inspire colleagues to adopt forward-thinking strategies and empower learners to approach AI with curiosity and creativity. Together, you will cultivate a culture of exploration, fostering resilience, sparking imagination, and preparing your community to thrive in a future shaped by AI.

Venturing Into a New Era

We are on the brink of an unprecedented transformation that parallels and may even surpass the monumental shifts of the previous Industrial Revolution (Kohnová & Salajová, 2019). The integration of AI into our daily lives represents a change like none we have ever witnessed. It is not merely an incremental step forward but a quantum leap, redefining how we learn, work, and interact. J. C. R. Licklider, a pioneer in computer science, envisioned the following in his seminal 1960 publication "Man-Computer Symbiosis":

> The hope is that, in not too many years, human brains and computing machines will be coupled together very tightly, and that the resulting partnership will think as no human brain has ever thought, and process data in a way not approached by the information-handling machines we know today. (p. 4)

Today, Licklider's vision is becoming a reality as we stand at the threshold of an era poised to revolutionize our societal, educational, and professional landscapes.

The tools and technologies available at the time of this writing are just the beginning, starting points on a journey that promises to unlock human potential and abundance in ways we are only beginning to imagine. Yet the unknown evokes many emotions: excitement for the possibilities, apprehension about the challenges, and fear of the unfamiliar. Recognizing these feelings as natural responses to profound change allows us to find comfort for ourselves and those we serve, embracing this transformation with resilience and courage.

Venturing deeper into this new frontier, we are not merely adopting a new technology—we are revolutionizing how we learn, create, and work. AI empowers us to break down barriers and provide personalized learning experiences, enhancing creativity and fostering critical thinking. AI-driven platforms can adapt to individual learning styles, offering customized feedback and resources tailored to each learner's unique needs. This journey is about building the skills needed to access these powerful tools, allowing every learner—whether in a classroom or pursuing personal growth—to reach new heights and achieve their fullest potential. By integrating AI into our educational frameworks, we not only enhance traditional teaching methods but also prepare learners for the challenges and opportunities of the future. To fully appreciate the role AI can play in transforming education, it's important to explore the specific benefits this technology offers. The following section highlights how AI supports learning experiences, empowers learners, and enhances instructional practices.

Accessing AI's Benefits for Learning

AI technologies offer numerous benefits that make them indispensable in modern education and personal learning journeys. They enhance personalized learning experiences by tailoring educational content to meet individual needs, fostering deeper understanding and engagement (Baidoo-Anu & Ansah, 2023). AI also increases efficiency in routine tasks, automating processes like scheduling and information management, thereby freeing up more time for creative and critical thinking activities. Additionally, AI provides advanced tools for data analysis and decision making, helping learners identify trends, assess progress, and make informed decisions to enhance their learning outcomes.

Integrating AI into educational settings requires thoughtful experimentation, discussion, and planning. It involves selecting AI tools that align with learning goals, providing training to effectively use these tools, and addressing ethical considerations and data privacy. By grounding AI integration in established educational theories, such as Jean Piaget's (1954) constructivist theory, which emphasizes active learning and discovery, and Lev S. Vygotsky's (1978) sociocultural theory, which focuses on the zone of proximal development and scaffolding, we can create enriched learning environments that promote active engagement, collaboration, and deeper understanding.

Vygotsky's (1978) sociocultural theory emphasizes zones of proximal development and scaffolding, where learning thrives through social interaction and guidance. AI can serve as an effective scaffolding tool by providing real-time feedback and support, enabling learners to achieve tasks they might not accomplish independently. For example, AI tools can expand a learner's abilities by guiding them from what they can achieve alone to what becomes possible with assistance. Beyond individual support, AI also fosters collaborative learning by encouraging learners to work with peers and technology to solve complex problems, enriching their experiences and skill development.

However, while AI offers significant opportunities for scaffolding, such as supporting language learners or providing immediate, personalized feedback, it cannot replicate the nuanced, adaptive guidance of human educators. Teachers bring empathy, context, and creativity that technology cannot fully replicate. Therefore, educators must design learning environments where AI complements their work, simulating scaffolding interactions within the zone of proximal development without replacing the critical role of human connection.

This book provides practical, hands-on experiments that help you explore and apply these ideas, offering concrete examples of how to use AI tools across contexts, content areas, and even in everyday life. Each experiment challenges you to engage deeply with AI, reflecting on how it enhances learning and how it can empower both educators and learners to achieve their full potential.

Engaging with AI tools also equips learners with essential digital literacy skills, empowering them to navigate technology confidently. Personalized AI systems adapt to learners' needs, enabling progress at their own pace and fostering an environment of continuous improvement. Additionally, AI can address diverse learning needs, offering tailored solutions for learners with disabilities, multilingual learners, or those who face other challenges. By leveraging AI's capabilities, educators can unlock the full intellectual potential of every learner, creating pathways for success that might otherwise remain inaccessible.

In this shared journey, equity and inclusivity must remain central. AI in education is not just about integrating technology: It is about ensuring that every learner, regardless of background, has access to transformative opportunities. Democratizing knowledge and distributing resources equitably are essential to realizing the full promise of this technological revolution. By bridging gaps, tailoring support, and fostering inclusivity, AI can create a more just and equitable educational landscape.

This journey requires a willingness to experiment, confront challenges, and embrace the unknown. Growth and transformation are rarely easy, but by engaging with the process, no matter how daunting, we cultivate resilience and achieve lasting success. Together, we can foster learning environments that spark curiosity, encourage creativity, and empower all learners to thrive in an AI-driven world. Building on that foundation, learners thrive in environments that promote ethical reflection and a spirit of inquiry—key elements for meaningful engagement with AI.

Creating a Supportive and Ethical Culture of Inquiry

Cultivating a curiosity-driven culture for all learners is essential. Perhaps you're guiding younger learners (under age thirteen) through teacher-facilitated, developmentally appropriate explorations, such as modeling the use of generative AI tools or engaging in concept-based discussions. Or maybe you're empowering older learners (ages thirteen and older, including adult lifelong learners) to explore and experiment independently. In either case, curiosity and questioning are foundational to meaningful engagement with AI technologies. In this shared journey, educators and learners alike are learning to integrate AI into daily processes, navigating its capabilities, modeling its use, and unlocking its potential to transform how we learn, teach, and innovate.

Supportive environments that encourage experimentation and exploration are key. Implementing experiential learning models that incorporate AI allows learners—whether in elementary classrooms, high school labs, or professional teams—to thrive through trial, error, and discovery rather than relying solely on traditional didactic methods. These approaches ignite creativity and resilience while equipping learners with skills that extend beyond the classroom.

By developing cross-disciplinary AI skills, learners can apply AI technologies across the arts, sciences, and humanities, fostering innovative applications and deeper understanding (Xie et al., 2024).

While the potential of AI is vast, it is crucial to approach its integration with mindfulness and responsibility. Addressing ethical considerations and safeguarding data privacy are paramount to creating safe and equitable learning environments. By embracing AI in education and personal learning, we are not simply adopting a new technology; we are transforming how we teach, learn, and grow, preparing ourselves and future generations for a world filled with possibilities.

At this juncture, ethical exploration is not just important—it is essential. Encouraging learners to think critically about the ethical dimensions of AI empowers them to consider the broader impact of technology on society and their personal lives. For educators, modeling this mindset is crucial. By demonstrating how to question assumptions, analyze biases, and evaluate the consequences of AI use, educators help build a culture of inquiry that extends beyond the classroom.

Professional development plays a vital role in equipping educators to stay current with AI advancements and innovative pedagogical strategies. Maintaining curiosity and competence in teaching AI-related content ensures that educators can guide learners effectively. Establishing innovation labs and committees within schools fosters collaborative exploration of AI technologies, enabling experimentation with new ideas and the development of practical solutions to real-world problems (AASA, ASCD, ISTE, NAESP, & NASSP, 2023).

We must approach AI with critical awareness and ethical resolve. By embedding these two principles into our teaching and professional practices, we prepare ourselves and those we serve to navigate a rapidly evolving technological landscape with confidence, creativity, and responsibility.

Encourage risk taking and embrace failures as valuable learning opportunities when experimenting with new technologies. Adopting an experimental mindset is essential as we integrate AI into our lives and education. By rethinking traditional pedagogies and embracing more holistic approaches to learning, we prepare ourselves and our learners to adapt to a rapidly evolving world.

The Virginia Department of Education (2024) notes:

> As we integrate these powerful tools into our schools and workplaces, we must urgently equip learners and workers with the skills, knowledge, and competencies to harness AI responsibly and effectively. Our education system must adapt to prepare a workforce that can leverage AI to its full potential while safeguarding against its risks.

This call to action invites us to rethink not only how we teach but also how we learn and grow in an AI-powered society.

The integration of AI challenges us to consider the broader implications of technology on our communities and the ethical responsibilities that come with it. By fostering curiosity, resilience, and critical thinking, we can prepare learners—and ourselves—not just to use AI effectively but to shape its development in ways that promote equity, innovation, and social good.

By fostering a culture of continuous learning and adaptability, educators prepare themselves—and their learners—to navigate an ever-evolving landscape with confidence and resilience. The skills and mindsets cultivated through AI-driven experiences will not only enhance professional practice but also empower learners to thrive in a rapidly changing world. The experiments in this book are designed to help educators customize discipline-specific lessons that teach learners these essential skills while modeling curiosity and innovation.

Collaborating With AI to Write This Book

This metacognitive AI journey reflects over two years of personal experimentation, skill building, and self-reflection. My experience with generative AI has been transformative; without it, this book would not exist. Generative AI has been my cocreator, helping me think about my thinking and working alongside me to refine my skills daily. Staying true to this work, I have infused generative AI throughout this resource, utilizing many of the skills highlighted in the experiments.

The reflections within this book mirror the ongoing dialogues I've had with fellow educators and learners, exploring how AI can support professional growth and inspire creative, intentional teaching. At times, I worked as an AI cyborg, seamlessly intertwining my expertise with AI's capabilities to push the boundaries of what we could achieve together. In their 2023 working paper *Navigating the Jagged Technological Frontier*, researchers Fabrizio Dell'Acqua and colleagues explain, "Cyborg users don't just delegate tasks; they intertwine their efforts with AI at the very frontier of capabilities" (p. 16). Other times, I adopted the role of an AI centaur, using AI strategically while letting human creativity lead the way (Dell'Acqua et al., 2023).

This dynamic interplay between human expertise and AI's potential is at the heart of this resource. I invite you to reflect on how you might combine your unique knowledge, skills, and creativity with AI tools to accelerate your growth, expand your capabilities, and transform your practice as an educator.

What to Expect in This Book

This book is designed to help educators learn about generative AI and integrate it into their teaching practices in meaningful ways. It is grounded in practical, hands-on experiments and discussions that emphasize the development of cross-cutting skills, such as analytical thinking, problem solving, creativity, collaboration, computational thinking, ethical reasoning, and digital literacy (Lansing-Stoeffler & Daley, 2022).

Throughout the book, you will find "Focus Skills" sections that spotlight key competencies learners need to thrive in an AI-influenced world. These recurring features help connect instructional practice to high-leverage skills and are designed to support both teacher and student growth. Some of the most important focus skills highlighted include critical thinking, analytical reasoning, collaboration, and digital fluency.

These focus skills (what Lansing-Stoeffler and Nola Daley call *cross-cutting skills*) are meant to emphasize the interdisciplinary, transferable nature of the competencies learners need to navigate emerging technologies and complex challenges. For example, critical thinking is the first and most consistently emphasized skill in each Focus Skills section, reinforcing its foundational importance across content areas and learning tasks. These skills are essential across disciplines, equipping learners with the tools they need to engage with diverse content and adapt to an evolving world.

The experiments and discussions in this book are intentionally crafted to develop these skills while offering practical applications for generative AI that deepen understanding and hone essential capabilities. This approach ensures the skills you develop through these experiments are durable and transferable, preparing both you and your learners for diverse contexts and future career paths.

In part 1 of this book, chapters 1 and 2 establish the foundation by introducing core concepts in AI and addressing ethical considerations for its use in educational settings. In part 2, chapters 3 through 6 present a scaffolded progression of experiments that increase in complexity, offering learners multiple entry points based on their experience and comfort level. These chapters contain discussion opportunities strategically placed to provide space to pause, reflect, and dive deeper into the conceptual, ethical, and practical dimensions of working with AI.

Levels of Experiments

The experiments are structured to support your learning, customization, and integration. Each begins with either a brief contextual narrative or an overarching "Big Question" that frames the metacognitive and real-world connection. The learning goals and focus skills support curricular and assessment planning. For experiments, educators should define evaluation criteria that align with these learning goals and incorporate content and technology standards as appropriate. As part of the planning process, educators should articulate this evaluation approach to learners, fostering clarity and engagement. Advanced utilization may include cocreating assessment criteria with learners to deepen their understanding and ownership of the learning process.

The experiments are grouped into four progressive levels, each designed to meet both educators and learners where they are, regardless of their current familiarity with AI.

1. **Entry-point experiments (chapter 3)** introduce foundational AI concepts and skills, helping you build confidence and curiosity. Entry-point experiments demystify AI, providing a starting point for exploring its potential in any subject or context.
2. **Elevated experiments (chapter 4)** build on foundational skills by engaging with more complex prompts and interdisciplinary applications. Elevated experiments encourage you to design creative and innovative learning experiences using AI.
3. **Experienced experiments (chapter 5)** focus on integrating AI into higher-order analytical and problem-solving tasks. Experienced experiments challenge you to develop discipline-specific lessons and guide learners through real-world applications of AI.
4. **Expert experiments (chapter 6)** explore advanced applications of AI, such as using code interpreters, conducting data assessments, and designing AI-driven solutions. Expert experiments push the boundaries of what AI can achieve in education, helping you and your learners unlock its full potential.

The experiments are hands-on and designed to work with a variety of generative AI tools. Educators should consult their district's approved tools for classroom use. At the time of publication, common options include ChatGPT (https://openai

.com/index/chatgpt), Gemini (https://gemini.google.com), Claude (https://claude.ai), Perplexity (www.perplexity.ai), and Khanmigo (www.khanmigo.ai). These tools vary in their capabilities and user interfaces; for example, some are optimized for conversational tasks while others excel in specific areas like coding, data analysis, or personalized learning. Exploring the features of each tool will help you identify the best fit for your learning goals and classroom needs. If access to these tools is limited, consider adapting activities by incorporating pregenerated AI outputs. Educators can create these outputs in advance by using any accessible AI tool to demonstrate the process or provide examples of AI-generated content that align with the experiment's goals. For example, an educator might use a tool like ChatGPT to generate a sample response to a prompt and share it with the class for critique, evaluation, or iterative refinement. This approach ensures all learners can engage meaningfully, even in environments with limited technology access.

Each chapter pairs experiments with discussions that shift in complexity as you progress on your AI learning journey, fostering critical thinking and deeper understanding. I describe these discussions in more detail in the following section.

Role of the Discussions

Each chapter includes discussion opportunities in the form of reproducible protocols designed to spark deeper reflection and conversation around AI-related topics. These tools offer structured ways to pause, engage with big ideas, and explore the ethical, conceptual, and practical dimensions of working with generative AI. Each reproducible includes a big question, learning goals, focus skills, and embedded AI prompts to help you tailor and extend the learning experience. Whether used for personal reflection, collaborative planning, or classroom dialogue, these discussions are designed to enrich the learning process and connect hands-on experimentation with critical inquiry. While the reproducibles are geared toward general use, educators can adapt their content to create developmentally appropriate experiences for learners of any age, opening opportunities to engage with foundational AI concepts through guided exploration and conceptual discussion. I designed the discussions to serve the following purposes.

- **Educators' reflection:** Use them to think critically about your own learning, assess AI's role in your practice, and explore ethical considerations.
- **Professional collaboration:** Share these prompts in team discussions to exchange ideas and strategies for integrating AI effectively.
- **Classroom engagement:** Adapt select discussions to guide learners in exploring the ethical and practical dimensions of AI, encouraging them to reflect on its societal impact and develop their critical thinking skills.

This versatility ensures the discussions are valuable whether used for personal growth, professional collaboration, or direct classroom application. Together with the hands-on experiments, these discussions provide a comprehensive approach to understanding and applying AI in educational settings while equipping educators and learners with critical skills for success in an increasingly technological world. While the discussions do not require direct learner access to technology, they tackle the broader ideas and concepts underpinning generative AI.

Purpose of the Prompts

The discussions and experiments contain a variety of generative AI prompts that serve as exemplars for both learners and educators. Prompts act as strategic instructions given to generative AI tools to guide their responses. Think of prompts as the inputs to an AI system—carefully crafted instructions that determine how the AI processes and generates its response. While crafting effective prompts is a foundational skill, it's equally important for learners to engage in an iterative feedback process to refine prompts and improve outcomes. Learners should critically evaluate the outputs produced by AI for factual accuracy, clarity, relevance, and potential biases. They use these evaluations to adjust their inputs, fostering continuous improvement and deeper learning. Through iterative refinement of prompts based on output quality, educators and learners can improve AI interactions while honing their analytical and critical thinking skills.

The prompts and activities in this book are designed to be flexible and adaptable to support differentiation. The text includes templates to help educators adjust tasks to accommodate diverse learning needs, from providing support for learners who require additional scaffolding to offering enrichment opportunities for those ready to engage at a deeper level. Educators should consider learners' cultural contexts when customizing experiments and discussions, ensuring that learning experiences are inclusive and relevant to learners' diverse backgrounds. By tailoring these activities to your discipline and your learners' unique needs, you can create engaging and meaningful experiences that maximize the potential of generative AI.

While we will delve deeper into the concepts of AI prompts, inputs and outputs, and iterative feedback, you can think of them now as both the foundation and framework for tailoring learning activities. Finally, you'll see curricular integration examples interwoven throughout to spark creativity and ideas as you embark on this learning journey within your classroom. ChatGPT generated these examples, which aim to inspire and guide you in tailoring the book's content to meet the unique needs of your learners.

Adapting AI Skills for Various Contexts

The skills in this book are adaptable to different grade levels and learning contexts. For learners younger than age thirteen, educators might introduce foundational AI concepts through discussion, modeling, guided exploration, and collaborative activities, using platforms permitted for this age group. For middle and high school learners over age thirteen, including adult learners, lessons can include more complex, independent applications of AI. Across all age groups, educators play a vital role in shaping how learners engage with AI, fostering ethical awareness, critical thinking, and problem-solving abilities.

To help you prepare your learners, this book emphasizes building the following critical AI understandings.

- **AI literacy** involves teaching learners the basics of AI: how it works and how it can be applied across fields.
- **Ethical implications** include guiding learners to think critically about the ethical use of AI, including privacy concerns, algorithmic bias, and broader societal impacts.
- **Data literacy** entails equipping learners with the skills to analyze and interpret data, as data is the foundation on which AI systems operate.
- **Coding and computational thinking** involve introducing learners to programming and computational thinking, which are crucial for developing and managing AI systems.
- **Creativity and innovation** look like encouraging learners to use AI as a tool for solving complex problems, fostering innovation across disciplines.
- **Emotional intelligence** includes helping learners develop interpersonal skills and self-awareness to complement AI's cognitive abilities.
- **Safety and security** look like teaching learners about cybersecurity, including how to protect systems and data from unauthorized access and why secure coding practices matter.
- **Critical thinking and problem solving** entail developing learners' ability to navigate complex challenges and make informed decisions when working with AI technologies.

By integrating these components into your teaching, you help learners understand and apply AI technology, enabling them to shape its development ethically and responsibly. As educators, your work ensures that the next generation is prepared not just to participate in an AI-driven world but to lead and innovate within it.

A Collaborative Call to Action

This journey is about more than using AI; it's about collaborating with it and combining your expertise with its capabilities to inspire creativity, foster critical thinking, and create meaningful change. Generative AI, when used thoughtfully, can amplify human intelligence and address some of the most pressing challenges in education and beyond.

Adopting a "human with machine" mindset, rather than a "human against machine" narrative, allows us to embrace AI as a tool to enhance our unique skills rather than replace them. Real-world applications like chess have demonstrated that collaboration between human intelligence and AI consistently outperforms either operating alone. Similarly, in education, thoughtful integration of AI can elevate both teaching and learning to unprecedented levels (Machajewski, 2024).

Socrates once criticized the advent of writing, believing it would weaken memory and critical engagement (Plato, 2013, original date 370 BC). AI now faces similar scrutiny. Socrates feared that relying on written texts would erode personal connections to knowledge. Just as books ultimately became indispensable for intellectual growth, AI also has the potential to revolutionize education and productivity. However, its success depends on our ability to approach it with a balanced perspective, addressing its challenges while harnessing its benefits with curiosity and ethical responsibility.

This book equips you with the tools to lead productive conversations about AI's role in education. How can we maximize its benefits while mitigating risks? How do we define its appropriate and inappropriate uses in the classroom? Through engaging in the experiments and discussions in this book, you'll gain insights into shaping a future where AI enhances, rather than diminishes, human ingenuity.

Collaboration is key. By fostering interdisciplinary cooperation and continuous feedback loops between educators, learners, and technology developers, we ensure that AI tools remain effective, ethical, and aligned with our educational goals. Ethical leadership plays a pivotal role in this transformation. As the IESE Business School at the University of Navarra (2020) notes, navigating today's volatile, uncertain, complex, and ambiguous world requires leaders who can diagnose challenges, overcome resistance, and seize opportunities for growth.

This is a moment of self-disruption—a necessary step for growth in an era where AI is constantly evolving. Lifelong learning and adaptability are essential for educators, as is cultivating an innovative mindset that views change as an opportunity for improvement and creativity. Thoughtfully applying AI in education is not just about adopting new technologies; it's about fostering a mindful, intentional integration that serves the greater good. As Carol S. Dweck (2016) reminds us, adopting a growth mindset is critical for embracing change and unlocking new possibilities. Educational systems must become agile and flexible, capable of responding to the needs of the workforce and society with speed and intention.

Let us step boldly into this new era of technological advancement. Together, we can create a future where every learner thrives. The potential for growth and creativity is limitless, and our collective imagination will drive us toward a brighter, more inclusive, and enlightened future. This is one of education's defining moments—let's experiment, reflect, and grow together.

PART 1

Foundations for AI Exploration

Part 1 lays the groundwork for working thoughtfully and responsibly with generative AI. Through key concepts, ethical considerations, and reflection-based discussion opportunities, we build a strong foundation for using AI in ways that support meaningful, inclusive, and critical learning experiences. Before stepping into experimentation, part 1 encourages you to consider not just what AI can do, but also how and why we choose to use it in educational settings—and how to do so in ways that are safe, ethical, and developmentally appropriate for all learners.

CHAPTER 1

Laying the Groundwork for AI Experiments

You wake up in the morning and ask your virtual assistant about the weather. Then you glance at your phone, which suggests the quickest route to work based on real-time traffic data. As you scroll through your social media feed, you notice an advertisement for a clothing item you were looking for online. The seamless integration of AI that has already taken root in our daily routines highlights its profound impact. AI is so ingrained in our everyday activities that we often don't realize the extent of its presence.

Have you ever paused to consider how you interact with AI, knowingly or unknowingly? What AI-powered tools do you use daily? How have those tools changed your routines or decision-making processes? Take a moment and reflect on your own AI encounters. Whether through voice assistants, personalized recommendations, or automated processes, AI is already at the core of many of our routines.

In this chapter, I share my story of becoming familiar with AI and ask you to tell yours. I give a brief overview of AI's evolution as well as the fundamentals of this technology. The chapter includes a series of discussions to guide your thinking on topics like supervised versus unsupervised learning, the ethics of human-AI collaboration, and staying informed and adaptable in seeking AI guidance

Sharing Our AI Stories

My AI story began in my basement chemistry lab filled with stuffed animals and my father's Apple IIe. From a young age, I was captivated by the possibilities of science and technology. I spent countless hours experimenting with early computer programs, cultivating a deep-seated curiosity and an eagerness to learn. As I entered the field of education as a high school science teacher, my affinity for technology became a valued asset. I quickly became the go-to person for explaining computers, software, email, and other tech-related initiatives to staff. My colleagues relied on me to demystify these new tools, and I enjoyed the challenge of integrating technology into the classroom to enhance learning experiences. As I transitioned into school leadership, I saw firsthand the potential of technology to streamline workflows, improve efficiency, and impact learning. I began developing rudimentary systems to manage administrative tasks, hoping to free up time for more meaningful activities. These early attempts were simple, but they laid the groundwork for a more profound engagement with technology.

One day, I noticed an intriguing pattern: Whenever I searched for something online—whether it was a gift or a product for my home—that item would later appear in unexpected places, such as ads on unrelated websites. This small but eye-opening realization showed me how interconnected and pervasive AI had become. Google Maps accompanied me in the car, suggesting the best routes, while Alexa seamlessly organized tasks and responded to my requests. These moments of convenience came with a quiet realization: If AI could anticipate my needs, how much of my personal data was driving those insights? As AI increasingly wove into my daily routines, I began to see both its remarkable potential and the important questions it raised about privacy and responsibility.

In the spring of 2022, at the ASU + GSV conference, a collaborative event between Arizona State University and Global Silicon Valley, I overheard a panel of superintendents discussing the rapid advancements in AI, almost as an afterthought to their broader conversation. One of them emphasized the importance of the 2035 Skills Imperative, which is a framework for guiding leaders on the skills learners need in an AI-driven world (Dickerson, Rossi, Bocock, Hillary, & Simcock, 2023). At the time, my team was launching Chicago's newest STEM high school, and the mention of AI captured my attention with laser precision. That conversation became a turning point. Curiosity sparked within me, and a palpable excitement about AI's potential began to take hold. I realized at that moment that understanding and leveraging AI would be critical for future success.

Not six months later, in the fall of 2022, ChatGPT 3.5 launched, accelerating AI advancements exponentially. I went all in, applying AI to every aspect of my work and personal life that I could imagine, from creating strategic plans to planning my garden to organizing vacation ideas. Brainstorming, outlining, customizing text, and more all became my go-to interactions with AI. I had crossed a threshold: I could now talk directly to my computer, have it understand me, and take actions to help. Within months, I began talking about AI so much that my friends and family tired of it. When their patience ran thin, I turned to creating content to support teachers, learners, and leaders in gaining these invaluable skills. The possibilities seemed endless, and each new application of AI opened my eyes to its transformative potential.

Use the following reproducible, "Write Your AI Story", to reflect on your evolving relationship with AI.

Write Your AI Story

Use the following reflection questions to reflect on your earliest interactions with technology and how your relationship with AI has evolved over time.

Where does your AI story start? What's your earliest memory of interacting with technology?

How has your relationship with technology—including AI—evolved over time?

What emotions does AI bring up for you? How do you see it showing up in your life?

In what ways has your relationship with AI shaped your views, values, or professional identity?

How might your relationship with AI shape your work or your interactions with peers, colleagues, or learners?

After reflecting on your responses, how would you describe your AI story in a few sentences?

As we transition from my personal journey to a broader exploration of AI, let's take a moment to examine how this technology has evolved and the fundamental principles that drive it. The profound impact AI has had on my journey is just the beginning—it will shape yours too. Understanding its origins and core principles is an essential foundation for our exploration. By tracing where AI began and how it continues to evolve, we can better grasp its current applications and future possibilities for society. Along this journey, ethical decisions will play a critical role, and having the right information will be key to navigating them responsibly.

Evolving Intelligence

Artificial intelligence was a dream long before it became a reality. The idea that machines could mimic human intelligence dates to ancient myths and stories (Shashkevich, 2019). However, it wasn't until the mid-20th century that AI began to take shape as a scientific discipline. In 1956, the term "artificial intelligence" was coined during the Dartmouth Conference, marking the official birth of AI as a field of study (Moor, 2006). Early AI research focused on problem solving and symbolic methods, leading to the development of the first AI programs capable of playing chess and solving mathematical problems (Anyoha, 2017).

In 2001, Google transformed web searching by introducing a simple form of machine learning aimed at supporting better spelling for web searches (Google, n.d.). This breakthrough marked a significant leap in AI's practical applications, embedding it into everyday life. By 2020, Google integrated its machine learning and AI division, DeepMind, into Google Maps for navigation route optimization, demonstrating AI's ability to enhance real-world tasks (Lange & Perez, 2020).

In 2022, OpenAI launched its generative AI large language model, ChatGPT 3.5, capable of producing human-like text and reasoning. This advancement marked a turning point in AI's evolution, rapidly expanding its creative and practical applications. Soon after, competing models began to emerge, further advancing the field and transforming how we interact with technology. These models not only revolutionized the technology landscape but also opened new pathways for innovation and creativity. As we explore these milestones, it becomes clear that AI is not merely a tool: It is a transformative force reshaping every aspect of our lives.

Understanding the Fundamentals of AI

From the moment you check your smartphone in the morning to the time you go to bed, AI is there, enhancing your experiences, streamlining your tasks, and shaping your interactions. But what exactly is AI, and how does it work?

At its core, *artificial intelligence* refers to computer systems designed to perform tasks that typically require human intelligence. These tasks include understanding natural language, recognizing patterns, making decisions, and learning from data (University of Illinois Chicago, 2024). Unlike traditional software, which relies on explicit, handcrafted code instructions, AI systems are trained to perform tasks through a process called *machine learning.* This training involves feeding the system vast amounts of data and iteratively adjusting its parameters to improve accuracy and performance.

Machine learning, the backbone of AI, allows systems to learn from experience, processing large datasets—collections of structured or unstructured information such as numbers, text, images, or audio. By identifying patterns, machine learning models can make predictions or decisions based on those patterns. This continuous learning process makes AI dynamic, capable of evolving and improving over time. Within machine learning lies a specialized subset called *deep learning*, which uses neural networks. *Neural networks* are computer systems designed to mimic how the human brain processes information by recognizing patterns and making connections across many layers. Deep learning leverages neural networks to analyze massive datasets with increasing complexity, enabling breakthroughs in areas such as image recognition, natural language processing, and autonomous systems.

Taking this one step further is *generative AI*—a cutting-edge subset of deep learning. Unlike other AI, generative AI not only recognizes patterns but also creates entirely new content based on the data it has learned (Brown, 2021). Generative AI powers platforms like ChatGPT and Google Gemini, enabling them to generate human-like text, create images, and even compose music (McKinsey & Company, 2024). These platforms rely on *large language models* (*LLMs*), a type of generative AI specifically designed to understand and produce text. LLMs are trained on diverse and extensive datasets, allowing them to comprehend context, answer questions, and engage in meaningful conversations with users (IBM, 2023).

The diagram in figure 1.1 depicts the relationship between these various forms of computing, illustrating how machine learning, deep learning, and generative AI are interrelated yet distinct in their capabilities.

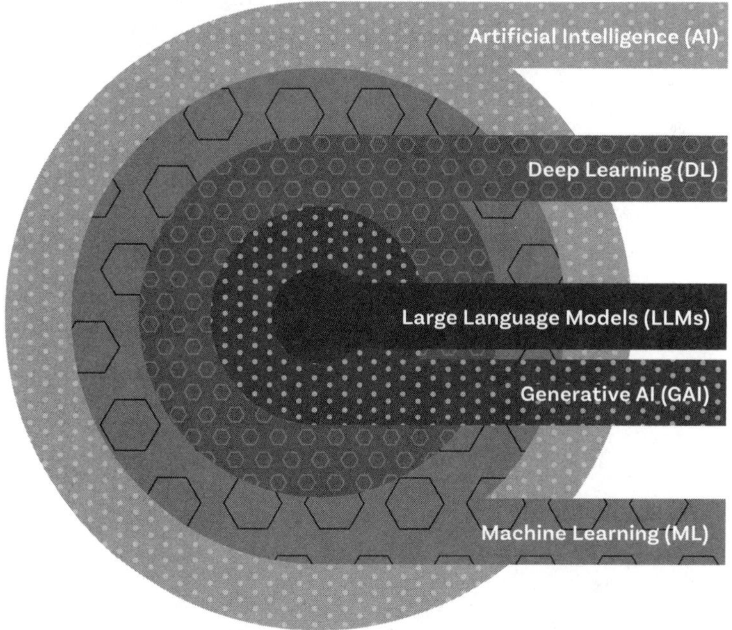

Source: © 2024 by TechEd Maven Consulting. Used with permission.

Figure 1.1: Core concepts in AI.

To better understand these relationships, think of AI as a dynamic learning ecosystem, with its components working together like the interconnected elements of a school. These acronyms are common in both educational and professional conversations about AI.

- **Artificial intelligence (AI)** is the overarching educational system that sets the framework for what is possible. Like a school campus, it houses and connects all the activities and programs inside.
- **Machine learning (ML)** represents the curriculum within this ecosystem. It provides the foundational program that "teaches" (data models) how to learn from examples and improve through practice—just as general classes build core knowledge and skills.
- **Deep learning (DL)** is the honors or Advanced Placement (AP) classes. These specialized courses tackle complex topics, requiring deeper thinking and more sophisticated tools, akin to the layered neural networks used in AI.
- **Generative AI (GAI)** is the school's innovation lab. It is where creativity comes to life, combining knowledge and skills from ML, DL, and LLMs to produce new and imaginative work, be it writing, visual art, or innovative solutions to challenges.
- **Large language models (LLMs)** are the star pupils of this system. These learners excel in communication and synthesis, generating clear and insightful responses by drawing on their extensive "studies" of language and context.

In this ecosystem, educators act as both mentors and architects, guiding learners on their journey through the interconnected layers of AI. Like the mentors in every great story, educators provide wisdom, tools, and encouragement while fostering the curiosity and courage needed to explore uncharted territory. Similarly, this book equips you with the knowledge and resources to support your learners as they navigate the complexities of AI.

By viewing AI through this lens, you'll gain a practical understanding of how its layers interact, empowering you to design educational experiences that align with both your teaching goals and your learners' needs.

The Artificial Intelligence (AI) for K–12 initiative (AI4K12; https://ai4k12.org) breaks down AI into five big ideas, offering a clear framework for understanding its foundational concepts. These ideas include the following.

1. **Perception:** AI systems perceive the world through sensors, such as cameras and microphones, allowing them to process and respond to real-world inputs.
2. **Representation and reasoning:** AI agents represent the world internally and use these representations to make informed decisions.

3. **Learning:** AI systems can learn from data to improve their performance over time, making them dynamic and adaptable.
4. **Natural interaction:** For AI to work effectively with humans, it must interact naturally through speech, gestures, and other forms of communication.
5. **Societal impact:** AI has far-reaching effects on society, influencing everything from healthcare and education to ethics and fairness, often raising both opportunities and challenges.

Within these big ideas, the AI4K12 initiative is developing K–12 standards for AI education. Because the integration of AI into education is evolving rapidly, educators should conduct their own research to stay informed about advancements and best practices.

The five big ideas can serve as a helpful framework as you engage with the experiments and discussions in this book. For example, the hands-on experiments often focus on how AI learns, interacts naturally, or processes inputs to generate meaningful outputs, while the discussions encourage reflection on broader societal impacts and ethical considerations. By drawing on these ideas, you can customize lessons to suit your learners' needs and guide them toward a holistic understanding of AI's potential and limitations.

One striking example of AI's capabilities is its role in representation and reasoning. AI systems analyze vast amounts of data to make informed decisions, such as predicting stock market trends or diagnosing health conditions. For instance, an AI-driven platform may assist doctors by analyzing patient data, identifying patterns, and suggesting potential treatments. This not only enhances the accuracy of medical decisions but also saves valuable time—an application that underscores AI's transformative potential (Bajwa, Munir, Nori, & Williams, 2021). AI has also revolutionized how we interact with technology through personalized recommendations. Streaming services like Netflix and Spotify use AI algorithms to analyze viewing and listening habits, curating suggestions that enhance user experience (Sahota, 2024). Similarly, in online shopping, AI tailors product recommendations based on browsing history and preferences, creating a customized experience for consumers (Power, 2024). Beyond entertainment and commerce, AI's predictive capabilities extend to fields such as weather forecasting, where it analyzes meteorological data to predict patterns with increasing accuracy (Zhu, 2024). Similarly, AI models predict trends in fields from stock market movements (Lin & Lobo Marques, 2024) to agricultural yields (Neethirajan, 2023), helping industries make proactive decisions.

These examples of representation, reasoning, and learning connect directly to the experiments and discussions you'll encounter throughout this book. While the experiments focus on building foundational AI skills—such as crafting prompts, evaluating AI outputs, and designing creative solutions—they also encourage learners to think critically, forge connections across their experiences, and envision AI's role in diverse industries. These hands-on activities nurture creativity and analytical thinking, empowering learners to approach challenges with an innovative mindset. Discussions complement this process by offering space for deeper reflection on the societal impacts and ethical dimensions of AI. For instance, you might facilitate explorations of AI's potential in fields like medicine or commerce while prompting learners to critically assess issues such as bias or limitations inherent in these systems.

Two Types of Machine Learning

To grasp how AI operates, it's essential to understand two major approaches to machine learning: supervised and unsupervised learning.

1. **Supervised learning:** This approach involves training AI on labeled data, where each example is paired with a correct output. For instance, a dataset used to teach an AI model to differentiate between cats and dogs would include labeled images, each identified as either cat or dog. This allows the model to learn the relationship between input data (the images) and the correct output (the labels; Sarker, 2021).
2. **Unsupervised learning:** In contrast, unsupervised learning analyzes unlabeled data to identify hidden patterns or structures. For example, an AI model might group news articles into categories based on content similarities without predefined labels. This method is often used for clustering, trend analysis, and exploratory purposes, helping reveal insights that might not be immediately apparent (Sarker, 2021).

These methods underpin many AI applications, from personalized recommendations to creative tools, providing a foundation for the innovations we'll explore in later chapters.

The Power and Potential of Generative AI

Building on the foundational principles of artificial intelligence, generative AI takes these concepts to an exciting new level. While traditional AI systems excel at recognizing patterns and making predictions, generative AI introduces a creative dimension, capable of producing entirely new and original content. This shift not only redefines the possibilities of AI but also amplifies its relevance in fields where innovation, creativity, and personalization are paramount.

Generative AI encompasses tools and technologies designed to create outputs such as text, images, music, or videos based on learned patterns in existing datasets (Digital Economy and Remote Work Applications Office, 2023). For educators and learners, this capability opens vast opportunities for exploration and problem solving. Imagine crafting lesson plans dynamically tailored to individual learner needs, designing visually engaging presentations, or using AI-generated story starters to spark creative writing. These tools transform routine tasks into opportunities for ingenuity and engagement.

Consider how generative AI might impact your specific discipline. In education, it offers the potential to revolutionize how you approach instruction, collaboration, and assessment. Beyond classrooms, it drives innovation in creative industries, healthcare, and engineering, offering solutions to challenges once considered too complex or resource intensive. As educators, our task is to harness AI's capabilities responsibly, helping learners navigate both the opportunities and challenges it presents.

For example, generative AI platforms like ChatGPT can generate realistic dialogue or explanations tailored to various reading levels, making complex topics more accessible. Similarly, many tools offer the ability to create visual or multimedia content with minimal technical expertise. These technologies inspire learners to explore their creative potential while reinforcing critical thinking skills as they evaluate AI-generated outputs.

Understanding what makes generative AI distinct helps frame why responsible use is so important. As the Los Angeles County Office of Education (2024) explains:

> Generative artificial intelligence . . . is a type of artificial intelligence that can create entirely new data, like text, images, or even music. It's distinct from other AI in that it's not just analyzing and understanding existing information, but rather using that knowledge to produce something original. (p. 3)

Educators must guide learners in considering the ethical implications of these technologies, from promoting academic integrity to addressing biases that might emerge in AI-generated content.

The Role of Algorithms and Ethical Considerations

At the heart of AI functionality are *algorithms*—sets of rules and instructions that guide AI systems in processing data and making decisions (Xu et al., 2021). In education, algorithms can tailor content to individual learning preferences, increasing engagement and improving outcomes. Adaptive learning platforms, for example, use algorithms to dynamically adjust lesson difficulty, ensuring learners are appropriately challenged and supported based on their progress.

For educators, this means carefully selecting AI tools that prioritize ethical considerations, such as data privacy and fairness. Parents, too, play a role by engaging their children in discussions about responsible AI use. These conversations lay the groundwork for understanding the broader societal implications of AI—a theme we will explore further in the chapters ahead.

Generative AI and the Role of Bias

Generative AI systems use large language models, which are trained on vast datasets primarily composed of human-generated content (Yu, Xu, Hu, & Deng, 2023). As a result, these models often inherit human and societal biases embedded in the data. The Arizona Institute for Education & the Economy's 2024 guide for generative AI in Arizona's K–12 school systems explains, "Generative AI systems use Large Language Models . . . [that] inherently incorporate human and societal biases into the applications and outputs they produce" (p. 18). Recognizing and addressing these biases is critical when deploying AI in any setting, especially education. Chapter 2 (page 39) explores this theme more deeply, and throughout the experimentation process, we'll keep a keen eye on identifying and responding to bias as we create with AI. For educators, this means guiding learners to critically evaluate AI-generated content, question its assumptions, and identify areas where biases might emerge.

Knowing Why These Fundamentals Matter

Understanding these fundamentals equips you with the knowledge to evaluate and implement AI tools effectively, enabling you to guide your learners confidently and responsibly. For educators, this foundation is more than technical know-how—it's a lens for shaping meaningful, innovative, and equitable learning experiences. By recognizing how algorithms personalize learning experiences while staying vigilant about potential biases, you can make informed choices about integrating AI into your practice.

These concepts are essential for navigating the experiments and discussions that follow in this book. For instance, crafting effective AI prompts or analyzing AI-generated outputs requires an appreciation of how AI processes and learns from data. Without this grounding, it's easy to focus solely on the "how-to" without understanding the "why" behind AI's responses or outputs, which means missing opportunities to critically assess and refine its use.

This foundational knowledge also ensures you can confidently address learners' questions and curiosity about AI's role in their lives, careers, and society. Whether you're exploring ethical considerations, fostering creativity, or helping learners draw connections across disciplines, your understanding of AI's inner workings helps you lead with clarity and purpose. Stay engaged with these fundamentals as you move forward. They're not just the building blocks of AI education—they're the compass for navigating the possibilities and challenges that lie ahead.

Applying this foundational understanding of AI also means leveraging machine learning tools to inspire creativity, foster collaboration, and address the diverse needs of your learners. By understanding how AI evolves and learns, you gain the confidence to navigate its complexities with intention. These foundational concepts are not just technical details; rather, they are the building blocks for using AI thoughtfully and responsibly in education and beyond.

Having established a foundational understanding of AI and its building blocks, including machine learning, it's time to delve deeper into two key approaches: supervised and unsupervised learning. These methodologies underpin many AI applications, from personalized recommendations to complex predictive systems. The following discussion, "Machine Learning: Supervised Versus Unsupervised" (page 26), invites you to explore their differences, applications, and implications, equipping you with insights that can inform both your teaching and your learners' understanding of these essential AI concepts.

Discussion: Machine Learning—Supervised Versus Unsupervised

Instructions: Use this protocol to plan and adapt a discussion that fits your audience, setting, and goals by reviewing the guidance and prompts prior to facilitating the discussion. This protocol is a flexible planning tool designed to help you frame the conversation, customize the experience, and support meaningful participation.

Big Question

What are the differences between supervised and unsupervised learning in machine learning, and how are they applied in various fields?

Introduction

Machine learning is a branch of artificial intelligence that helps computers learn from data. Think of it like teaching a computer to make decisions or predictions based on examples we provide. There are two main types of machine learning: supervised and unsupervised learning.

- **Supervised learning:** This is like having a teacher. We give the computer labeled data, meaning we provide examples with the correct answers. The computer learns from these examples to make predictions or decisions. For instance, teaching a computer to recognize cats in photos by showing it many pictures labeled *cat* or *not cat*.
- **Unsupervised learning:** This is more like exploring on your own. The computer is given data without labels and must find patterns and relationships by itself. For example, if we give the computer a collection of photos without any labels, it might group them based on similarities, such as sorting animals by their shapes or colors.
- **Generative AI:** Generative AI uses both supervised and unsupervised learning techniques to create new content. For example, it can generate realistic images, write coherent text, or even compose music by learning from large datasets. Understanding how these two types of learning work helps us see how to use generative AI responsibly and effectively in various applications.

Understanding these approaches is crucial for knowing how to use machine learning to solve different problems, whether it's predicting trends, organizing information, or creating new technologies.

Learning Goals

- Understand the basic principles of supervised and unsupervised learning.
- Explore the types of problems each method is best suited for.
- Analyze the benefits and drawbacks of supervised and unsupervised learning.
- Evaluate real-world applications of both methods in various fields.
- Develop critical thinking about choosing the right machine learning method for different tasks.

Focus Skills

Critical Thinking	Ethical Reasoning	Research Skills
Technological Literacy	Decision Making	Evaluation and Synthesis
Communication	Strategic Thinking	Problem Solving

Discussion Customization AI Prompt

How can I customize a discussion for my [grade] [subject] class focused on understanding the differences between supervised and unsupervised learning?

For example:

> How can I customize a discussion for a high school computer science class focused on the technical aspects and algorithms of supervised and unsupervised learning?

Discussion Differentiation AI Prompt

> How can I adjust a discussion for [grade] [content] learners who [specific needs] and need [specific support] to understand supervised and unsupervised learning?

For example:

> How can I adjust a discussion for sixth-grade science learners who are English learners and need audio summaries to understand supervised and unsupervised learning?

Discussion Extension AI Prompt

> How can I extend a discussion to challenge advanced [grade] [content] learners and deepen their understanding of supervised and unsupervised learning?

For example:

> How can I extend a discussion for high school computer science learners who enjoy real-world problem solving to propose improvements to supervised and unsupervised learning applications?

Working With AI: The Human-in-the-Loop Approach

At the heart of our technological journey lies a critical principle: maintaining a symbiotic relationship between humans and machines. Licklider (1960) foresaw the immense value of integrating the positive characteristics of both humans and computers. He observed that "a symbiotic cooperation, if successful in integrating the positive characteristics of men and computers, would be of great value" (Licklider, 1960, p. 6). According to Ethan Mollick (2024), professor of innovation and entrepreneurship at the Wharton School of the University of Pennsylvania, "The key is to keep humans firmly in the loop—to use AI as an assistive tool, not as a crutch" (p. 52).

The human-in-the-loop (HITL) approach means that people stay involved at important points when using AI. In education, this approach takes on profound significance. For example, an educator might use AI-driven software to analyze learner performance data. While the software provides insights, it is the teacher's interpretation and professional judgment that tailor instructional strategies to meet learners' unique needs. This active engagement helps educators sharpen their skills and adapt to innovative ways of problem solving.

This idea extends beyond the classroom. Parents might use AI-powered apps to track their child's developmental milestones, but their intuition and understanding of their child guide decisions about care. Similarly, in business, managers may analyze market trends using AI yet rely on their expertise to shape strategies that align with organizational goals. These examples reinforce the broader application of human oversight in AI-powered tools across domains.

The necessity of human oversight becomes clear when considering potential pitfalls. Imagine an AI system generates a report summarizing the latest educational trends, only to include a factually inaccurate claim. As the Digital Economy and Remote Work Applications Office (2023) of the United Arab Emirates' Minister of State for Artificial Intelligence explains, "Generative AI applications rely solely on self-learning to generate text. So while they may produce text that is grammatically correct, it may not always be factually accurate, or can be misleading. Therefore, human supervision is crucial" (p. 8). Without such oversight, misinformation can easily spread, underlining the importance of critical human intervention.

In education specifically, the HITL approach ensures that AI tools complement rather than supplant educators. This ensures that teachers, not just technology, are the ones making key decisions, using AI as a tool to support, not replace, their professional judgment. For instance, a teacher using AI to assess learning might rely on the system to identify patterns, but they remain at the helm, making instructional decisions informed by professional judgment and classroom context. As the U.S. Department of Education's Office of Educational Technology (2023) emphasizes, "people are part of the process of noticing patterns in an educational system and assigning meaning to those patterns. It also means that teachers remain at the helm of major instructional decisions" (p. 17).

The HITL concept encompasses three critical loops: (1) moment-to-moment teaching decisions; (2) planning and reflection; and (3) participation in the design, selection, and evaluation of AI-enabled technologies (Office of Educational Technology, 2023). These loops highlight educators' multifaceted roles in shaping AI's integration into classrooms. Imagine a planning session where educators collaborate with AI developers to align technology with real classroom needs: This partnership exemplifies HITL in action.

Beyond education, HITL aligns with broader principles such as human-centered AI and AI for social good. The Office of Educational Technology (2023) explains the following in their *Artificial Intelligence and the Future of Teaching and Learning* report:

> The idea of humans in the loop is part of our broader discussions happening about AI and society, not just AI in education. Interested readers could look for more on human-centered AI, responsible AI, value-sensitive AI, AI for social good, and other similar terms that ally with humans in the loop. (p. 17)

These principles emphasize ethical considerations and human oversight to ensure responsible AI use.

A guide on human-centered AI in K–12 schools produced by the Washington Office of Superintendent of Public Instruction (2024) further reinforces this point: "AI should aid in (not replace) decision-making, creativity, learning, development, growth, and productivity" (p. 10). This ensures that AI enhances human capabilities while keeping critical decisions firmly under human control.

To implement AI effectively, educators must develop *AI literacy*, the ability to critically assess and ethically create and apply AI-generated content. The Arizona Institute for Education & the Economy (2024) highlights, "AI literacy equips teachers and leaders to provide informed human oversight for AI implementation" (p. 11). This understanding empowers educators to critically evaluate and guide AI's use in their practice. Ethical considerations also come into play, such as mitigating biases in AI systems and balancing data-driven insights with privacy concerns.

In conclusion, the HITL concept is foundational to the responsible and ethical integration of AI in education and beyond. By maintaining human oversight, we ensure that AI complements and enhances human skills and decision making. This approach not only preserves the central role of educators but also fosters a more ethical and effective use of AI across various domains.

The concept of keeping humans in the loop is not just a technical necessity—it's a deeply ethical and practical consideration that impacts education, work, and society. As we reflect on how AI and humans collaborate, it's essential to explore how this partnership shapes decision making, accountability, and innovation. Use the following discussion, "Human-AI Collaboration—Ethics and Practice," to critically examine what it means to maintain human oversight in AI applications, both in your classroom and in the world at large.

Discussion: Human-AI Collaboration—Ethics and Practice

Instructions: Use this protocol to plan and adapt a discussion that fits your audience, setting, and goals by reviewing the guidance and prompts prior to facilitating the discussion. This protocol serves as a flexible planning tool designed to help you frame the conversation, customize the experience, and support meaningful participation.

Big Question

What does it mean to keep humans in the loop with AI in our classroom and in the world at large?

Learning Goals

- Understand the concept of "human in the loop" in AI systems.
- Identify the benefits and challenges of integrating human oversight in AI applications.
- Explore the impact of human oversight on AI decision making in educational settings and beyond.
- Discuss ethical considerations related to human involvement in AI processes.
- Investigate the roles of transparency, accountability, and responsibility in human-AI collaboration.
- Develop strategies for effectively keeping humans in the loop in AI applications.
- Examine the balance between automation and human control in various AI systems.
- Explore the implications of human-AI collaboration on future job roles and skills.

Focus Skills

Critical Thinking	Ethical Reasoning	Research Skills
Technological Literacy	Decision Making	Evaluation and Synthesis
Communication	Strategic Thinking	Problem Solving

Discussion Customization AI Prompt

> How can I customize a discussion for my [grade] [subject] class focused on keeping humans in the loop with AI in our classroom and in the world at large?

For example:

> How can I customize a discussion in a tenth-grade social studies class on the importance of human oversight in AI applications used in civic systems?

Discussion Differentiation AI Prompt

> How can I adjust a discussion for [grade] [content] learners who [specific needs] and need support in understanding what it means to keep humans in the loop with AI in our classroom and in the world at large?

For example:

> How can I adjust a discussion for eighth-grade English learners who need sentence starters and guided questions to express ideas about human-AI responsibility?

Discussion Extension AI Prompt

> How can I extend a discussion to challenge advanced [grade] [content] learners and deepen their understanding of the ethical use of AI in education and everyday life?

For example:

> How can I adjust a discussion for eighth-grade English learners who need sentence starters and guided questions to express ideas about human-AI responsibility?

Adapting as AI Evolves

The rapid evolution of AI in education presents both opportunities and challenges. Across universities, governmental agencies, nonprofits, and school districts, leaders are researching and developing guidance on integrating AI responsibly. Even as this book is published, countless new resources and use cases are emerging. In this dynamic, collaborative effort is crucial. As the North Carolina Department of Public Instruction (2024) emphasizes, schools and districts "must continuously review and adapt their AI guidelines to keep pace with the rapid evolution of AI technologies" (p. 32). Ongoing assessments of practices, risks, and trends are vital to maintaining ethical and effective AI integration.

This chapter provides a snapshot of the many organizations and thought leaders contributing to this work, offering a starting point for deeper exploration. The resources I cite represent just a fraction of the insights available. As you begin or continue your study, use these references as a foundation. Dive into their cited materials, conduct your own research, and encourage your learners to critically evaluate the credibility and relevance of the sources they encounter. The discussion "AI Guidance—Staying Informed and Adaptable" included in this chapter (page 34) is designed to support these efforts, helping you and your team reflect on the ongoing development of AI literacy and policy.

Collaboration plays a central role in crafting effective AI policies. The Oregon Department of Education (2023) reminds us that these discussions must extend beyond the classroom, reflecting the broader societal impact of AI. As they explain, "It is important to acknowledge the prevalence of AI being used outside of the education system" (p. 10). This perspective ensures that educational AI strategies align with the larger digital ecosystem, preparing learners to navigate a world increasingly influenced by AI.

Developing AI literacy is foundational to this preparation. According to the Washington Office of Superintendent of Public Instruction (2024), learners must understand "the concepts, applications, and implications of AI in various domains" to effectively use it as a tool for learning and problem solving (p. 7). Beyond individual classrooms, AI literacy empowers people to engage in critical conversations about the technology's societal impact. As the North Carolina Department of Public Instruction (2024) observes, "AI literacy empowers individuals to be informed decision-makers" and prepares them to participate meaningfully in discussions about ethical AI development and use (p. 15).

As educators, your engagement in collaborative discussions with colleagues, learners, and stakeholders is essential. These conversations shape AI's evolving role in education, ensuring its responsible and effective use while fostering innovative and equitable learning environments. Each step you take in exploring and implementing

AI contributes to a broader narrative that has the potential to reshape the future of education.

While the path ahead may be complex, it is filled with opportunities for growth and collaboration. By embracing shared wisdom and collective effort, we can navigate this transformative moment together and ensure AI serves as a force for good in our classrooms and beyond.

The dynamic nature of AI requires educators to not only adapt to emerging tools but to also critically evaluate the policies and guidance that influence its integration. Use the following discussion, "AI Guidance—Staying Informed and Adaptable" (page 34), to explore how ongoing collaboration, adaptability, and reflection can inform responsible AI use in education and the world at large.

Discussion: AI Guidance—Staying Informed and Adaptable

Instructions: Use this protocol to plan and adapt a discussion that fits your audience, setting, and goals by reviewing the guidance and prompts prior to facilitating the discussion. This protocol serves as a flexible planning tool designed to help you frame the conversation, customize the experience, and support meaningful participation.

Big Question

How can we stay informed and adapt our practices with the continuous advancements in AI technology?

Introduction

The rapid advancements in AI technology require continuous monitoring and regular updates to AI policies to ensure they remain relevant and effective. The Virginia Department of Education (2024) highlights the importance of these actions as follows:

> Be constantly discerning and responsive to the continuous expansion of AI capabilities and uses: This is not a one-and-done. The guidelines, best practices, and tools available will constantly need to be revisited to keep pace with the changes brought by the exponential growth of AI and technology advancements in our world. (p. 2)

This discussion invites participants to review and analyze various sources of AI guidance and policies, understand their implications, and develop strategies to remain adaptable in the ever-evolving AI landscape. By engaging in this dialogue, we can ensure that our practices align with ethical considerations and emerging innovations.

Learning Goals

- Understand the importance of continuously monitoring and updating AI policies.
- Explore various sources of guidance and best practices for AI usage.
- Analyze the differences and similarities in AI policies across different sectors.
- Evaluate the effectiveness of current AI guidance documents in addressing new challenges and opportunities.
- Develop critical thinking about the dynamic nature of AI and the need for adaptable policies.

Focus Skills

Critical Thinking	Ethical Reasoning	Decision Making
Technological Literacy	Information Literacy	Evaluation and Synthesis
Communication	Strategic Thinking	Policy Analysis

Discussion Customization AI Prompt

> How can I customize a discussion for my [grade] [subject] class focused on reviewing and understanding AI guidance documents?

For example:

> How can I customize a discussion for tenth-grade global studies learners comparing national AI regulations and their social impact?

Discussion Differentiation AI Prompt

> How can I adjust a discussion for [grade] [content] learners who [specific needs] and need [specific support] to understand AI guidance documents?

For example:

> How can I adjust a discussion for seventh-grade social studies learners who need reading support by using visuals, sentence frames, and summaries to understand AI guidance documents?

Discussion Extension AI Prompt

> How can I extend a discussion to challenge advanced [grade] [content] learners and deepen their understanding of AI guidance documents?

For example:

> How can I extend a discussion for university-level ethics learners who develop and present a mock AI governance proposal based on global trends?

Reference

Virginia Department of Education. (2024). *Guidelines for AI integration throughout education in the Commonwealth of Virginia.* Author. Accessed at_www.education.virginia.gov/media/governorvirginiagov/secretary-of-education/pdf/AI-Education-Guidelines.pdf on February 27, 2025.

Reflecting and Taking Action

Every meaningful journey begins with a foundation of gaining the tools, knowledge, and mindset necessary to navigate new frontiers. In this chapter, you took the first steps toward understanding AI's transformative role in education and beyond. As you step into the role of an AI experimenter, consider how these foundational ideas will guide your next steps. Just as an explorer learns to navigate unfamiliar terrain, your journey with AI requires curiosity, resilience, and a commitment to thoughtful experimentation. To embrace this mindset, reflect on the following steps as you prepare to move forward.

1. Equip yourself with knowledge.
    a. Revisit key concepts such as machine learning, generative AI, and the HITL approach.
    b. Reflect on how these ideas align with your unique context and goals as an educator, leader, or learner.
2. Engage in collaborative exploration.
    a. Use the discussions in this chapter to spark dialogue with colleagues and learners.
    b. Share insights and questions, building a culture of shared learning and experimentation.
3. Embrace experimentation.
    a. Begin applying AI tools in small, manageable ways to test their potential in your practice.
    b. Treat each experiment as a learning opportunity, whether it succeeds or reveals areas for growth.
4. Pursue continued learning.
    a. Dive deeper into the resources cited in this chapter, using them as a springboard for further research.
    b. Encourage learners and colleagues to do the same, fostering critical thinking about AI's possibilities and limitations.
5. Reflect on your role as a guide.
    a. Consider how your expertise and unique perspective can shape AI's integration in your classroom, school, or organization.
    b. Ask yourself how you can inspire those you serve to approach AI with curiosity, ethics, and creativity.

Consider the following questions to guide your thinking.

- What steps can you take to balance human expertise with AI tools in your role as an educator or leader?
- How might experimentation with AI transform not only your practices but also the learning experiences of your learners or colleagues?
- In what ways can you embody the explorer's mindset, guiding others to navigate the opportunities and challenges of this evolving landscape?

With this chapter, you have built the foundation for AI exploration. Now it's time to think critically about its impact. The next step in your journey focuses on AI's ethical dimensions: privacy, bias, and responsible use. As AI becomes a more prominent force in learning and work, the question is not just how we use AI but why and to what end. We must find ways to ensure AI remains a tool for empowerment rather than division. Just as every experiment begins with a question, your journey is fueled by curiosity and action. Together, we will continue exploring this exciting frontier, empowering you to lead with confidence, creativity, and integrity.

CHAPTER 2

Foundations for Ethical AI Experiments

Envisioning a future where robots would operate safely and ethically alongside humans, writer Isaac Asimov (1950) introduced his Three Laws of Robotics:

1. A robot may not injure a human being or, through inaction, allow a human being to come to harm.
2. A robot must obey orders given it by human beings except where such orders would conflict with the First Law.
3. A robot must protect its own existence as long as such protection does not conflict with the First or Second Law. (Auburn University, n.d.)

These fictional laws, though written decades ago, remain a touchstone in conversations about AI ethics, highlighting the need to prioritize human values in technological advancement. As we stand at the threshold of the AI age, these principles are more relevant than ever.

Mollick (2024) captures this urgency, observing, "The reality is that we are already living in the early days of the AI Age, and we need to make some very important decisions about what that actually means" (p. 32). The choices we make today about how to integrate AI into education will shape the future—not just of classrooms but of society at large.

In this chapter, we explore the ethical dimensions of AI through the lenses of safety, privacy, equity, and societal impact. By understanding these foundational principles, you will be better equipped to lead conversations, design experiments, and implement AI practices that align with your values and those of your learning community. Together, we examine best practices for establishing productive relationships with AI tools, structuring effective conversations, and incorporating AI feedback into teaching practice. We'll also address how to overcome challenges and limitations. The goal is to help you integrate AI into your work in ways that enhance teaching and learning while maintaining a human-centered approach that prioritizes ethics, equity, and the indispensable role of educators. By the end of this chapter, you'll have the tools to start crafting ethical AI policies for your classroom, school, district, or organization, ensuring that this ever-evolving technology is used thoughtfully and equitably.

Guiding Learners in Ethical AI Use

As an educator, you've likely engaged in conversations about classroom rules or digital citizenship policies. Integrating AI into education calls for similar discussions, but on a broader scale. These ethical conversations ensure AI supports critical thinking, creativity, and human connection without replacing them. The California Department of Education (2024) emphasizes that ethical guidelines for AI should involve students, teachers, and administrators alike. When learners help shape these rules, they don't just follow them—they understand and own the responsibility of using AI thoughtfully.

Imagine introducing an AI tool to provide instant feedback on learner essays. How do you ensure learners see it as a learning aid rather than a shortcut? By engaging them in conversations about responsible AI use, you build their capacity to think critically about these tools, reinforcing their role as active participants in their education.

AI opens new doors for innovation in the classroom, but it also comes with challenges like inequity and overreliance on technology. The Los Angeles County Office of Education (2024) stresses the importance of thoughtful integration to address these challenges effectively. Educators must ensure that AI tools enhance rather than undermine human relationships in the classroom. Thoughtful use of AI helps maintain the balance between leveraging technology's benefits and preserving the essential human connection that makes learning meaningful.

Ensuring equitable access to AI tools is essential for preparing learners for the future. The Arizona Institute for Education & the Economy (2024) warns that unequal access to these technologies could deepen existing divides, positioning some learners to excel while others are left behind. Addressing this gap isn't just about resources; it's about equity. Providing opportunities for every learner to engage with AI ensures that no one is excluded from the careers and possibilities of tomorrow.

The stakes of AI extend beyond the classroom. The World Economic Forum (2024) highlights that unchecked AI growth could reshape economies and societies in profound ways—both for better and worse. This might feel distant, but as educators, you're at the forefront of this shift. By helping learners think critically about AI's role in their lives, you're equipping them to navigate and shape its future responsibly.

Your work is more than teaching about technology; it's about empowering learners to use AI as a tool for good. With thoughtful integration, we can ensure that AI fosters equity, creativity, and curiosity in every classroom. Together, we can shape a future where every learner has the tools to thrive and the understanding to lead.

Developing AI Literacy

Developing AI literacy is essential for preparing learners to engage thoughtfully and responsibly with these technologies. The Washington Office of Superintendent Public Instruction (2024) highlights this necessity, emphasizing that fostering AI literacy empowers learners to understand AI's concepts, applications, and implications while using it as a tool for problem solving and innovation.

Engaging stakeholders—educators, families, and communities—in conversations about AI's ethical deployment is equally important. The Los Angeles County Office of Education (2024) underscores this point, noting that ensuring districts, educators, and families are prepared to harness AI's benefits will be critical in the years to come. These discussions provide the foundation for shared AI policies that can evolve as AI technologies continue to advance.

Providing ethical, unbiased, and equitable learning opportunities requires a proactive approach to AI design and implementation. Developers must intentionally curate high-quality data while remaining vigilant about potential unconscious biases embedded in algorithms (EDSAFE AI Alliance, 2023). When we prioritize these practices, AI becomes a tool that enhances human capabilities, with critical decisions staying under human control.

However, achieving this balance demands collaboration. How can we engage stakeholders in conversations to ensure AI serves the greater good? What steps can we take across sectors—education, technology, and beyond—to keep AI rooted in the human values we cherish most? These questions challenge us to think deeply about the ethical dimensions of AI and its role in shaping education and society.

The following discussion, "Ethics of AI in Education and Life" (page 42), invites you to dive into these complex ideas, fostering thoughtful collaboration and exploration. By engaging with the prompts and learning goals provided, you will be equipped to consider both the possibilities and the responsibilities tied to integrating AI. Together, let's ensure that the adoption of AI isn't just innovative but also intentional, ethical, and human-centered.

Discussion: Ethics of AI in Education and Life

Instructions: Use this protocol to plan and adapt a discussion that fits your audience, setting, and goals by reviewing the guidance and prompts prior to facilitating the discussion. This protocol serves as a flexible planning tool designed to help you frame the conversation, customize the experience, and support meaningful participation.

Big Question

How should we ethically use AI in education and in our everyday lives?

Learning Goals

- Understand key ethical principles for AI usage across educational and personal contexts.
- Identify potential benefits and challenges of AI, particularly in fostering equitable access and maintaining transparency.
- Explore the impact of AI on learning, teacher practices, and daily activities.
- Discuss the importance of transparency and fairness in AI algorithms.
- Investigate the role of consent and data privacy in AI applications.
- Develop guidelines for responsible AI usage in education and personal contexts.
- Examine the role of AI in reducing or exacerbating inequalities.
- Explore the ethical considerations of AI decision-making processes in different areas of life.

Focus Skills

Critical Thinking	Ethical Reasoning	Research Skills
Technological Literacy	Decision Making	Evaluation and Synthesis
Communication	Strategic Thinking	Problem Solving

Discussion Customization AI Prompt

> How can I customize a discussion for my [grade] [subject] class focused on the ethical use of AI in education and everyday life?

For example:

> How can I customize a Socratic circle discussion in a fourth-grade social studies class where learners explore how using AI in school affects fairness, privacy, and decision making?

Discussion Differentiation AI Prompt

> How can I adjust a discussion for [grade] [content] learners who [specific needs] and need support in understanding how to maintain privacy while using AI inside and outside the classroom?

For example:

> How can I adjust a discussion for eighth-grade technology learners who benefit from structure by using small-group prompts and visuals to explore data privacy and AI use?

Discussion Extension AI Prompt

> How can I extend a discussion to challenge advanced [grade] [content] learners and deepen their understanding of the ethical use of AI in education and everyday life?

For example:

> How can I extend a discussion in a ninth-grade English class on the ethical boundaries of AI use in schools, using real-world examples to support their arguments?

Supporting Safety

How will you know what to believe when AI can twist the truth? Can you trust your own eyes in a world where videos lie? What happens when AI turns your private data against you? Will AI bring us closer together or tear us apart? These questions highlight the pressing need for educators to address misinformation, deepfakes, cybersecurity risks, and the intrapersonal and interpersonal implications of AI in their classrooms. Mollick (2024) captures the unsettling reality of our times: "When machines can pass for humans, even for people who know they are speaking to machines, weird things happen" (p. 88). Safe experimentation, rooted in informed awareness, can help educators guide learners in navigating these complexities responsibly.

In the early stages of our AI journey, educators face a world where even the fabric of reality can be manipulated. This isn't a future dystopia—it's happening now, as AI accelerates the creation of synthetic content and misinformation. The United States federal government, in its 2023 executive order Safe, Secure, and Trustworthy Development and Use of Artificial Intelligence, addresses the issue as follows:

> Responsible AI use has the potential to help solve urgent challenges while making our world more prosperous, productive, innovative, and secure. At the same time, irresponsible use could exacerbate societal harms such as fraud, discrimination, bias, and disinformation. (Exec. Order No. 14110, 2023)

The decisions we make about how to introduce AI in our classrooms will profoundly influence the next generation's ability to critically assess and navigate this complex landscape. The classroom becomes the testing ground for critical thinking and digital literacy—key elements in preparing the next generation for thoughtful engagement with AI tools.

One of the most significant challenges we face is the rise of deepfake technology. In a 2024 article, researcher Matthew Groh and colleagues write, "Recent advances in technology for algorithmically applying hyper-realistic manipulations to video are simultaneously enabling new forms of interpersonal communication and posing a threat to traditional standards of evidence and trust in media" (Groh et al., 2024, p. 1). The ability to create hyper-realistic manipulated videos undermines trust in media and the authenticity of visual evidence. Educators must ask, "How do you spot a deepfake? How well can ordinary people tell the difference between a video manipulated by AI and a normal, non-altered video?" (Groh, n.d.). Addressing these questions in classrooms equips learners with the tools to critically assess digital content. Without these skills, learners may fall victim to misinformation, with consequences that include cyberbullying through fabricated media, which has already led to instances of self-harm and violence. Educators have a vital role in guiding learners to recognize and resist these manipulations.

AI's intersection with cybercrime is another pressing concern. Easy-to-use interfaces for large-scale AI models have enabled a surge in falsified information, voice cloning, and counterfeit websites (World Economic Forum, 2024). These tools make it easier than ever for malicious actors to exploit personal data, leading to identity theft or ransomware attacks. Schools must remain vigilant, implementing strict safeguards to protect learner privacy and fostering digital literacy. Encouraging a culture of safety and proactive experimentation with AI can provide valuable insights while maintaining boundaries that protect both educators and learners.

Beyond technical risks, the mental health implications of AI integration warrant attention. Mollick (2024) predicts that "not only will we have chatbots that feel like interacting with people—they will make us feel better" (p. 90). While AI offers potential for meaningful support, such as mental health assistance, it can also lead to emotional dependencies. Vulnerable learners may substitute AI interactions for genuine human relationships, deepening feelings of isolation or anxiety (Arizona Institute for Education & the Economy, 2024). Moreover, efficiency-driven automation risks replacing human connections in education, from teacher-learner interactions to peer collaboration. As concerns grow about AI's emotional and developmental impact on youth—including lawsuits from the mid-2020s from parents over harm linked to certain tools—these conversations take on greater urgency. They underscore the importance of educators modeling responsible use to ensure AI supports rather than replaces meaningful human relationships.

How can educators use AI to enhance teaching while safeguarding against these risks? By embedding lessons on critical thinking, digital literacy, and intrapersonal and interpersonal awareness into their classrooms, teachers can guide learners in navigating AI's complexities. These lessons will equip learners to use AI responsibly, ensuring it enhances their lives rather than compromises their trust or well-being.

Addressing the safety challenges of AI requires vigilance, collaboration, and proactive education. By fostering critical discussions, teaching practical skills, and encouraging ethical reflection, educators can empower learners to engage with AI thoughtfully and intentionally. Just as experiments allow us to test, learn, and refine, approaching AI in the classroom with a mindset of safe experimentation ensures that its integration is measured, mindful, and aligned with educational goals.

As we delve deeper into this topic, it's time to pause and consider the potential dangers of AI and how we can mitigate these risks to ensure its safe and ethical use. Use the following discussion, "Potential Dangers of AI," to engage learners and colleagues in unpacking these essential concerns. Let's experiment and explore together, ensuring AI serves humanity while preserving trust, connection, and integrity in the digital age.

Discussion: Potential Dangers of AI

Instructions: Use this protocol to plan and adapt a discussion that fits your audience, setting, and goals by reviewing the guidance and prompts prior to facilitating the discussion. This protocol serves as a flexible planning tool designed to help you frame the conversation, customize the experience, and support meaningful participation.

Big Question

What are the potential dangers of AI, and how can we mitigate these risks to ensure safe and ethical use of AI?

Learning Goals

- Identify and understand the various risks associated with the development and deployment of AI technologies.
- Examine the intrapersonal and interpersonal implications of AI, such as its impact on relationships, mental health, and well-being.
- Explore the ethical concerns and biases inherent in AI systems.
- Analyze the potential impact of AI on privacy and surveillance.
- Evaluate the threats AI poses to employment and economic stability.
- Examine the role of AI in security and surveillance.
- Discuss the possibility of AI leading to increased inequality and societal disruption.
- Develop strategies and policies to mitigate the dangers of AI.
- Develop critical thinking regarding the regulation and control of AI technologies.
- Promote ethical reasoning and critical thinking about AI development and usage.

Focus Skills

Critical Thinking	Ethical Reasoning	Relational Awareness
Technological Literacy	Information Literacy	Evaluation and Synthesis
Communication	Strategic Thinking	Decision Making

Discussion Customization AI Prompt

How can I customize a discussion for my [grade] [subject] class focused on the dangers of AI?

For example:

How can I customize a discussion in an eleventh-grade philosophy class where learners apply ethical theories like utilitarianism or deontology to examine the moral implications of AI in surveillance, warfare, or decision making?

Discussion Differentiation AI Prompt

How can I adjust a discussion for [grade] [content] learners who [specific needs] and need [specific support] to understand the dangers of AI?

For example:

How can I, as a school counselor, lead a discussion for third-grade learners with tech anxiety using picture books and guided conversation to safely explore AI's risks?

Discussion Extension AI Prompt

How can I extend a discussion to challenge advanced [grade] [content] learners and deepen their understanding of the dangers of AI?

For example:

How can I extend a discussion in an eighth-grade technology class where learners role-play various stakeholders to argue for or against stricter regulation of AI technologies?

Protecting Privacy

To frame this conversation, the federal Office of Science and Technology Policy's *Blueprint for an AI Bill of Rights*, originally published in October 2022 and archived in January 2025, outlines foundational protections for individuals in an AI-driven world. It emphasizes, "You should be protected from abusive data practices via built-in protections and you should have agency over how data about you is used" (Office of Science and Technology Policy, 2022). In today's world, where data is continuously collected and analyzed, the question becomes personal: How much do you value your privacy? For educators, this question extends to the learners they serve, whose data is often entrusted to digital tools and platforms.

Ensuring the protection of personal information is not just a legal requirement but a moral imperative, as the Digital Economy and Remote Work Applications Office (2023) describes:

> Data privacy refers to the protection of an individual's personal information or data, including sensitive information such as financial and health data, from unauthorized access, use, or disclosure. It involves controlling how data is collected, used, stored, shared, and disposed of by organizations or entities that collect or process that data. Data privacy is an essential component of information security and is governed by various laws, regulations, and best practices aimed at ensuring the confidentiality, integrity, and availability of personal information. (p. 4)

As AI becomes more ingrained in classrooms and administrative systems, robust privacy measures are crucial not only for compliance but also for maintaining trust among learners, families, and educators.

The integration of AI technologies in education raises significant questions about the ethical and legal implications of data sharing. As the Office of Educational Technology (2023) notes, "How will users understand the legal and ethical implications of sharing data with AI-enabled technologies and how to mitigate privacy risks?" (p. 50). Awareness and proactive mitigation strategies are essential to protect learner privacy, ensuring that AI technologies are implemented in ways that prioritize security and ethical responsibility. Educators and administrators play a critical role in shaping these practices, making their understanding of these issues a cornerstone of responsible AI integration.

AI's ability to predict learner behavior and preferences through predictive analytics offers exciting possibilities for personalized education. These technologies can identify learners' needs, enhance tailored support, and improve intervention strategies for learners requiring emotional or academic assistance, such as those with learning disabilities (Individuals With Disabilities Education Act [IDEA], 2004). However, while these benefits are substantial, they must be balanced against ethical concerns about how personal data is collected, analyzed, and used. Educators must remain vigilant, ensuring that AI enhances learning without compromising privacy or well-being.

Regulatory frameworks such as IDEA, CIPA (Children's Internet Protection Act), COPPA (Children's Online Privacy Protection Act), and FERPA (Family Educational Rights and Privacy Act) provide essential guidelines to protect learner data and form the foundation of privacy commitments in educational settings. For example, COPPA mandates security measures to safeguard the "confidentiality, security, and integrity of personal information collected from children" (Federal Trade Commission, n.d.). FERPA ensures transparency and gives families control over student records, while IDEA upholds the rights of learners with disabilities, helping ensure that AI tools used in schools remain inclusive and compliant.

The Children's Internet Protection Act was enacted by Congress in 2000 to address concerns about children's access to harmful or obscene online content. CIPA places specific requirements on schools and libraries that receive discounted internet services through the E-Rate program, ensuring that institutions implement appropriate filters and safeguards (Federal Communications Commission, 2019). Adhering to CIPA highlights the dual responsibility of protecting children from harmful content while ensuring equitable access to necessary digital resources. Teachers, librarians, and administrators must work together to create safe online environments that support learning without exposing learners to risks.

In addition to adhering to regulatory frameworks, educators must exercise caution when using AI tools in the classroom. As the Canadian Centre for Cyber Security (2023) warns, users may unknowingly provide sensitive data in their interactions with AI systems. This information could be exploited by threat actors to impersonate individuals or disseminate false information. The rapid rise in cybercrime associated with AI, including impersonation and ransomware attacks, underscores the need for robust cybersecurity measures to protect both individuals and institutions. For educators, this highlights the importance of critical thinking and digital literacy in equipping learners to navigate these risks responsibly. Teachers and learners should be careful to never enter identifying or confidential information into AI programs without express consent and adherence to district technology-use policies. For example, COPPA specifies that learners under thirteen should not use AI chatbots unless they are COPPA compliant and authorized by the district. For learners over thirteen, parental permission and district approval are generally required for the use of common chatbots such as ChatGPT. Teachers, as the direct users of these tools, play a key role in ensuring that these guidelines are followed. This vigilance helps protect learner data from misuse while fostering a safer digital environment.

Globally, approaches to data privacy vary widely. The European Union has implemented stringent regulations on data protection and privacy, often restricting AI training on data without explicit permission. Conversely, the United States allows more freedom in data collection and use but leaves room for legal recourse in cases of misuse. Japan has taken a radically different approach, permitting unrestricted use of data for AI training, regardless of its origin or the associated copyright concerns (Mollick, 2024). These international perspectives offer valuable insights for educators and administrators as they shape data privacy practices in their schools. Awareness of these differing global standards can help educators make informed decisions and advocate for policies that align with ethical and legal best practices.

Ultimately, addressing privacy concerns requires constant vigilance and a proactive approach. By fostering a culture of privacy awareness and ethical consideration, educators and administrators can guide their communities in navigating the complexities of AI responsibly. The following discussion, "Privacy in the Age of AI," offers an opportunity to deepen understanding and collaborate on effective strategies for safeguarding personal information. Together, we can ensure that AI serves humanity while protecting our learners' privacy and security.

Discussion: Privacy in the Age of AI

Instructions: Use this protocol to plan and adapt a discussion that fits your audience, setting, and goals by reviewing the guidance and prompts prior to facilitating the discussion. This protocol serves as a flexible planning tool designed to help you frame the conversation, customize the experience, and support meaningful participation.

Big Question

How can we maintain privacy while using AI inside and outside the classroom?

Learning Goals

- Understand the principles of data privacy and protection.
- Explore the ethical implications of using AI in educational settings.
- Identify best practices for ensuring learner privacy when using AI tools.
- Analyze the potential risks and benefits of AI in education.
- Develop strategies to mitigate privacy risks associated with AI.
- Evaluate the impact of AI on learner trust and classroom dynamics.
- Examine how global perspectives on data privacy influence local educational practices.

Focus Skills

Critical Thinking	Information Literacy	Research Skills
Technological Literacy	Data Analysis	Ethical Reasoning
Communication	Strategic Thinking	Problem Solving

Discussion Customization AI Prompt

> How can I customize a discussion for my [grade] [subject] class focused on maintaining privacy while using AI inside and outside the classroom?

For example:

> How can I customize a discussion for fourth-grade digital citizenship learners using role-play to explore basic privacy concerns with AI and classroom technology?

Discussion Differentiation AI Prompt

> How can I adjust a discussion for [grade] [content] learners who [specific needs] and need support in understanding how to maintain privacy while using AI inside and outside the classroom?

For example:

> How can I adjust a discussion for seventh-grade social studies learners who benefit from collaboration and need structured practice to explain AI privacy with real-world examples?

Discussion Extension AI Prompt

> How can I extend a discussion to challenge advanced [grade] [content] learners and deepen their understanding of maintaining privacy while using AI inside and outside the classroom?

For example:

> How can I extend a discussion for tenth-grade computer science learners ready for research who need a chance to apply knowledge about AI privacy in real-world scenarios?

Navigating Bias

Imagine AI tools that, despite their power, inadvertently perpetuate the very biases we strive to eliminate. Consider a middle school teacher who is excited to incorporate a new AI-driven tool into her classroom to help with grading essays. She hopes this tool will save her time and provide objective assessments. However, she soon notices a troubling pattern: Learners from traditionally marginalized ethnicities receive consistently lower scores. Computer scientists Joy Buolamwini and Timnit Gebru (2018) write, "Recent studies demonstrate that machine learning algorithms can discriminate based on classes like race and gender" (p. 1). This raises a critical question: How can we ensure these tools serve as unbiased allies in our quest for fairness, equality, and equity?

Generative AI systems rely on large datasets collected from the internet, which inherently carry societal biases. These biases are often subtle, embedded in the data that AI systems learn from. For example, the Oregon Department of Education (2023) notes that algorithms often privilege certain language variations, exhibit racial and gender biases, and provide a limited or United States–centric lens. These systemic issues highlight the need for educators to approach AI outputs with critical evaluation to prevent the reinforcement of historical inequities in the classroom.

Understanding the origins of these biases is essential for developing strategies to mitigate them. Training data for generative AI systems play a significant role in shaping their outputs. Guidance from Northern Arizona University (2023) states, "Generative AI systems use Large Language Models . . . trained on extensive datasets, primarily consisting of human-generated content. Consequently, these models inherently incorporate human and societal biases" (Arizona Institute for Education & the Economy, 2024, p. 18). This means educators must question whether AI-generated content promotes fairness and equity rather than perpetuates harmful stereotypes.

Bias within AI tools can manifest in multiple ways, from allocative harms, where opportunities are distributed unfairly, to representational harms, which reinforce harmful stereotypes (Maslej et al., 2023). For instance, AI detectors may falsely identify work by non-native English writers as AI-generated, leading to unjust consequences and amplifying systemic inequities (Liang, Yuksekgonul, Mao, Wu, & Zou, 2023). Educators should actively scrutinize these tools and advocate for their equitable development to avoid exacerbating disparities.

Moreover, these challenges remind us of the importance of maintaining a human-in-the-loop approach, as discussed in chapter 1 (page 28). Human oversight ensures that AI complements diverse perspectives and aligns with ethical considerations. Critical thinking and robust evaluation skills are vital in combating algorithmic bias. For educators, this means using AI tools cautiously and always verifying their outputs for accuracy (Washington Office of Superintendent of Public Instruction, 2024, p. 14).

Reflecting on bias is a vital part of our AI exploration. In the following discussion, "AI Algorithmic Bias: Understanding the Impact" (page 52), you'll deepen your understanding and identification of bias. As you delve into the experiments in part 2, you will encounter the BIAS Identification Framework (page 77). The framework helps learners to critically analyze and evaluate AI-produced content, fostering a thoughtful, inclusive mindset. Rooted in widely accepted educational theory and practice, the BIAS Identification Framework prompts learners to consider how bias might appear in subtle or systemic ways and informs educators how to help learners recognize and respond to these patterns.

By applying this approach, educators and learners can collaborate to examine biases, identify errors, and reflect on emotional responses to AI outputs. These practices not only support critical thinking and ethical consideration but also empower AI users to experiment responsibly and guide learners in navigating its complexities. Together, we create a learning environment that values equity, reflection, and informed decision making.

Discussion: AI Algorithmic Bias—Understanding the Impact

Instructions: Use this protocol to plan and adapt a discussion that fits your audience, setting, and goals by reviewing the guidance and prompts prior to facilitating the discussion. This protocol serves as a flexible planning tool designed to help you frame the conversation, customize the experience, and support meaningful participation.

Big Question

What is AI algorithmic bias, who does it affect, where does it occur, when is it most prevalent, and why does it matter?

Introduction

AI algorithmic bias refers to the systematic discrimination that arises from the algorithms used in AI systems. The U.S. Department of Education's Office of Educational Technology (2023) explains the issue as follows:

> Datasets are used to develop AI, and when they are non-representative or contain undesired associations or patterns, resulting AI models may act unfairly in how they detect patterns or automate decisions. Systematic, unwanted unfairness in how a computer detects patterns or automates decisions is called "algorithmic bias." (p. 11)

As AI becomes an integral part of society, its potential to amplify inequalities is a critical issue. Algorithmic bias can lead to unfair outcomes in hiring processes, educational assessments, healthcare decisions, and even legal proceedings. Recognizing and mitigating these biases are essential steps in ensuring AI systems align with principles of fairness, equity, and justice. This discussion invites participants to explore these dimensions of AI bias, its impact, and strategies for creating more ethical systems.

Learning Goals

- Understand the causes and consequences of AI algorithmic bias.
- Identify which groups and sectors are most affected by AI bias.
- Analyze real-world case studies to evaluate where and why biases occur.
- Explore ethical and social implications of AI bias in practical settings.
- Develop strategies to identify, measure, and reduce AI biases.
- Promote fairness and equity in the design and use of AI systems.

Focus Skills

Critical Thinking	Information Literacy	Evaluation and Synthesis
Technological Literacy	Data Analysis	Ethical Reasoning
Communication	Strategic Thinking	Decision Making

Discussion Customization AI Prompt

> How can I customize a discussion for my [grade] [subject] class focused on understanding AI algorithmic bias?

For example:

> How can I customize a discussion for first-grade media literacy learners exploring fairness by comparing how computers make choices and why humans should stay involved?

Discussion Differentiation AI Prompt

> How can I adjust a discussion for [grade] [content] learners who [specific needs] and need [specific support] to understand AI algorithmic bias?

For example:

> How can I adjust a discussion for high school computer science learners who benefit from visuals and need concrete examples to understand bias in data?

Discussion Extension AI Prompt

> How can I extend a discussion to challenge advanced [grade] [content] learners and deepen their understanding of AI algorithmic bias?

For example:

> How can I extend a discussion for sixth-grade English language arts learners ready for inquiry who need a chance to apply ethical reasoning to real-world bias issues?

Reference

Office of Educational Technology. (2023). *Artificial intelligence and the future of teaching and learning: Insights and recommendations.* The U.S. Department of Education. Accessed at https://www.ed.gov/sites/ed/files/documents/ai-report/ai-report.pdf on February 27, 2025.

Ensuring Equity and Access

Reflecting on my early experiences as a STEM teacher on Chicago's West Side, I witnessed firsthand how systemic disparities in underserved communities restricted opportunities and stifled potential. Many of my students, predominantly African American and living in nearby low-income public housing, arrived in my freshman biology class without prior exposure to quality STEM programming. As the U.S. Equal Employment Opportunity Commission (2019) notes, "Students from minority ethnic groups are less likely to have access to high school math and science courses that allow them to build the skills necessary for STEM degrees." These disparities start early; many of my students shared stories of elementary schools without science teachers or where instructional time was diverted to focus on literacy and mathematics. Even when STEM extracurricular programs were available, they often failed to bridge the gap in foundational knowledge.

This lack of access is not just a statistic for me; it is a lived reality. I vividly recall being the only woman of color in most of my undergraduate STEM courses. Statistics from the National Science Foundation's National Center for Science and Engineering Statistics' 2023 report on diversity and STEM provide a stark reminder of the broader inequities. While STEM roles account for 24 percent of positions in the U.S. job market, only 18 percent of those roles are held by individuals identifying as female or African American. This reflects a 25 percent underrepresentation compared to the general population. Disparities deepen when considering intersectional identities—such as women of color, women with disabilities, or individuals of color with disabilities—whose experiences remain underexplored yet are profoundly impacted.

Income disparities further underscore the challenges. Women of color, particularly Black and Hispanic women, earn the lowest wages among their peers in STEM fields, averaging only $57,000 annually compared to $103,300 for Asian men or $90,600 for White men (Fry, Kennedy, & Funk, 2021). These figures reveal not only the unequal access to STEM careers but also the stark inequalities in economic outcomes within the field. For women of color in STEM, this represents a double burden of underrepresentation and undercompensation, compounding barriers to advancement and equity.

Addressing these inequities requires more than individual effort; it demands systemic change. The California Department of Education (2024) emphasizes the importance of "building AI understanding for all learners, regardless of zip code, race, gender, or socioeconomic status, to diversify the STEM pipeline by breaking down barriers and biases in tech fields." Equitable access to AI and emerging technologies offers a chance to close these gaps, ensuring that future generations are better equipped to succeed in an increasingly technological world. By bridging these divides, we can foster a more just and inclusive society.

The digital access divide remains a pressing issue in education, shaping learners' opportunities and future prospects. The Arizona Institute for Education & the Economy (2024) highlights the following:

> Teachers and students in some communities have far better access than others to the devices, internet connectivity, and resources that GenAI requires. Differences in exposure and use of GenAI tools can position some students to gain skills and competencies they will need to thrive in future workplaces while leaving others behind. A lack of AI skills could potentially limit students' career opportunities. (p. 21)

This stark divide underscores the urgent need to address inequities in access to technology.

The Office of Educational Technology's (2024) *National Educational Technology Plan* identifies several dimensions of this digital divide.

- **Technological access** refers to the gap between those who have access to modern technology, such as computers and smartphones, and those who do not.
- **Software accessibility** refers to the variances in access to advanced software and tools critical for learning and navigating the digital age.
- **Skill gaps** refer to the differences in digital literacy and technical proficiency that hinder some individuals from effectively leveraging technology.
- **Internet connectivity** refers to the divide between those with reliable high-speed internet and those with limited or no access.
- **Educational resources** refer to the inequities in access to the educational content and tools that support digital learning and skill development.

More than two decades after I stepped into my biology classroom at Crane High School, the digital divide continues to persist. While the tools and technologies may have evolved, the inequities remain entrenched. The California Department of Education (2024) notes the following:

> Educators and learners who have the skills to leverage AI safely and efficiently will benefit from increased productivity. Conversely, communities who lack access to skill-building experiences with AI at home may not have the opportunity to gain proficiency with this emerging technology if the skills are not also addressed in the school setting.

However, AI also offers powerful solutions to help bridge these gaps. Tools such as language translation for multilingual learners, voice typing for individuals with disabilities, and organizational aids for those needing executive processing support provide opportunities to level the playing field (California Department of Education, 2024). These advancements can enhance learning experiences for marginalized populations, making education more accessible and equitable.

Despite these potential benefits, disparities in access to AI tools and digital resources continue to create barriers to future opportunities for many learners. Addressing this divide requires intentionality, resources, and collaboration, ensuring all learners can build the skills needed to thrive in an increasingly digital world.

Without intentional efforts to promote equitable access to AI technologies, the societal impacts could be catastrophic. The World Economic Forum (2024) warns:

> The convergence of technological advances and geopolitical dynamics will likely create a new set of winners and losers across advanced and developing economies alike. If commercial incentives and geopolitical imperatives, rather than public interest, remain the primary drivers of the development of artificial intelligence (AI) and other frontier technologies, the digital gap between high- and low-income countries will drive a stark disparity in the distribution of related benefits—and risks. (p. 8)

This highlights the urgent need for global cooperation and policies focused on the public good rather than commercial or political priorities. Without such intentionality, these disparities will not only persist but also deepen, creating stark divides in opportunity and prosperity.

One of the most pressing manifestations of these disparities is technological (digital) redlining. *Technological redlining* refers to the discriminatory practice of systematically denying certain groups or communities access to technology and digital services based on factors such as socioeconomic status, race, or geography. Such practices perpetuate existing inequalities and create new barriers to opportunity. As AI and other technologies become more pervasive in our daily lives, addressing technological redlining is not just a moral imperative—it is essential for fostering equity and inclusion.

In engaging with this critical issue, educators, policymakers, and community leaders must explore the multifaceted dimensions of digital inequity, its far-reaching impacts, and actionable strategies to mitigate its effects. The following discussion, "Technological Redlining," provides a structured framework to delve deeper into these challenges and develop solutions that promote fairness in the age of AI.

Discussion: Technological Redlining

Instructions: Use this protocol to plan and adapt a discussion that fits your audience, setting, and goals by reviewing the guidance and prompts prior to facilitating the discussion. This protocol serves as a flexible planning tool designed to help you frame the conversation, customize the experience, and support meaningful participation.

Big Question

How does technological redlining manifest in society, and what are its implications for different communities?

Introduction

Technological (digital) redlining refers to the discriminatory practice where certain groups or communities are systematically denied access to technology and digital services based on socioeconomic status, race, or other factors. This can occur when broadband companies avoid expanding high-speed internet to low-income neighborhoods or when algorithms prioritize ads and digital content for certain demographics, leaving others underserved. Such practices perpetuate existing inequalities and create new barriers to opportunity. As AI and other technologies become more integrated into everyday life, understanding and addressing technological redlining are essential for fostering equity and inclusion. In this discussion, we will examine the systemic impacts of digital inequity and explore strategies to dismantle these barriers.

Learning Goals

- Understand what technological redlining is and how it manifests.
- Explore the different groups and sectors affected by technological redlining.
- Analyze case studies to identify where and when technological redlining occurs.
- Evaluate the ethical and social implications of technological redlining.
- Investigate strategies to identify, measure, and mitigate technological redlining.
- Develop critical thinking about the importance of digital equity and inclusion.

Focus Skills

Critical Thinking	Information Literacy	Evaluation and Synthesis
Technological Literacy	Data Analysis	Ethical Reasoning
Communication	Strategic Thinking	Decision Making

Discussion Customization AI Prompt

How can I customize a discussion for my [grade] [subject] class focused on understanding technological redlining?

For example:

How can I customize a discussion for high school U.S. history learners exploring redlining's roots and its modern form through case studies on broadband access?

Discussion Differentiation AI Prompt

How can I adjust a discussion for [grade] [content] learners who [specific needs] and need [specific support] to understand technological redlining?

For example:

How can I adjust a discussion for university-level civics learners who benefit from active formats and need small-group simulations to explore technological redlining?

Discussion Extension AI Prompt

> How can I extend a discussion to challenge advanced [grade] [content] learners and deepen their understanding of technological redlining?

For example:

> How can I extend a discussion for sixth-grade humanities learners eager for real-world problem solving who need a challenge to explore civic responses to technological redlining?

Setting Norms for AI Use

Establishing clear and thoughtful policies around educational AI usage is a priority. Creating norms for safety, ethics, bias, and acceptable use is not just a formality but a necessary step to ensure that AI integration enhances life and learning while safeguarding liberty. As Mollick (2024) notes, "We need agreed-upon norms and standards for AI's ethical development and use, shaped through an inclusive process representing diverse voices" (p. 44). For educators, this can begin at the classroom level. By involving learners in conversations about ethical AI use and collaboratively setting norms, teachers create an opportunity for learners to take ownership of how AI is used in their learning environment. Small-scale actions—such as guiding learners to develop classroom-specific AI agreements or participating in grade-level discussions—can ripple outward, informing broader practices. This approach complements the broader need for collaborative policy development, ensuring that those directly impacted by these technologies—teachers and learners—have a voice in shaping how AI is used. As the Office of Educational Technology (2023) asserts, "The people most affected by the use of AI in education must be part of the development of the AI model, system, or tool, even if this slows the pace of adoption" (p. 10).

Effective AI policies must balance the drive for advances with the need to mitigate risks. The Office of Educational Technology (2023) notes:

> Policies should focus on the most valuable educational advances while mitigating risks. Trust and safeguarding are particularly important in education because we have an obligation to keep students out of harm's way and safeguard their learning experiences. (p. 10)

This balancing act is familiar to educators, who already manage classroom norms that support both engagement and accountability. Much like classroom norms guide learners' behavior and interactions, thoughtful AI policies can provide clear expectations for using technology to support learning while minimizing harm.

An inclusive approach is critical for creating effective policies. This policy from the Arizona Institute for Education & the Economy (2024) is one example:

> Together, think through the shared values of the community to develop organizational stances on AI integration. Include all stakeholder groups in the development of guiding principles including district leaders, school staff, parents, learners, community partners, tribal leaders, etc. (p. 24)

This mirrors how teachers collaborate with learners to set expectations for classroom conduct, involving learners in the process to ensure buy-in and understanding. Similarly, the California Department of Education (2024) emphasizes the value of involving learners directly, stating, "Involve students in discussions when developing ethical use guidelines at the district, school site, and classroom level" (p. 8).

These collaborative processes ensure that policies and norms are not just top-down directives but are cocreated by those directly impacted.

Teachers already establish classroom norms that foster safe, respectful, and productive learning environments. Consider how educators work with learners to define rules for group work, appropriate technology use, or even behavior during experiments in a science lab. These discussions encourage learners to take ownership of the learning environment and build essential relational skills like accountability and collaboration. Applying this same practice to AI norms allows learners to understand its potential and boundaries, fostering responsible and ethical usage from an early age.

Educators, school leaders, and communities must think critically and work together to shape the future of AI in education. Just as teachers hold conversations about shared expectations with their learners, schools can engage broader communities in discussions about AI's role, forming committees and developing comprehensive policies that reflect shared values. This collaborative, inclusive process ensures AI serves humanity in a way that fosters a safer, more equitable, and innovative learning environment.

As we explore how to craft shared norms and policies for AI usage, it's important to consider the varied contexts where these discussions might occur. For teachers, this could mean working directly with learners to establish classroom-specific guidelines for ethical AI use, paralleling existing practices for creating behavior norms or technology-use agreements. For collaborative teams or administrators, these discussions might take the form of planning meetings or policy committees aimed at aligning AI implementation with broader institutional values.

To provide clarity, this discussion protocol is designed to be adaptable. It can guide educators in framing conversations with their learners, facilitating dialogue among professional teams or communities, or engaging school leadership in strategic planning. Regardless of the setting, the goal is to create a shared understanding of how to use AI ethically and effectively while addressing the unique needs of each context. Engage with the following discussion, "Shared Norms and Policies for AI Experimentation," to reflect on how you can contribute to shaping the norms and policies that will guide AI usage in your classroom, school, or community.

Discussion: Shared Norms and Policies for AI Experimentation

Instructions: Use this protocol to plan and adapt a discussion that fits your audience, setting, and goals by reviewing the guidance and prompts prior to facilitating the discussion. This protocol serves as a flexible planning tool designed to help you frame the conversation, customize the experience, and support meaningful participation.

Big Question

How can we create shared norms and policies for the ethical use of generative AI in our classroom or organization?

Introduction

As generative AI becomes increasingly integrated into educational and organizational settings, educators and leaders must develop clear norms and policies to guide its use. These norms should align with familiar classroom practices, such as setting behavior expectations or establishing collaborative guidelines, and must include input from a diverse range of stakeholders. Involving learners, parents, educators, and administrators ensures that the resulting policies are both inclusive and practical. This process should occur at multiple levels—classroom, school, and district—to ensure consistency and scalability while addressing the unique needs of each context. These policies must tackle ethical considerations, potential biases, privacy concerns, and academic honesty. Crafting these shared norms ensures that generative AI is used responsibly and effectively, fostering environments of trust and innovation. This discussion examines critical elements to consider when developing norms and policies, including when, where, how, by whom, for what purpose, and why generative AI can and should be used.

Learning Goals

- Understand the importance of shared norms and policies for the use of generative AI.
- Explore the ethical, social, and legal considerations involved in experimenting with generative AI.
- Analyze the elements that contribute to effective and responsible use of generative AI.
- Evaluate the impact of these norms and policies on academic honesty, bias, privacy, and ethics.
- Develop strategies to implement and monitor these norms and policies within the classroom or organization.

Focus Skills

Critical Thinking	Information Literacy	Evaluation and Synthesis
Technological Literacy	Collaboration	Ethical Reasoning
Communication	Strategic Thinking	Policy Analysis

Discussion Customization AI Prompt

> How can I customize a discussion for my [grade] [subject] class focused on creating shared norms and policies for the use of generative AI?

For example:

> How can I customize a discussion for ninth-grade algebra learners exploring generative AI in mathematics and creating classroom norms with input from educators, learners, and families?

Discussion Differentiation AI Prompt

How can I adjust a discussion for [grade] [content] learners who [specific needs] and need [specific support] to understand the importance of creating shared norms and policies for generative AI use?

For example:

How can I adjust a discussion for twelfth-grade career and technical education architecture learners new to AI who need scaffolded language to understand shared norms and policies for generative AI?

Discussion Extension AI Prompt

How can I extend a discussion to challenge advanced [grade] [content] learners and deepen their understanding of creating shared norms and policies for generative AI use?

For example:

How can I extend a discussion for sixth-grade library science learners who enjoy collaboration and need a chance to explore diverse perspectives on AI norms and policies?

Reflecting and Taking Action

Every challenge in a hero's journey brings a test of values, a moment for reflection, and an opportunity for growth. In this chapter, you examined the ethical dimensions of AI and grappled with issues of safety, privacy, equity, and responsible decision making. These principles are not just guidelines; they are the foundation for ensuring AI serves as a tool for empowerment rather than harm.

As a leader in education, your role extends beyond implementation. Rather, it is about inspiring others to navigate this transformative era with thoughtfulness, integrity, and a commitment to ethical exploration. To embody this spirit of ethical AI experimentation, reflect on the following steps as you prepare to move forward.

1. Equip yourself with ethical foundations.
    a. Revisit the core principles explored in this chapter, such as responsible data use, equitable access, and bias mitigation.
    b. Reflect on how these principles align with your values and goals as an educator, leader, or learner.
    c. Identify areas within your practice where these ethical dimensions are most critical.
2. Engage in collaborative norm setting.
    a. Use the tools and discussions from this chapter to initiate conversations with learners, colleagues, and community stakeholders.
    b. Work together to create shared norms and policies for AI integration, ensuring inclusivity and mutual understanding.
    c. Recognize that collective dialogue strengthens accountability and empowers diverse perspectives.
3. Experiment with intention.
    a. Begin applying ethical frameworks to small-scale AI experiments in your classroom or organization.
    b. Approach each experiment as a learning opportunity, using both successes and failures to refine your practices.
    c. Stay vigilant about unintended outcomes and adapt thoughtfully to uphold ethical standards.
4. Pursue ongoing learning.
    a. Dive deeper into resources provided in this chapter, using them to expand your understanding of AI's potential and limitations.
    b. Encourage learners and colleagues to critically engage with these ideas, fostering a culture of ethical inquiry and exploration.
    c. Stay attuned to emerging developments in AI and education, positioning yourself as a lifelong learner in this evolving landscape.
5. Reflect on your leadership role.

a. Embrace your role as a guide, shaping how your learning community approaches AI experimentation and ethical integration.
b. Consider how you can inspire others to see AI not as a replacement for human connection but as a tool to enhance it.
c. Commit to leading with integrity, ensuring AI's role in education remains equitable, safe, and aligned with shared values.

Consider the following questions to guide your thinking.

- How can you integrate ethical practices into your AI experiments to address safety, equity, and bias concerns?
- In what ways can involving stakeholders—learners, families, and colleagues—enrich the norms and policies guiding AI use in your context?
- How can experimentation with AI deepen not only your teaching practices but also your role as a leader in education?

Now, it's time to move from principles to practice, bridging the gap between ethical awareness and hands-on experimentation. In the next chapter, you will explore entry-level AI experiments that introduce practical techniques for prompting, evaluating, and refining AI outputs. These foundational skills will set the stage for more advanced AI integration, ensuring that experimentation remains both purposeful and ethical.

Just as every experiment begins with a question, every hero's journey is propelled by discovery and collaboration. Together, we will continue exploring this exciting frontier, building a future where AI serves humanity and education thrives through ethical innovation.

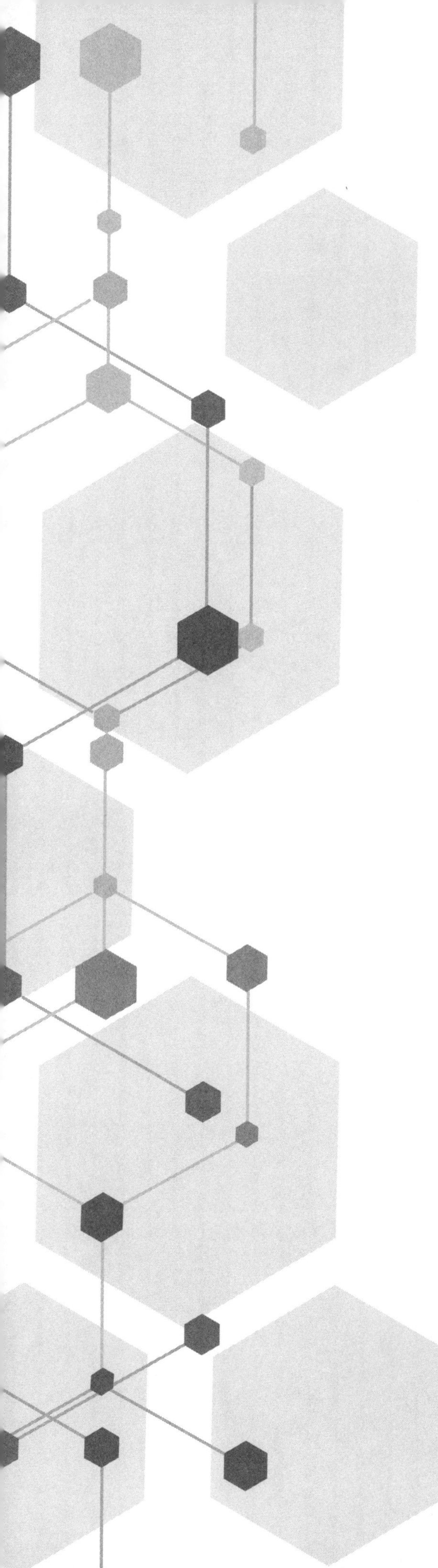

PART 2

Experimenting With AI

Now that part 1 of this book has provided you with a solid foundation, part 2 invites you into the hands-on work of experimenting with generative AI. These scaffolded activities are designed to support creativity, critical thinking, and purposeful use, whether you're just getting started or looking to push further. Each experiment offers adaptable entry points and includes opportunities to reflect, iterate, and explore how AI can enhance learning, collaboration, and classroom engagement.

CHAPTER 3

Entry-Point AI Experiments

Now, let's get ready to experiment with AI! These cross-disciplinary learning experiences introduce generative AI skills through engaging experiments that are adaptable for diverse settings. Each experiment includes clear learning goals, targeted skills, a high-level experimental or instructional protocol, and customizable generative AI prompts. You can customize these experiments and the associated prompts to fit specific content areas, learner ages, and educational goals. They're also suitable for classrooms, professional learning teams, or individual exploration. Additionally, the customizable protocols are designed with cultural uniqueness and differentiation in mind, enabling instructors to meet learners where they are and create meaningful, inclusive experiences.

The experiments and discussions build technical fluency and empower learners with critical thinking, ethical reasoning, and collaborative problem-solving skills. By engaging with these activities, you are preparing learners—and yourself—for meaningful participation in a world increasingly influenced by generative AI.

Building generative AI skills is not just about mastering technology—it's about stepping into the role of a hero in the evolving digital age. Like the hero on a journey, educators and learners must navigate uncharted territories, using curiosity, resilience, and a commitment to ethical action as their guide. Teachers can seamlessly integrate these skills into daily tasks and routines, helping learners build fluency and confidence in navigating this powerful technology. Even for tasks where generative AI might not seem immediately necessary, experimenting with it can unlock opportunities for innovation and deeper engagement. The California Department of Education (2024) writes, "As educators and students learn about AI, they are better able to promote ethical use with attention to potential bias, social impacts, and equity. Education about AI enhances responsible digital citizenship" (p. 3). By embedding generative AI education into everyday activities, teachers equip learners to embrace their own hero's journey—leading responsibly, navigating challenges with integrity, and contributing to a more equitable and informed society. For educators, this integration offers a pathway to model ethical, creative, and purposeful use of technology, inspiring their learners to do the same.

Generative AI is a new frontier for everyone, and these experiments provide a practical way to learn AI by doing, developing skills alongside colleagues, students, or even family members. Educators can use the experiments to cocreate AI-integrative lessons during team planning sessions, modeling usage and sharing learning collegially. Beyond the classroom, these activities can help deepen understanding of AI's potential to enrich personal projects, enhance workflows, and support lifelong learning. By approaching these experiments and discussions flexibly, you can tailor the activities to align with your specific goals, whether fostering engagement, enhancing professional practice, or exploring AI independently.

In classroom settings, you might organize learners into small groups to foster collaboration and shared learning. For workshops or professional learning communities, these experiments can inspire rich discussions and hands-on exploration with generative AI tools. Their open-ended structure enables you to adjust the sequence, tasks, or skill focus, ensuring alignment with your goals and learners' needs.

In this chapter, learners begin their AI journey by building essential skills for understanding and interacting with AI tools. These entry-point experiments focus on foundational concepts like crafting effective prompts, identifying bias, and evaluating AI-generated content for clarity and fairness. Just as every journey begins with orientation and early discovery, this chapter helps learners build confidence, develop critical habits, and establish ethical approaches that will guide deeper exploration ahead.

Introducing the Experiments

This section introduces key tools developed by TechEd Maven Consulting to support your journey as an AI educator and to empower your learners in mastering foundational AI skills. These tools include the following.

- **The PROMPT Recipe** is a step-by-step framework for crafting thoughtful, precise prompts to guide meaningful interactions with AI tools. It is in the section titled "Engineering the AI Prompt Recipe" (page 70).
- **The CHECK AI Framework** is a systematic approach to critically evaluating AI-generated outputs for clarity, accuracy, and ethical considerations. It is in the section titled "Applying the CHECK AI Framework" (page 73).
- **The BIAS Identification Framework** is a practical guide for identifying and addressing biases in AI outputs, promoting fairness and inclusivity. It is in the section titled "Identifying and Addressing Bias in AI" (page 77).

These three tools are interwoven into the experiment protocols throughout the book, providing consistent support for your explorations. Additionally, they serve as reference points for extending experimentation beyond the book's structured activities. Downloadable versions of these tools are available at www.TechEdMaven.com/ai-skills, offering further resources to customize and adapt the experiments to your specific needs.

Interwoven throughout the experiments are key discussions designed to deepen understanding, provoke critical thinking, and encourage ethical reflection. While the text suggests placements for these discussions, consider adapting them to the natural flow of your learning journey. As the leader of your learning community, your insight and creativity play a vital role in tailoring these activities to maximize their relevance and impact.

To begin your learning journey, you will develop foundational skills in crafting effective prompts by mastering the PROMPT Recipe. This method will set the stage for consistently creating high-quality prompts, a crucial factor in maximizing your interactions with AI. It's equally important to examine AI responses critically, for accuracy, bias, and fairness. The California Department of Education (2024) recommends embedding "prompt engineering and fact-checking skills into digital literacy lessons" (p. 13). To support this critical analysis, we will also explore the CHECK AI Framework and BIAS Identification Framework, equipping you to evaluate AI-generated content with a focus on clarity, accuracy, and ethical considerations.

When working with AI tools, learners must also engage in the iterative feedback process to improve outputs. This involves providing the AI with refined instructions based on its initial responses, creating a cycle of improvement that mirrors effective learning practices. Learners can use the CHECK AI and BIAS Identification frameworks to screen for areas requiring feedback, such as factual accuracy, clarity, or bias. Additionally, they should rely on their own intuition and professional judgment to identify other areas for refinement. This iterative approach not only enhances the quality of AI outputs but also deepens learners' analytical and critical thinking skills, fostering a more thoughtful and effective use of AI tools.

These activities are designed to be dynamic and adaptable. Whether you're leading a middle school classroom, facilitating a professional development workshop, or exploring AI independently, you can tailor these protocols to suit the unique needs and goals of your learning environment. This resource interweaves experiments and discussions at natural points in the learning journey. These flexible activities empower you to customize tasks and align them with your learners' needs, ensuring AI integration enhances their educational experience. As the architect of your learning community's AI strategy, you can chart a purposeful path that supports every learner. Together, we can explore, innovate, and lead with integrity.

EXPERIMENT

Engineering the AI PROMPT Recipe

In this experiment, participants dive into the AI PROMPT Recipe, which is a structured method for creating effective AI prompts. By mastering this recipe, learners develop essential skills in prompt engineering and iterative refinement, equipping them to navigate AI as a dynamic tool for education, creativity, and professional problem solving.

Whether you're guiding learners in classroom activities, collaborating on curriculum design, or applying AI to solve everyday challenges, this foundational experiment equips you with the tools and insights you need to integrate AI meaningfully.

Introduction to the PROMPT Recipe

The PROMPT Recipe is a step-by-step guide to crafting high-quality AI prompts that lead to meaningful and effective interactions. Each component of the recipe builds the foundation for clear, focused, and creative communication with AI.

- **Purpose:** Clearly define the purpose of your prompts to guide your interactions and ensure focused and purposeful responses from AI.
- **Relevant information:** Provide context and guidance to AI by including relevant details, key words, and background information in your prompts.
- **Open-endedness:** Keep your prompts open-ended to encourage thoughtful and creative responses from AI, fostering a deeper exploration of ideas.
- **Meaning and clarity:** Craft prompts that are clear and meaningful, using concise and precise language to ensure AI understands your intentions accurately.
- **Personalization:** Infuse your unique voice and style into your prompts, creating engaging and authentic conversations with AI.
- **Thought-provoking:** Spark curiosity and stimulate deeper thinking with thought-provoking prompts that encourage AI to explore complex ideas, share opinions, and imagine new scenarios.

The objective of this experiment is to help learners develop the ability to use the PROMPT Recipe to create effective AI prompts, improve their evaluation and critical thinking skills, and foster an appreciation for the importance of iterative feedback in optimizing AI outputs.

Learning Goals

This experiment aligns with the following learning objectives.

- Understand the role and capabilities of generative AI in responding to well-crafted prompts.

- Develop skills in using the PROMPT Recipe to create high-quality AI prompts.
- Enhance communication and prompt engineering skills through AI-assisted prompt creation and evaluation.

Focus Skills

Critical Thinking	Prompt Engineering	Problem Solving
Digital Literacy	Evaluation and Synthesis	Communication
Strategic Planning	Reflective Thinking	Analytical Thinking

Experiment Protocol

Use the following steps to engage with this experiment.

1. Introduce the AI PROMPT Recipe and provide a detailed explanation of each component.
2. Model for learners how to use the generative AI tool, including the utilization of the PROMPT Recipe.
3. Discuss the importance of well-crafted prompts in effective AI interactions. Highlight examples of successful prompt engineering.
4. Have learners work independently or in small groups (for example, two to four participants) based on their needs and the available resources, ensuring each participant or group has access to the generative AI tool of your choice.
5. Explain how you will evaluate learners. Share the evaluation criteria (for example, clarity, alignment with goals, creativity) and clarify whether feedback will come from peers, the educator, or both.
6. Assign learners or groups a simple task related to your current instructional goals, such as generating an AI response to a basic question, summarizing a concept, or drafting creative ideas. The goal is to practice applying the PROMPT Recipe to create effective prompts.
7. Have learners use the AI tool to generate responses based on their prompts.
8. Instruct learners to critically evaluate the AI-generated responses, checking for clarity, accuracy, and feasibility.
9. Ask learners to provide iterative feedback to the AI, refining their prompts based on the evaluation to improve the quality of the AI-generated responses.
10. Facilitate a discussion on the effectiveness of the PROMPT Recipe and iterative feedback in creating high-quality AI prompts, addressing any challenges or improvements.

Experiment Customization AI Prompt

Customize the following prompt to collaborate with AI

How can I customize an AI-assisted prompt creation and evaluation learning experiment for my [grade] [subject] class focused on [specific task]? The learning experiment involves learners working individually or in groups with access to a generative AI tool to create effective prompts using the PROMPT Recipe. They will specify the task, generate prompts, use the AI to provide responses, and evaluate the AI-generated outputs. The PROMPT Recipe includes the following elements:

- **P**urpose: Clearly define the purpose of your prompts to guide your interactions and ensure focused and purposeful responses from AI.
- **R**elevant Information: Provide context and guidance to AI by including relevant details, key words, and background information in your prompts.
- **O**pen-Endedness: Keep your prompts open-ended to encourage thoughtful and creative responses from AI, fostering a deeper exploration of ideas.
- **M**eaningful and Clear: Craft prompts that are clear and meaningful, using concise and precise language to ensure AI understands your intentions accurately.
- **P**ersonalization: Infuse your unique voice and style into your prompts, creating engaging and authentic conversations with AI.
- **T**hought-Provoking: Spark curiosity and stimulate deeper thinking with thought-provoking prompts that encourage AI to explore complex ideas, share opinions, and imagine new scenarios.

Adapt the learning objectives, activities, and assessments to fit my classroom context. Consider intrapersonal and interpersonal skill development along with cultural uniqueness.

Experiment Differentiation AI Prompt

Customize the following prompt to collaboratively differentiate with AI.

How can I adjust a generative AI-assisted prompt creation and evaluation learning experiment for [grade] [content] learners who [specific needs] and need [specific support]? The current activity entails learners working individually or in groups with access to a generative AI tool to create effective prompts using the PROMPT Recipe. They will specify the task, generate prompts, use the AI to provide responses, and evaluate the AI-generated outputs. The PROMPT Recipe includes the following.

- **P**urpose: Clearly define the purpose of your prompts to guide your interactions and ensure focused and purposeful responses from AI.
- **R**elevant Information: Provide context and guidance to AI by including relevant details, key words, and background information in your prompts.

- **O**pen-Endedness: Keep your prompts open-ended to encourage thoughtful and creative responses from AI, fostering a deeper exploration of ideas.
- **M**eaningful and Clear: Craft prompts that are clear and meaningful, using concise and precise language to ensure AI understands your intentions accurately.
- **P**ersonalization: Infuse your unique voice and style into your prompts, creating engaging and authentic conversations with AI.
- **T**hought-Provoking: Spark curiosity and stimulate deeper thinking with thought-provoking prompts that encourage AI to explore complex ideas, share opinions, and imagine new scenarios.

Integration Examples

Explore integration examples across various learning contexts.

- **English:** Learners use the PROMPT Recipe to craft prompts for a creative story. They analyze AI-generated ideas for clarity and creativity, refining prompts to improve specificity and engagement.
- **Elementary social studies:** Learners use the PROMPT Recipe to create prompts asking AI to summarize a classroom topic or event. The teacher models AI use, and learners refine prompts to improve clarity and relevance.
- **Science:** Learners use the PROMPT Recipe to craft prompts for generating scientific problem-solving ideas. They refine prompts to focus on practicality and feasibility in AI-generated suggestions.
- **Health education:** Learners use the PROMPT Recipe to create prompts for generating strategies to promote healthy habits. They refine prompts to align with relevance and clarity in health-related outputs.
- **Professional learning:** Educators use the PROMPT Recipe to craft prompts for generating ideas to improve learner engagement. They iteratively refine prompts to enhance alignment with instructional goals.

EXPERIMENT

Applying the CHECK AI Framework

In a world increasingly shaped by AI, it's more important than ever that users are able to evaluate its outputs. This experiment empowers learners to assess AI responses with rigor, sharpening their critical thinking while enhancing their understanding of effective AI communication. These foundational skills are essential for navigating the evolving role of AI in education, work, and beyond.

Introduction to the CHECK AI Framework

The CHECK AI Framework is a practical tool designed to elevate the quality of AI interactions. By focusing on clarity, helpfulness, ethics, consistency, and knowledgeability, this structured approach ensures learners can evaluate and refine AI-generated content, fostering reliability and trust in AI tools. This framework should be utilized to review content created by generative AI before accepting or applying the output.

- **Clear:** Is the AI answer easy to understand? Make sure it is straightforward and free from confusion.
- **Helpful:** Does the AI answer provide useful information and thoroughly cover the prompt's requirements?
- **Ethical:** Is the AI answer fair and respectful? Ensure it avoids biases and respects privacy.
- **Consistent:** Does the AI answer remain the same when asked similar questions? Check consistency and reliability.
- **Knowledgeable:** Is the AI answer based on accurate information? Verify the facts and the usefulness of the response.

By applying the CHECK AI Framework, learners develop a structured approach to evaluating AI-generated content, focusing on clarity, ethics, and accuracy. This hands-on practice not only improves the quality of AI outputs but also fosters critical evaluation skills essential for navigating AI-driven tools effectively across educational and professional contexts.

Learning Goals

This experiment aligns with the following learning objectives.

- Understand the role and capabilities of generative AI in responding to prompts.
- Learn to use the CHECK AI Framework to evaluate the clarity, helpfulness, ethics, consistency, and knowledgeability of AI-generated responses.
- Enhance critical evaluation and communication skills through AI-assisted content refinement.

Focus Skills

Critical Thinking	Prompt Engineering	Problem Solving
Digital Literacy	Evaluation and Synthesis	Communication
Ethical Reasoning	Reflective Thinking	Analytical Thinking

Experiment Protocol

Use the following steps to engage with this experiment.

1. If necessary, model how to use the generative AI tool and review how to use the PROMPT Recipe Framework.
2. Introduce the CHECK AI Framework and provide a detailed explanation of each component.
3. Discuss the importance of evaluating AI responses for clarity, helpfulness, ethics, consistency, and knowledgeability. Highlight examples of successful AI evaluations.
4. Have learners work independently or in small groups (for example, two to four participants) based on their needs and the available resources, ensuring each participant or group has access to the generative AI tool of your choice.
5. Explain how you will evaluate learners. Share the evaluation criteria (for example, clarity, alignment with goals, creativity) and clarify whether feedback will come from peers, the educator, or both.
6. Assign each learner or group a specific task to create AI prompts using the PROMPT Recipe. This could include writing prompts, project planning prompts, problem-solving prompts, and so on.
7. Have learners use the AI tool to generate responses based on their prompts.
8. Learners should use the CHECK AI Framework to evaluate the AI-generated output, then provide iterative feedback by refining their prompts and responses based on that evaluation to improve overall quality.
9. Facilitate a discussion on the effectiveness of the CHECK AI Framework in creating high-quality AI interactions, addressing any challenges or improvements.

Experiment Customization AI Prompt

Customize the following prompt to collaborate with AI.

> How can I customize an AI-assisted evaluation and refinement learning experiment for my [grade] [subject] class focused on [specific task]? The learning experiment involves learners working individually or in groups with access to a generative AI tool to evaluate and refine AI-generated responses using the CHECK AI Framework. The CHECK AI Framework includes the following elements.
>
> - **C**lear: Is the AI answer easy to understand? Make sure it is straightforward and free from confusion.
> - **H**elpful: Does the AI answer provide useful information and thoroughly cover the prompt's requirements?

- **E**thical: Is the AI answer fair and respectful? Ensure it avoids biases and respects privacy.
- **C**onsistent: Does the AI answer remain the same when asked similar questions? Check consistency and reliability.
- **K**nowledgeable: Is the AI answer based on accurate information? Verify the facts and the usefulness of the response.

Adapt the learning objectives, activities, and assessments to fit my classroom context. Consider intrapersonal and interpersonal skill development along with cultural uniqueness.

Experiment Differentiation AI Prompt

Customize the following prompt to collaboratively differentiate with AI.

How can I adjust a generative AI-assisted evaluation and refinement activity for [grade] [content] learners who [specific needs] and need [specific support]? The current activity entails learners working individually or in groups with access to a generative AI tool to evaluate and refine AI-generated responses using the CHECK AI Framework. The CHECK AI Framework includes the following elements.

- **C**lear: Is the AI answer easy to understand? Make sure it is straightforward and free from confusion.
- **H**elpful: Does the AI answer provide useful information and thoroughly cover the prompt's requirements?
- **E**thical: Is the AI answer fair and respectful? Ensure it avoids biases and respects privacy.
- **C**onsistent: Does the AI answer remain the same when asked similar questions? Check consistency and reliability.
- **K**nowledgeable: Is the AI answer based on accurate information? Verify the facts and the usefulness of the response.

Integration Examples

Explore integration examples across various learning contexts.

- **Social studies:** Learners apply the CHECK AI Framework to analyze AI-generated policy recommendations. They evaluate the recommendations for ethical considerations, relevance, and potential societal impact, refining prompts for deeper insights.
- **Mathematics:** Learners use the CHECK AI Framework to evaluate AI-generated solutions to mathematical problems. They assess responses for logical flow, accuracy, and clarity, refining prompts to improve outputs.

- **Elementary visual arts:** Learners apply the CHECK AI Framework to evaluate teacher-generated AI ideas for a class art project. They assess the ideas for creativity and clarity, suggesting refinements to improve the prompt.
- **Psychology:** Learners use the CHECK AI Framework to evaluate AI-generated psychological study designs. They assess the designs for clarity, ethical considerations, and validity, refining prompts and outputs as needed.
- **Professional learning:** Educators use the CHECK AI Framework to evaluate AI-generated ideas for interdisciplinary lesson planning. They assess the ideas for clarity, alignment with standards, and ethical inclusivity, refining prompts collaboratively.

EXPERIMENT

Identifying and Addressing Bias in AI

Bias in AI-generated content affects fairness, inclusivity, and trust in technology. This experiment empowers learners to uncover and address these biases by combining practical tools with critical thinking. Using the PROMPT Recipe and the CHECK AI Framework, participants will evaluate AI responses for clarity, consistency, and fairness. They will also apply the BIAS Identification Framework to recognize subtle biases and develop strategies for reducing their impact.

Through this hands-on activity, educators will gain insights into identifying and addressing biases that may influence their own use of AI tools in instructional design, assessment, or classroom interactions. This process encourages reflective practice, equipping educators to ensure their applications of AI foster equity and inclusivity. By developing these skills, both educators and learners will be better prepared to engage with AI responsibly across educational and societal contexts.

Introduction to the BIAS Identification Framework

The BIAS Identification Framework empowers users to recognize and address biases in AI-generated content. By applying this framework, participants critically examine AI outputs and refine their processes to create responses that reflect greater fairness and inclusivity.

- **Be aware:** The first step is understanding and recognizing different types of bias. It's important to be mindful of common biases such as gender, racial, and confirmation bias. By becoming aware of these biases, stakeholders can better anticipate and mitigate their impact on AI outputs.
- **Identify:** Users should spot potential biases in AI responses. This includes looking for biased language, unfair treatment of certain groups, or the

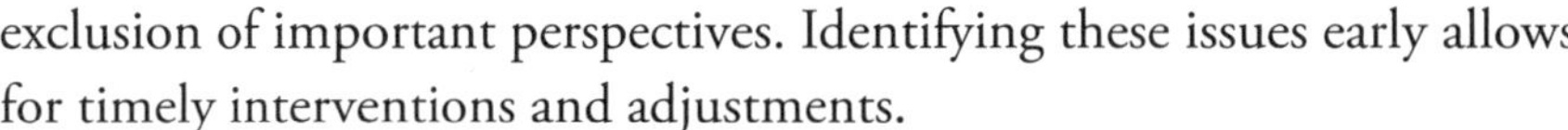

exclusion of important perspectives. Identifying these issues early allows for timely interventions and adjustments.

- **Analyze:** Users must critically examine AI outputs. Ask questions like, "Who benefits or is harmed by this output? Does the output reinforce any stereotypes?" This analytical approach helps learners understand the broader implications of AI decisions and promotes fairness.
- **Seek solutions:** Finally, find ways to reduce bias. This involves revising AI prompts, using inclusive data, and considering diverse viewpoints. By seeking solutions, users can improve the fairness and inclusivity of AI systems.

By the end of this experiment, participants will be equipped to critically evaluate AI-generated contcnt, rccognizc bias, and apply practical strategies to promote fairness and inclusivity in their AI interactions.

Learning Goals

This experiment aligns with the following learning objectives.

- Understand the role and capabilities of generative AI in responding to well-crafted prompts.
- Develop skills in using the PROMPT Recipe to create high-quality AI prompts.
- Learn to use the CHECK AI Framework to evaluate the clarity, helpfulness, ethics, consistency, and knowledgeability of AI-generated responses.
- Apply the BIAS Identification Framework to identify and address biases in AI-generated content.
- Enhance communication and prompt engineering, critical evaluation, and ethical reasoning skills through comprehensive AI-assisted content creation and refinement.

Focus Skills

Critical Thinking	Prompt Engineering	Problem Solving
Digital Literacy	Evaluation and Synthesis	Communication
Ethical Reasoning	Reflective Thinking	Analytical Thinking

Experiment Protocol

Use the following steps to engage with this experiment.

1. If necessary, model how to use the generative AI tool as well as the PROMPT Recipe and CHECK AI Framework.

2. Introduce the BIAS Identification Framework and explain each component in detail.
3. Have learners work independently or in small groups (for example, two to four participants) based on their needs and the available resources, ensuring each participant or group has access to the generative AI tool of your choice.
4. Explain how you will evaluate learners. Share the evaluation criteria (for example, clarity, alignment with goals, creativity) and clarify whether feedback will come from peers, the educator, or both.
5. Assign each learner or group a specific task to create AI prompts using the PROMPT Recipe. This could include writing prompts, project planning prompts, problem-solving prompts, and so on.
6. Have learners use the AI tool to generate responses based on their prompts.
7. Instruct learners to critically evaluate the AI-generated responses using the CHECK AI Framework, checking for clarity, helpfulness, ethics, consistency, and knowledgeability.
8. Guide learners in applying the BIAS Identification Framework to identify and address any biases in the AI-generated content.
9. Ask learners to provide iterative feedback to the AI, refining their prompts and responses based on the evaluation to improve the quality of the AI-generated outputs.
10. Facilitate a discussion on the effectiveness of the PROMPT Recipe, CHECK AI Framework, and BIAS Identification Framework in creating high-quality and ethical AI interactions, addressing any challenges or improvements.

Experiment Customization AI Prompt

Customize the following prompt to collaborate with AI.

> How can I customize an AI-assisted prompt creation, evaluation, and bias identification learning experiment for my [grade] [subject] class focused on [specific task]? The activity entails learners working individually or in groups with access to a generative AI tool to create effective prompts. Learners will evaluate the AI-generated outputs using the BIAS Identification Framework.
>
> The BIAS Identification Framework includes the following elements.
>
> - **B**e Aware: Understand and recognize different types of bias.
> - **I**dentify: Spot potential biases in AI responses.
> - **A**nalyze: Critically examine AI outputs to understand broader implications.
> - **S**eek Solutions: Find ways to reduce bias and improve fairness.
>
> Adapt the learning objectives, activities, and assessments to fit my classroom context. Consider intrapersonal and interpersonal skill development along with cultural uniqueness.

Experiment Differentiation AI Prompt

Customize the following prompt to collaboratively differentiate with AI.

How can I adjust a generative AI-assisted prompt creation, evaluation, and bias identification activity for [grade] [content] learners who [specific needs] and need [specific support]? The activity entails learners working individually or in groups with access to a generative AI tool to create effective prompts. Learners will evaluate the AI-generated outputs using the BIAS Identification Framework.

The BIAS Identification Framework includes the following elements.

- **B**e Aware: Understand and recognize different types of bias.
- **I**dentify: Spot potential biases in AI responses.
- **A**nalyze: Critically examine AI outputs to understand broader implications.
- **S**eek Solutions: Find ways to reduce bias and improve fairness.

Integration Examples

Explore integration examples across various learning contexts.

- **History:** Learners use the BIAS Identification Framework to analyze AI-generated summaries of primary or secondary sources on a historical event. They identify biases in the representation of perspectives and refine prompts to achieve more balanced outputs.
- **Elementary media studies:** The teacher models how AI generates image descriptions or search results. Learners apply the BIAS Identification Framework to identify biased representations and discuss how to improve prompts or outputs for inclusivity.
- **Physical education:** Learners evaluate AI-generated fitness plans for inclusivity and accessibility. They apply the BIAS Identification Framework to identify biases in suggested activities, such as favoring able-bodied individuals, and revise prompts to address diverse physical needs.
- **Business:** Learners use the BIAS Identification Framework to evaluate AI-generated marketing strategies for inclusivity and fairness. They identify potential biases, such as targeting specific demographics while excluding others, and refine prompts to develop more equitable approaches.
- **Professional learning:** Educators use the BIAS Identification Framework to analyze AI-generated assessment ideas for fairness and equity. They identify biases that might affect different learner groups and collaboratively refine prompts to create more inclusive assessments.

In the following discussion, "AI and Human Emotions—Benefits and Risks," learners consider how AI can sharpen their skills and creativity without replacing their own thinking.

Discussion: AI and Human Emotions—Benefits and Risks

Instructions: Use this protocol to plan and adapt a discussion that fits your audience, setting, and goals by reviewing the guidance and prompts prior to facilitating the discussion. This protocol serves as a flexible planning tool designed to help you frame the conversation, customize the experience, and support meaningful participation.

Big Question

How might AI positively or negatively impact human emotions and feelings in our classroom and in the world at large?

Learning Goals

- Understand how AI can influence human emotions and feelings.
- Identify the potential positive and negative emotional impacts of AI in various contexts.
- Explore the role of AI in enhancing emotional well-being and mental health.
- Discuss ethical considerations related to AI's influence on emotions.
- Investigate the importance of empathy and emotional intelligence in AI design.
- Develop strategies for using AI to support emotional well-being in educational and personal settings.
- Examine the psychological risks associated with AI interactions.
- Explore the balance between technological benefits and emotional health in AI usage.

Focus Skills

Critical Thinking	Decision Making	Research Skills
Technological Literacy	Emotional Intelligence	Ethical Reasoning
Communication	Strategic Thinking	Problem Solving

Discussion Customization AI Prompt

> How can I customize a discussion for my [grade] [subject] class focused on how AI might positively or negatively impact human emotions and feelings in our classroom and in the world at large?

For example:

> How can I customize a discussion for fifth-grade health learners exploring emotions and digital tools who need a creative way to imagine how AI could support well-being?

Discussion Differentiation AI Prompt

> How can I adjust a discussion for [grade] [content] learners who [specific needs] and need support in understanding how AI might positively or negatively impact human emotions and feelings in our classroom and in the world at large?

For example:

> How can I adjust a discussion for eleventh-grade occupational skill learners who benefit from creative expression and need options to show understanding of AI's emotional impact?

Discussion Extension AI Prompt

How can I extend a discussion to challenge advanced [grade] [content] learners and deepen their understanding of how AI might positively or negatively impact human emotions and feelings in our classroom and in the world at large?

For example:

How can I extend a discussion for seventh-grade English language arts learners who are curious about current events and emerging technologies and need a structured opportunity to compare viewpoints about AI and emotions?

EXPERIMENT

Brainstorming With AI

Collaboration with AI is transforming how we approach creativity and innovation. In this experiment, learners team up with AI tools to brainstorm solutions to challenges across disciplines—from art and literature to science and technology. This introductory activity sets the stage for ongoing idea generation and can be seamlessly integrated into any subject area or real-world context.

Educators also gain insight into how AI can support brainstorming in lesson planning, interdisciplinary projects, and professional development. By engaging with this experiment, participants build the foundational skills needed to collaborate effectively with AI in both personal and professional settings.

Learning Goals

This experiment aligns with the following learning objectives.

- Understand the basics of generative AI and its applications.
- Develop skills in brainstorming with AI tools.
- Learn to use the PROMPT Recipe for effective AI interaction.
- Apply the CHECK AI Framework to review and refine AI-generated content.
- Identify and address biases using the BIAS Identification Framework.

Focus Skills

Critical Thinking	Creativity	Problem Solving
Digital Literacy	Collaboration	Communication
Reflective Thinking	Ethical Reasoning	Analytical Thinking

Experiment Protocol

Use the following steps to engage with this experiment.

1. If necessary, model how to use the generative AI tool as well as the PROMPT Recipe, CHECK AI, and BIAS Identification frameworks.
2. Have learners work independently or in small groups (for example, two to four participants) based on their needs and the available resources, ensuring each participant or group has access to the generative AI tool of your choice.
3. Assign each group a specific area or topic as the focus for their brainstorming.
4. Explain how you will evaluate learners. Share the evaluation criteria (for example, clarity, alignment with goals, creativity) and clarify whether feedback will come from peers, the educator, or both.

5. Remind learners to apply the PROMPT Recipe to ensure their prompt inputs are comprehensive and clear. Direct them to use the generative AI tool to brainstorm ideas and document the resulting outputs effectively.
6. Learners should critically evaluate and iteratively refine the AI-generated content, checking for accuracy, relevance, and potential biases. Encourage learners to apply the CHECK AI and BIAS Identification frameworks to ensure clarity, accuracy, and ethical considerations in their outputs.
7. Groups can select their top responses, along with a review of their thoughts on the process, to share with the class.
8. Facilitate a discussion on the feasibility, creativity, and ethical considerations of learners' ideas.

Experiment Customization AI Prompt

Customize the following prompt to collaborate with AI.

> How can I customize an AI brainstorming learning experiment for my [grade] [subject] class focused on [topic]? The learning experiment involves learners working in small groups with access to a generative AI tool to brainstorm and document ideas. I plan to divide learners into small groups and assign each group a specific topic. Groups will select their top ideas and review their thought process to share with the class. In closing, I plan to facilitate a discussion on feasibility, creativity, and ethical considerations, and provide constructive feedback from teachers or peers. Adapt the learning objectives, activities, and assessments to fit my classroom context. Consider intrapersonal and interpersonal skill development along with cultural uniqueness.

Experiment Differentiation AI Prompt

Customize the following prompt to collaboratively differentiate with AI.

> How can I adjust an AI brainstorming activity for [grade] [content] learners who [specific needs] and need [specific support]? The current activity entails learners working in small groups with access to a generative AI tool, brainstorming ideas within a specific topic, and documenting their outputs. The current process includes a tutorial on using the AI tool, group discussions to share top ideas, and a class presentation with feedback on feasibility, creativity, and ethical considerations.

Integration Examples

Explore integration examples across various learning contexts.

- **Economics:** Learners brainstorm with AI to generate creative budgeting strategies for personal or community needs. They evaluate ideas for feasibility, ethical considerations, and inclusivity, sharing refined solutions with the class.

- **Elementary mathematics:** The teacher models brainstorming with AI to explore ways mathematics helps solve everyday problems, like sharing snacks fairly or organizing classroom jobs. Learners discuss and refine ideas based on fairness, logic, and practicality.
- **Visual art:** Learners use generative AI to brainstorm ideas for a public art installation representing community values. They refine and evaluate ideas for creativity, inclusivity, and feasibility, sharing their final concepts with peers for feedback.
- **Media studies:** Learners collaborate with AI to brainstorm concepts for social media campaigns, addressing topics like mental health or environmental awareness. They evaluate ideas for originality, inclusivity, and potential impact, selecting their top campaigns to present.
- **Professional learning:** Educators collaborate with AI to brainstorm interdisciplinary project ideas, integrating topics across science, art, and social studies. They evaluate the AI-generated ideas for alignment with curriculum goals, feasibility, and inclusivity, refining them into actionable plans.

EXPERIMENT

Testing AI Versus Human Creativity

This experiment challenges learners to test their creativity and problem-solving skills against AI. By engaging in the Remote Associates Test (RAT), a classic psychological measure of creative association, learners will explore their cognitive processes and compare them with AI's capabilities. This activity highlights the interplay between human ingenuity and machine learning, fostering a deeper understanding of both.

The RAT, developed by Sarnoff A. Mednick and Martha T. Mednick in 1967, evaluates creative convergent thinking by asking participants to connect three unrelated words (for example, *cake*, *blue*, and *cottage*) with a fourth word (for example, *cheese*) that forms a compound word or common phrase. It has been a cornerstone in psychological research on creativity and associative thinking (Mednick, 1968).

For learners, this experiment offers a unique opportunity to examine the nature of creativity and intelligence. For educators, it serves as a tool to inspire learners while showcasing the potential of AI as a collaborator in cognitive exploration and critical thinking.

Learning Goals

This experiment aligns with the following learning objectives.

- Understand the basics of the Remote Associates Test and the testing outcomes of humans versus AI.

- Develop skills in using AI tools to perform creative tasks.
- Learn to use the PROMPT Recipe for effective AI interaction.
- Apply the CHECK AI Framework to review and refine AI-generated content.
- Identify and address biases in AI using the BIAS Identification Framework.

Focus Skills

Critical Thinking	Creativity	Digital Literacy
Problem Solving	Communication	Collaboration
Reflective Thinking	Analytical Thinking	Ethical Reasoning

Experiment Protocol

Use the following steps to engage with this experiment.

1. If necessary, model how to use the generative AI tool as well as the PROMPT Recipe, CHECK AI, and BIAS Identification frameworks.
2. Provide a brief introduction to the RAT and its significance in cognitive psychology. Utilize AI to assist you in preparation, appropriate to your learners.
3. Have learners work independently or in small groups (for example, two to four participants) based on their needs and the available resources, ensuring each participant or group has access to the generative AI tool of your choice.
4. Explain how you will evaluate learners. Share the evaluation criteria (for example, clarity, alignment with goals, creativity) and clarify whether feedback will come from peers, the educator, or both.
5. Assign each group a set of RAT problems to solve without AI assistance. Utilize AI to assist in creating the RAT words.
6. Remind learners to apply the PROMPT Recipe to ensure their prompt inputs are comprehensive and clear. Direct them to use the generative AI tool to solve the same set of RAT problems.
7. Have learners document their own solutions and the AI-generated solutions for comparison.
8. Ask learners to critically evaluate and iteratively refine the AI-generated content, checking for accuracy, relevance, and potential biases. Encourage learners to apply the CHECK AI and BIAS Identification frameworks to ensure clarity, accuracy, and ethical considerations in their outputs.
9. Facilitate a discussion comparing the performance, creativity, and approaches of humans versus AI.

Experiment Customization AI Prompt

Customize the following prompt to collaborate with AI.

> How can I customize a Remote Associates Test (RAT) learning experiment for my [grade] [subject] class focused on comparing human and AI performance focused on [specific topic]? The learning experiment involves learners working in small groups to solve RAT problems and then using a generative AI tool to solve the same problems. Learners will compare their solutions with the AI's and discuss the results. Adapt the learning objectives, activities, and assessments to fit my classroom context. Consider intrapersonal and interpersonal skill development along with cultural uniqueness.

Experiment Differentiation AI Prompt

Customize the following prompt to collaboratively differentiate with AI.

> How can I adjust a Remote Associates Test (RAT) learning experiment for [grade] [content] focused on [specific topic] for learners who [specific needs] and need [specific support]? The current activity entails learners working in small groups to solve RAT problems and then using a generative AI tool to solve the same problems. Learners will compare their solutions with the AI's and discuss the results. The process includes a tutorial on using the AI tool, group discussions, and a class presentation with feedback on creativity and problem-solving approaches.

Integration Examples

Explore integration examples across various learning contexts.

- **English:** Learners solve RAT problems (for example, connect *light*, *book*, and *match* to *fire*) to brainstorm creative story elements. They use the AI tool to generate alternative associations for the same RAT problems, comparing how their ideas and the AI's inspire different themes, symbols, or plot points.
- **Engineering:** Learners use RAT prompts (for example, connect *paper*, *metal*, and *stand* to *clip*) to brainstorm innovative product designs. They compare their solutions with AI-generated outputs for creativity, feasibility, and alignment with engineering principles, refining their ideas collaboratively.
- **Visual art:** Learners solve RAT-style prompts (for example, connect *cloud*, *train*, and *glass* to *steam*) to brainstorm artistic concepts. They then use AI to generate additional ideas and compare outputs for originality, practical application in art projects, and inclusivity.
- **Elementary physical education:** Learners brainstorm game ideas using RAT-style prompts (for example, connect *circle*, *rope*, and *jump* to *hoop*)

independent of technology. The teacher then models how AI responds to the same prompts. Together, the class compares human and AI-generated ideas to explore creative, inclusive ways to stay active.

- **Professional learning:** Educators solve RAT-style prompts (for example, connect *light*, *board*, and *project* to *idea*) to brainstorm interdisciplinary lesson ideas. They compare their solutions with AI-generated outputs, focusing on creativity, practicality, and alignment with diverse learner needs.

EXPERIMENT

Crafting Summaries

In this experiment, learners become knowledge curators, leveraging AI to master the art of summarization. With the help of generative AI tools, they'll learn to identify key points, analyze text structures, and create clear, concise summaries of various types of texts. This hands-on process builds foundational skills in distillation and synthesis, essential for academic and professional communication.

For educators, this experiment offers dual benefits. It provides a practical way to teach the principles of summarizing texts while also introducing learners to the collaborative potential of AI. Additionally, educators can apply these same AI-assisted summarization techniques in their own research and studies, making the task of condensing complex information more efficient and accurate. By mentoring learners through this activity, educators empower them to become effective communicators while modeling how AI can enhance both teaching and scholarly work.

Learning Goals

This experiment aligns with the following learning objectives.

- Understand the principles of summarizing texts.
- Develop skills in identifying key points and main ideas.
- Learn to use AI tools to assist in summarizing various types of texts.
- Learn to use the PROMPT Recipe for effective AI interaction.
- Apply the CHECK AI Framework to review and refine AI-generated content.
- Identify and address biases in AI using the BIAS Identification Framework.
- Enhance critical thinking and information processing skills.

Focus Skills

Critical Thinking	Summarization	Digital Literacy
Information Processing	Communication	Analytical Thinking
Reflective Thinking	Attention to Detail	Time Management

Experiment Protocol

Use the following steps to engage with this experiment.

1. If necessary, model how to use the generative AI tool as well as the PROMPT Recipe, CHECK AI, and BIAS Identification frameworks.
2. Explain the purpose and importance of summarizing texts. Discuss different types of summaries (for example, abstract, executive summary, synopsis) and their uses.
3. Have learners work independently or in small groups (for example, two to four participants) based on their needs and the available resources, ensuring each participant or group has access to the generative AI tool of your choice.
4. Explain how you will evaluate learners. Share the evaluation criteria (for example, clarity, alignment with goals, creativity) and clarify whether feedback will come from peers, the educator, or both.
5. Assign each group a different type of text to summarize (for example, article, book chapter, research paper, news report).
6. Have each group attempt to create a summary of their assigned text without the use of AI tools. Guide learners to identify key points, main ideas, and essential details in the text during their manual summarization process.
7. Remind learners to apply the PROMPT Recipe to ensure their prompt inputs are comprehensive and clear. Direct them to use the generative AI tool to summarize the text and document the resulting outputs effectively. Some AI tools will allow uploading while others will require cutting and pasting text.
8. Encourage learners to apply the CHECK AI and BIAS Identification frameworks as part of their iterative refinement process to ensure clarity, accuracy, and ethical considerations in their outputs.
9. Compare the AI-generated summary with learners' manual summaries, identifying strengths and areas for improvement in both versions.
10. Groups exchange their AI-generated summaries with another group for feedback and suggestions for improvement. Learners revise their summaries based on peer feedback and further AI assistance.
11. Each group presents their summarized text to the class, highlighting the key points and the process they used to create the summary.

12. Learners write a brief reflection on what they learned from the summarization process and how they can improve, including their experience with both manual and AI-assisted methods.
13. Facilitate a class discussion on the experience of creating and refining summaries using AI. Discuss the benefits and challenges encountered.

Experiment Customization AI Prompt

Customize the following prompt to collaborate with AI.

> How can I customize a learning experiment where learners use generative AI to summarize texts in my [grade] [subject] class focused on [specific topic]? The experiment involves learners working in small groups to summarize different types of texts with the help of AI. Groups will also participate in peer reviews, presentations, and class discussions to reflect on the process. Adapt the learning objectives, activities, and assessments to fit my classroom context. Consider intrapersonal and interpersonal skill development along with cultural uniqueness.

Experiment Differentiation AI Prompt

Customize the following prompt to collaboratively differentiate with AI.

> How can I adjust a learning experiment where learners use generative AI to summarize texts for [grade] [content] learners who [specific needs] and need [specific support]? The current activity entails learners working in small groups to summarize different types of texts with the help of AI. The current process includes peer reviews, presentations, and class discussions to reflect on the process.

Integration Examples

Explore integration examples across various learning contexts.

- **Science:** Learners use generative AI to summarize scientific research articles, focusing on identifying key findings, methodologies, and implications. They compare their manually written summaries with AI-generated versions, evaluating clarity and completeness before presenting the key takeaways to the class.
- **Computer science:** Learners use generative AI to summarize technical manuals, software documentation, or articles on emerging technologies. They compare AI-generated summaries with their manual attempts, evaluating for clarity, precision, and relevance before presenting key features and challenges.
- **World language:** Learners use generative AI to summarize texts in the target language, highlighting main ideas, vocabulary, and cultural insights. They compare manual and AI-generated summaries, refining

for linguistic accuracy and cultural appropriateness, and present their findings to the class.

- **Elementary social studies:** Learners read a short historical passage and work together to summarize the key ideas without using technology. The teacher then prompts generative AI to summarize the same passage as if explaining it to a [grade level] learner. The class compares both summaries to explore clarity, completeness, and perspective.
- **Professional learning:** Educators use generative AI to summarize educational research articles or reports. They compare AI-generated summaries with their own to identify efficiencies and improvements in summarizing complex information for use in lesson planning or professional development.

EXPERIMENT

Simplifying Complexity

Learners take on the challenge of simplifying complexity with the help of generative AI tools. Using prompts like "explain cryptocurrency in a way a seven-year-old could understand," they break down intricate topics into accessible explanations. This activity sharpens their ability to paraphrase, summarize, and distill complex ideas while fostering skills in evaluating AI-generated content for accuracy and biases.

For educators, the activity offers practical tools to communicate difficult concepts with clarity and precision. Beyond supporting learners, AI-assisted techniques can streamline educators' own research, enhance presentations, and improve professional communication. By engaging in this process, both learners and educators build critical skills to navigate an increasingly AI-driven world effectively and responsibly.

Learning Goals

This experiment aligns with the following learning objectives.

- Understand how to use generative AI to simplify complex concepts.
- Develop skills in paraphrasing and summarizing complex information.
- Learn to use the PROMPT Recipe for effective AI interaction.
- Apply the CHECK AI Framework to review and refine AI-generated content.
- Identify and address biases in AI using the BIAS Identification Framework.

Focus Skills

Critical Thinking	Creativity	Digital Literacy
Problem Solving	Communication	Reflective Thinking
Adaptability	Analytical Thinking	Ethical Reasoning

Experiment Protocol

Use the following steps to engage with this experiment.

1. If necessary, model how to use the generative AI tool as well as the PROMPT Recipe, CHECK AI, and BIAS Identification frameworks.
2. Provide a brief introduction to the importance of simplifying complex concepts and how AI can assist in this process. Utilize AI to assist you in preparation, appropriate to your learners.
3. Have learners work independently or in small groups (for example, two to four participants) based on their needs and the available resources, ensuring each participant or group has access to the generative AI tool of your choice.
4. Explain how you will evaluate learners. Share the evaluation criteria (for example, clarity, alignment with goals, creativity) and clarify whether feedback will come from peers, the educator, or both.
5. Assign each group a complex concept to break down (for example, quantum mechanics, economic theories, historical events)—initially without using generative AI.
6. Remind learners to apply the PROMPT Recipe to ensure their prompt inputs are comprehensive and clear. Direct them to use the generative AI tool to generate simplified explanations of their assigned concepts and document the resulting outputs effectively.
7. Encourage learners to apply the CHECK AI and BIAS Identification frameworks as part of their iterative refinement process to ensure clarity, accuracy, and ethical considerations in their outputs.
8. Learners should compare the AI-generated explanations with their own explanations and document the differences and similarities.
9. Facilitate a discussion on the effectiveness of the AI-generated explanations and how they compare to the learners' understanding.

Experiment Customization AI Prompt

Customize the following prompt to collaborate with AI.

> How can I customize a learning experiment for my [grade] [subject] class where learners use AI to simplify complex concepts related to [topic]? The learning experiment involves learners working in small groups to generate simplified explanations

of complex topics using a generative AI tool, then comparing and discussing the results. Adapt the learning objectives, activities, and assessments to fit my classroom context. Consider intrapersonal and interpersonal skill development along with cultural uniqueness.

Experiment Differentiation AI Prompt

Customize the following prompt to collaboratively differentiate with AI.

How can I adjust a learning experiment for [grade] [content] learners who [specific needs] and need [specific support]? The current activity entails learners working in small groups to use a generative AI tool to simplify complex concepts and compare the results. The process includes a tutorial on using the AI tool, group discussions, and a class presentation with feedback on clarity and comprehension.

Integration Examples

Explore integration examples across various learning contexts.

- **Biology:** Learners use generative AI to simplify complex biological processes, such as DNA replication or photosynthesis, into accessible explanations. They compare AI-generated versions with their own, discussing clarity, accuracy, and the educational value of each.
- **Elementary health:** Learners explore a health-related topic, such as the digestive system or healthy eating, and create simple explanations. The teacher uses generative AI to produce a version written at the learners' grade level, and together they compare it with their own to evaluate clarity and understanding.
- **Music:** Learners use generative AI to simplify complex music theory concepts, such as harmony or counterpoint, into explanations suitable for beginners. They compare AI-generated outputs with their own, discussing accuracy and educational value.
- **Visual art:** Learners use generative AI to simplify sophisticated art movements or techniques, such as cubism or surrealism, into beginner-friendly explanations. They compare AI's summaries with their own, refining for clarity, inclusivity, and cultural sensitivity.
- **Professional learning:** Educators use generative AI to simplify challenging educational concepts, such as Universal Design for Learning or culturally responsive teaching. They compare AI-generated outputs with their own explanations, discussing how the process improves their ability to present material effectively to diverse learners.

EXPERIMENT

AI-Powered Analogy Creation Workshop

Analogies are powerful tools for making the unfamiliar familiar, and in this workshop, learners harness AI to master this art. Learners work with AI to create meaningful analogies for complex topics, such as comparing the internet to a library that never closes. This process challenges learners to think critically and creatively while enhancing their understanding of challenging concepts.

For educators, this activity provides a unique opportunity to explore how AI can improve both teaching and professional communication. Whether clarifying ideas for learners, crafting impactful presentations, or finding fresh ways to explain complex concepts, educators can leverage AI to refine their own analogy-making skills. By engaging with AI tools, learners and educators alike will sharpen their ability to foster connections, communicate effectively, and think outside the box.

Learning Goals

This experiment aligns with the following learning objectives.

- Understand the role and capabilities of generative AI in creating analogies.
- Develop skills in using AI tools to craft analogies for various topics.
- Learn to use the PROMPT Recipe for effective AI interaction in analogy creation.
- Apply the CHECK AI Framework to ensure the clarity and appropriateness of AI-generated analogies.
- Identify and address biases in AI-generated content using the BIAS Identification Framework.
- Enhance comprehension of complex concepts using analogies.
- Foster creativity and effective communication through analogy creation.

Focus Skills

Critical Thinking	Communication	Digital Literacy
Creativity	Analytical Thinking	Reflective Thinking
Problem Solving	Cognitive Flexibility	Ethical Reasoning

Experiment Protocol

Use the following steps to engage with this experiment.

1. If necessary, model how to use the generative AI tool as well as the PROMPT Recipe, CHECK AI, and BIAS Identification frameworks.

2. Discuss the importance and use of analogies in learning and communication. Highlight examples of effective analogies in various contexts.
3. Have learners work independently or in small groups (for example, two to four participants) based on their needs and the available resources, ensuring each participant or group has access to the generative AI tool of your choice.
4. Explain how you will evaluate learners. Share the evaluation criteria (for example, clarity, alignment with goals, creativity) and clarify whether feedback will come from peers, the educator, or both.
5. Assign each learner or group a specific topic or concept related to the course content. This could include scientific theories, historical events, mathematical principles, literary themes, or any other subject matter.
6. Remind learners to apply the PROMPT Recipe to ensure their prompt inputs are comprehensive and clear. Direct them to use the generative AI tool to create analogies for their assigned topic, specifying the elements of the analogy in their prompt and documenting the resulting outputs effectively.
7. Encourage learners to apply the CHECK AI and BIAS Identification frameworks as part of their iterative refinement process to ensure clarity, accuracy, and ethical considerations in their outputs.
8. Learners should refine and document their AI-generated analogies to ensure clarity, appropriateness, and effectiveness.
9. Facilitate a discussion on the effectiveness of the AI-generated analogies, addressing any challenges or improvements.

Experiment Customization AI Prompt

Customize the following prompt to collaborate with AI.

> How can I customize an AI-assisted analogy creation learning experiment for my [grade] [subject] class focused on [concept]? The learning experiment involves learners working individually or in groups with access to a generative AI tool to create analogies for various topics. They will specify the elements of their analogies and evaluate the AI-generated content for clarity, appropriateness, and effectiveness. Adapt the learning objectives, activities, and assessments to fit my classroom context. Consider intrapersonal and interpersonal skill development along with cultural uniqueness.

Experiment Differentiation AI Prompt

Customize the following prompt to collaboratively differentiate with AI.

How can I adjust an AI-assisted analogy creation activity for [grade] [content] learners who [specific needs] and need [specific support]? The current activity entails learners working individually or in groups with access to a generative AI tool to create analogies for various topics. They will specify the elements of their analogies and evaluate the AI-generated content for clarity, appropriateness, and effectiveness.

Integration Examples

Explore integration examples across various learning contexts.

- **Science:** Learners use generative AI to create analogies that explain natural processes, such as describing the water cycle as a recycling system. They refine AI outputs for clarity, accuracy, and relevance, presenting their final analogy to the class.
- **Elementary English language arts:** Learners brainstorm analogies to describe story elements, such as comparing a character's journey to climbing a mountain. The teacher uses generative AI to create similar analogies written at the learners' grade level. Together, they evaluate and refine the results for clarity and meaning before sharing with the class.
- **Social studies:** Learners use generative AI to create analogies that connect political systems to familiar structures, like describing democracy as a group decision made at a potluck. They refine their analogies for depth and appropriateness, discussing their insights in class.
- **Mathematics:** Learners use generative AI to develop analogies for explaining abstract mathematical concepts. For example, they might compare solving algebraic equations to solving a puzzle where every piece must fit. They refine their ideas for clarity and comprehensibility before presenting their work.
- **Professional learning:** Educators use generative AI to craft analogies for explaining teaching strategies, such as likening scaffolding to building a bridge step by step to support learning. They refine AI outputs to ensure relevance and clarity for professional use.

EXPERIMENT

Tailoring Texts

Language is a powerful tool, and this experiment invites learners to explore how tone, voice, and style can transform the meaning and resonance of any text. Using generative AI tools, they'll practice reframing content for different audiences and purposes, whether it's rewriting the U.S. Constitution in a robotic video gamer tone or converting an informal email into a polished professional message. This hands-on activity sharpens learners' ability to adapt language creatively and effectively, helping them excel in diverse communication scenarios.

For educators, this experiment offers a practical way to demonstrate the art of tailoring communication to specific audiences, an essential skill in teaching, leadership, and collaboration. Outside the classroom, educators can use AI tools to reframe complex ideas for team discussions, adapt communication for different stakeholders, or even craft innovative ways to engage learners. By embracing this activity, both learners and educators gain a deeper appreciation for the nuances of language and its potential to connect, inform, and inspire.

Learning Goals

This experiment aligns with the following learning objectives.

- Understand how to use generative AI to reframe language in different tones, voices, and styles.
- Develop skills in adapting language for various audiences and purposes.
- Learn to use the PROMPT Recipe for effective AI interaction.
- Apply the CHECK AI Framework to review and refine AI-generated content.
- Identify and address biases in AI-generated content using the BIAS Identification Framework.

Focus Skills

Critical Thinking	Creativity	Digital Literacy
Cultural Awareness	Communication	Reflective Thinking
Adaptability	Analytical Thinking	Ethical Reasoning

Experiment Protocol

Use the following steps to engage with this experiment.

1. If necessary, model how to use the generative AI tool as well as the PROMPT Recipe, CHECK AI, and BIAS Identification frameworks.
2. Provide a brief introduction to the importance of adapting language to different audiences and purposes. Utilize AI to assist you in preparation, appropriate to your learners.
3. Have learners work independently or in small groups (for example, two to four) based on their needs and the available resources, ensuring each participant or group has access to the generative AI tool of your choice.
4. Explain how you will evaluate learners. Share the evaluation criteria (for example, clarity, alignment with goals, creativity) and clarify whether feedback will come from peers, the educator, or both.
5. Assign each group a text to reframe (for example, the U.S. Constitution, a casual email, a formal report) and request they manually attempt to

reframe the text in different tones, voices, or styles (such as robotic gamer tone, hip-hop style, professional, excited, serious).

6. Remind learners to apply the PROMPT Recipe to ensure their prompt inputs are comprehensive and clear. Direct them to use the generative AI tool to reframe the text and document the resulting outputs effectively.
7. Encourage learners to apply the CHECK AI and BIAS Identification frameworks as part of their iterative refinement process to ensure clarity, accuracy, and ethical considerations in their outputs.
8. Learners should compare the AI-generated versions with their own attempts and discuss the differences and similarities.
9. Facilitate a discussion on the effectiveness of the AI-generated reframings and how they compare to the learners' versions.

Experiment Customization AI Prompt

Customize the following prompt to collaborate with AI.

How can I customize a learning experiment for my [grade] [subject] class where learners use AI to reframe language related to [topic]? The learning experiment involves learners working in small groups to reframe various texts using a generative AI tool, then comparing and discussing the results. Adapt the learning objectives, activities, and assessments to fit my classroom context. Consider intrapersonal and interpersonal skill development along with cultural uniqueness.

Experiment Differentiation AI Prompt

Customize the following prompt to collaboratively differentiate with AI.

How can I adjust a learning experiment for [grade] [content] learners who [specific needs] and need [specific support]? The current activity entails learners working in small groups to use a generative AI tool to reframe language and compare the results. The process includes a tutorial on using the AI tool, group discussions, and a class presentation with feedback on effectiveness and adaptability.

Integration Examples

Explore integration examples across various learning contexts.

- **English:** Learners use generative AI to rewrite classic texts, such as transforming a Shakespearean sonnet into contemporary lyrics. They compare the AI-generated reframing with their own, evaluating the effectiveness in maintaining meaning while adapting tone and style.
- **Elementary music:** Learners discuss how to explain a music concept like rhythm to a friend. The teacher uses generative AI to model different versions of the explanation, such as a rhyme, a short story, or a friendly letter. Together, they evaluate which version is clearest and most fun, refining it as a class.

- **Business:** Learners use generative AI to rewrite business proposals or marketing materials, adjusting for different audiences and tones, such as professional, enthusiastic, or formal. They evaluate the AI-generated versions for clarity and persuasiveness.
- **History:** Learners use generative AI to reframe historical documents, such as rewriting the Gettysburg Address as a motivational speech. They refine the AI-generated versions for accuracy and relevance, discussing how tone and style affect interpretation.
- **Professional learning:** Educators use generative AI to adapt lesson plans or professional communication, such as converting an academic article into a clear and engaging presentation. They refine the AI outputs for alignment with instructional goals and accessibility.

EXPERIMENT

Formatting Content

The ability to organize and present information effectively is a critical skill in any field. In this experiment, learners use generative AI tools to transform written content into various user-defined formats, such as tables, structured outlines, or professional email templates. By working hands-on with AI, learners will refine their ability to manage and present content clearly and effectively, preparing them for academic, professional, and creative challenges.

For educators, this activity highlights how AI can simplify content organization and improve communication. Whether creating structured lesson plans, drafting actionable plans for projects, or formatting public data into tables for clarity, AI tools offer valuable support. By guiding learners through this process, educators can model effective content presentation strategies while also enhancing their own proficiency in organizing and sharing ideas across diverse contexts.

Learning Goals

This experiment aligns with the following learning objectives.

- Understand the role and capabilities of generative AI in organizing and presenting written content.
- Develop skills in using AI tools to transform written information into specific formats such as tables, structured documents, and templates.
- Learn to use the PROMPT Recipe for effective AI interaction in content organization.
- Apply the CHECK AI Framework to ensure the clarity and accuracy of AI-generated content outputs.

- Identify and address biases in AI-generated content using the BIAS Identification Framework.
- Enhance content management and presentation skills using AI-generated outputs.

Focus Skills

Critical Thinking	Content Literacy	Digital Literacy
Organizational Skills	Analytical Thinking	Reflective Thinking
Strategic Planning	Evaluation and Synthesis	Information Visualization

Experiment Protocol

Use the following steps to engage with this experiment.

1. If necessary, model how to use the generative AI tool as well as the PROMPT Recipe, CHECK AI, and BIAS Identification frameworks.
2. Discuss the importance of content organization and presentation in personal and academic success. Highlight examples of effective content outputs.
3. Have learners work independently or in small groups (for example, two to four participants) based on their needs and the available resources, ensuring each participant or group has access to the generative AI tool of your choice.
4. Explain how you will evaluate learners. Share the evaluation criteria (for example, clarity, alignment with goals, creativity) and clarify whether feedback will come from peers, the educator, or both.
5. Assign each learner or group a specific task involving written content and instruct them to specify the desired output format (for example, table, structured document, flowchart) in their prompt.
6. Remind learners to apply the PROMPT Recipe to ensure their prompt inputs are comprehensive and clear. Direct them to use the generative AI tool to transform the written content into the specified format and document the resulting outputs effectively.
7. Encourage learners to apply the CHECK AI and BIAS Identification frameworks as part of their iterative refinement process to ensure clarity, accuracy, and ethical considerations in their outputs.
8. Have learners document their content outputs and the AI feedback, making necessary adjustments to refine their presentations.
9. Facilitate a discussion on the effectiveness of AI-generated content organization, addressing any challenges or improvements.

Experiment Customization AI Prompt

Customize the following prompt to collaborate with AI.

> How can I customize an AI-assisted content organization learning experiment for my [grade] [subject] class focused on [specific content format]? The learning experiment involves learners working individually with access to a generative AI tool to transform written content into specific formats. They will specify the desired output format and evaluate the AI-generated outputs for clarity, accuracy, and effectiveness. Adapt the learning objectives, activities, and assessments to fit my classroom context. Consider intrapersonal and interpersonal skill development along with cultural uniqueness.

Experiment Differentiation AI Prompt

Customize the following prompt to collaboratively differentiate with AI.

> How can I adjust an AI-assisted content organization activity for [grade] [content] learners who [specific needs] and need [specific support]? The current activity entails learners working individually with access to a generative AI tool to transform written content into specific formats. They will specify the desired output format and evaluate the AI-generated outputs for clarity, accuracy, and effectiveness.

Integration Examples

Explore integration examples across various learning contexts.

- **English:** Learners use generative AI to transform written analyses or ideas into structured formats, such as haiku, sonnets, or acrostics. They refine AI-generated outputs to ensure adherence to the required structure and creative integrity.
- **Elementary science:** Learners investigate a topic, like the water cycle or plant growth, via hands-on activities or readings. The teacher uses generative AI to model how to format information into a flowchart. Learners review and discuss the flowchart to evaluate how well it supports their understanding.
- **Mathematics:** Learners use generative AI to organize problem-solving strategies into bulleted lists or tables, presenting different methods and solutions for a given mathematical problem. They refine the AI-generated formats for clarity, accuracy, and logical flow.
- **Visual art:** Learners use generative AI to create tables comparing art movements, such as cubism and surrealism, based on criteria like techniques, themes, and key figures. They refine the AI-generated tables for accuracy and visual appeal.
- **Professional learning:** Educators use generative AI to create bulleted checklists for classroom management strategies, such as setting routines, addressing disruptive behavior, and organizing resources. They refine the AI outputs to ensure practicality and applicability.

EXPERIMENT

Enhancing Inquiry

Great questions lead to great discoveries, and this experiment encourages learners to sharpen their inquiry skills by collaborating with AI. Starting with a topic of interest, learners pose initial questions, analyze the AI's responses, and craft thoughtful follow-ups to dig deeper into the subject. Each interaction challenges them to think critically, refine their approach, and uncover richer insights while fostering a mindset of curiosity and exploration.

For educators, this activity demonstrates the value of follow-up questions in teaching, research, and professional growth. By modeling effective questioning strategies, educators guide learners toward deeper comprehension while also applying these techniques in their own work, whether designing thought-provoking lessons, leading discussions, or exploring complex ideas collaboratively. This hands-on process equips both learners and educators with essential tools for continuous inquiry and growth.

Learning Goals

This experiment aligns with the following learning objectives.

- Understand the importance of follow-up questions in enhancing comprehension and exploration of topics.
- Develop skills in crafting effective and meaningful follow-up questions.
- Learn to use the PROMPT Recipe for effective AI interaction.
- Apply the CHECK AI Framework to review and refine AI-generated content.
- Identify and address biases in AI-generated content using the BIAS Identification Framework.

Focus Skills

Critical Thinking	Inquiry	Digital Literacy
Problem Solving	Communication	Reflective Thinking
Adaptability	Analytical Thinking	Ethical Reasoning

Experiment Protocol

Use the following steps to engage with this experiment.

1. If necessary, model how to use the generative AI tool as well as the PROMPT Recipe, CHECK AI, and BIAS Identification frameworks.
2. Provide a brief introduction to the significance of follow-up questions and how they can deepen understanding. Utilize AI to assist you in preparation, appropriate to your learners.

3. Have learners work independently or in small groups (for example, two to four participants) based on their needs and the available resources, ensuring each participant or group has access to the generative AI tool of your choice.
4. Explain how you will evaluate learners. Share the evaluation criteria (for example, clarity, alignment with goals, creativity) and clarify whether feedback will come from peers, the educator, or both.
5. Assign each group a primary question to ask the AI tool on a chosen topic (for example, climate change, historical events, scientific theories).
6. Remind learners to apply the PROMPT Recipe to ensure their prompt inputs are comprehensive and clear. Direct them to use the generative AI tool to receive initial responses to their primary question and document the resulting outputs effectively.
7. Encourage learners to apply the CHECK AI and BIAS Identification frameworks as part of their iterative refinement process to ensure clarity, accuracy, and ethical considerations in their outputs.
8. Guide learners in manually crafting follow-up questions based on the AI's initial responses, aiming for deeper exploration and understanding. Next, have learners ask the generative AI tool, "What follow-up questions should I ask?"
9. Have learners compare their follow-up questions with those suggested by the AI, documenting the differences and similarities.
10. Facilitate a discussion on the effectiveness of the follow-up questions and how they can improve learners' questioning techniques.

Experiment Customization AI Prompt

Customize the following prompt to collaborate with AI.

How can I customize a learning experiment for my [grade] [subject] class where learners use AI to practice crafting and asking follow-up questions related to [topic]? The learning experiment involves learners working in small groups to develop follow-up questions based on AI-generated responses to a primary question. The learners will then craft follow-up questions independently and then with generative AI. They will compare and discuss the results. Adapt the learning objectives, activities, and assessments to fit my classroom context. Consider intrapersonal and interpersonal skill development along with cultural uniqueness.

Experiment Differentiation AI Prompt

Customize the following prompt to collaboratively differentiate with AI.

How can I adjust a learning experiment for [grade] [content] learners who [specific needs] and need [specific support]? The current activity entails learners working in small groups to use a generative AI tool to answer a primary question. They will then craft follow-up questions independently and then with generative AI. They will compare and discuss the results. The process includes a tutorial on using the AI tool, group discussions, and a class presentation with feedback on effectiveness and depth.

Integration Examples

Explore integration examples across various learning contexts.

- **Philosophy:** Learners use a generative AI tool to ask follow-up questions about philosophical arguments, such as the ethics of artificial intelligence, exploring implications and counterarguments to enhance their understanding.
- **Science:** Learners use a generative AI tool to further inquire about scientific concepts or experiments, aiming to gain a deeper understanding of the principles involved. They compare their follow-up questions with those suggested by the AI, discussing the clarity and comprehensiveness.
- **English:** Learners use a generative AI tool to ask follow-up questions about themes, symbolism, or character development in a novel or poem, refining their analysis through deeper exploration.
- **Elementary social studies:** Learners investigate a topic like community helpers or local landmarks through stories and class discussion. The teacher uses generative AI to model how to ask follow-up questions that deepen understanding, such as "Why are firefighters important?" or "How did this place get its name?" Learners evaluate and discuss the questions to guide their own inquiry.
- **Professional learning:** Educators use generative AI to ask follow-up questions about lesson design, such as how to incorporate inquiry-based learning into diverse subjects, refining questions to support deeper engagement with learners.

EXPERIMENT

Fact-Checking Generative AI Outputs

Academic integrity is a cornerstone of meaningful research, and this experiment challenges learners to uphold it while collaborating with AI. Starting with a topic of interest, learners use generative AI to produce content, then rigorously fact-check the output against credible academic sources. This process sharpens their ability to evaluate information for accuracy and reliability, fostering critical thinking and an appreciation for the research process.

For educators, this activity offers a way to guide learners through the nuances of academic integrity in the age of AI. Beyond teaching learners to validate sources, educators can use these skills in their own scholarly work, ensuring rigor and credibility when incorporating AI-generated insights. By engaging in this experiment, both learners and educators build essential research and evaluation skills, equipping them to navigate a complex information landscape with confidence and integrity.

Learning Goals

This experiment aligns with the following learning objectives.

- Understand the role and capabilities of generative AI in academic research.
- Develop skills in using AI tools for generating research content.
- Learn to use the PROMPT Recipe for effective AI interaction.
- Apply the CHECK AI Framework to ensure the accuracy and credibility of AI-generated content.
- Identify and address biases in AI-generated content using the BIAS Identification Framework.

Focus Skills

Critical Thinking	Information Literacy	Digital Literacy
Research Skills	Problem Solving	Ethical Reasoning
Verification and Validation	Analytical Thinking	Evaluation and Synthesis

Experiment Protocol

Use the following steps to engage with this experiment.

1. If necessary, model how to use the generative AI tool as well as the PROMPT Recipe, CHECK AI, and BIAS Identification frameworks.
2. Discuss the significance of verifying the accuracy of information and using credible sources from the internet. Emphasize that not all information found online is reliable and teach learners how to identify trustworthy academic sources. (You can also prepare examples using personal generative AI findings of inaccuracy.)
3. Have learners work independently or in small groups (for example, two to four participants) based on their needs and the available resources, ensuring each participant or group has access to the generative AI tool of your choice.
4. Explain how you will evaluate learners. Share the evaluation criteria (for example, clarity, alignment with goals, creativity) and clarify whether feedback will come from peers, the educator, or both.

5. Assign each group a specific research topic related to the course content, or allow them to select their own. Specify they should focus on directing their AI tool toward academic sources and citing whenever possible.
6. Remind learners to apply the PROMPT Recipe to ensure their prompt inputs are comprehensive and clear. Direct them to use the generative AI tool to gather information and generate preliminary research, documenting the resulting outputs effectively.
7. Encourage learners to apply the CHECK AI and BIAS Identification frameworks as part of their iterative refinement process to ensure clarity, accuracy, and ethical considerations in their outputs.
8. Have groups document their findings, noting discrepancies and confirming facts with reliable academic references.
9. Facilitate a discussion on the reliability, accuracy, and ethical considerations of the AI-generated content.

Experiment Customization AI Prompt

Customize the following prompt to collaborate with AI.

> How can I customize an AI-assisted academic research and fact-checking learning experiment for my [grade] [subject] class focused on [topic]? The learning experiment involves learners working in small groups with access to a generative AI tool to generate and verify research content. Groups will share their findings, noting discrepancies and confirming facts with reliable academic references. Adapt the learning objectives, activities, and assessments to fit my classroom context. Consider intrapersonal and interpersonal skill development along with cultural uniqueness.

Experiment Differentiation AI Prompt

Customize the following prompt to collaboratively differentiate with AI.

> How can I adjust an AI-assisted academic research activity for [grade] [content] learners who [specific needs] and need [specific support]? The current activity entails learners working in small groups with access to a generative AI tool to generate and verify research content. The process includes a tutorial on using the AI tool, group discussions to share findings, and a class presentation with feedback on the accuracy and credibility of the information.

Integration Examples

Explore integration examples across various learning contexts.

- **Elementary science:** Learners explore a topic like animal habitats or plant life cycles through books and class discussions. The teacher uses generative AI to model how to find and verify facts, comparing AI outputs with information from trusted science texts or educational websites. Learners discuss which facts are accurate and why source checking matters.

- **English:** Learners use generative AI to analyze themes in classic novels, such as *To Kill a Mockingbird* (Lee, 1960) or *1984* (Orwell, 1949). They fact-check AI-generated insights with established literary critiques, refining their analysis before presenting conclusions.
- **Psychology:** Learners use generative AI to investigate psychological theories, such as Maslow's hierarchy of needs or cognitive dissonance. They cross-check AI-generated information with peer-reviewed journals and present their findings.
- **Business:** Learners use generative AI to analyze market trends and strategies, such as the rise of e-commerce or cryptocurrency adoption. They verify AI-generated insights with data from reputable business publications, refining their analysis for accuracy.
- **Professional learning:** Educators use generative AI to gather information on educational trends, such as culturally responsive teaching or flipped classrooms. They validate AI-generated content with peer-reviewed studies and use the findings in professional discussions or articles.

EXPERIMENT

Refining Ideas

Refining ideas is an essential skill, and in this experiment, learners explore how AI can assist in the iterative improvement process. Learners engage in a dialogue with generative AI, asking, "What should I ask you to improve your response?" By doing so, learners uncover the power of refining prompts to achieve progressively better outputs. Each interaction challenges them to think critically, experiment with language, and optimize results, cultivating a mindset of continuous improvement.

For educators, this activity offers insights into how iterative refinement can enhance both teaching and professional tasks. Whether drafting clearer instructions, troubleshooting lesson plans, or improving communication with diverse audiences, AI tools provide a powerful ally in achieving precision and clarity. By guiding learners through this process, educators not only model effective AI use but also deepen their own skills in iterative thinking and prompt engineering.

Learning Goals

This experiment aligns with the following learning objectives.

- Understand the role and capabilities of generative AI in iterative improvement.

- Develop skills in using AI tools to refine prompts and improve AI-generated responses.
- Learn to use the PROMPT Recipe for effective AI interaction in iterative refinement.
- Apply the CHECK AI Framework to ensure the clarity and accuracy of AI-generated improvements.
- Identify and address biases in AI-generated content using the BIAS Identification Framework.
- Enhance critical thinking and prompt engineering skills through AI-assisted iterative improvement.

Focus Skills

Critical Thinking	Information Literacy	Digital Literacy
Prompt Engineering	Problem Solving	Reflective Thinking
Iterative Refinement	Analytical Thinking	Evaluation and Synthesis

Experiment Protocol

Use the following steps to engage with this experiment.

1. If necessary, model how to use the generative AI tool as well as the PROMPT Recipe, CHECK AI, and BIAS Identification frameworks.
2. Discuss the importance of iterative refinement in AI interactions. Highlight examples of successful iterative improvements.
3. Have learners work independently or in small groups (for example, two to four participants) based on their needs and the available resources, ensuring each participant or group has access to the generative AI tool of your choice.
4. Explain how you will evaluate learners. Share the evaluation criteria (for example, clarity, alignment with goals, creativity) and clarify whether feedback will come from peers, the educator, or both.
5. Assign each learner or group a specific task to generate content using the AI tool. This could include writing, data analysis, problem-solving tasks, and so on.
6. Remind learners to apply the PROMPT Recipe to ensure their prompt inputs are comprehensive and clear. Direct them to ask the generative AI tool, "What should I ask you to improve your response?" and document the resulting outputs effectively.
7. Encourage learners to apply the CHECK AI and BIAS Identification frameworks as part of their iterative refinement process to ensure clarity, accuracy, and ethical considerations in their outputs.

8. Have learners document their initial prompts, AI suggestions, refined prompts, and the improved responses, making necessary adjustments to refine their approaches.
9. Facilitate a discussion on the effectiveness of AI-generated iterative improvements, addressing any challenges or improvements.

Experiment Customization AI Prompt

Customize the following prompt to collaborate with AI.

> How can I customize an AI-assisted iterative improvement learning experiment for my [grade] [subject] class focused on [specific task]? The learning experiment involves learners working individually or in groups with access to a generative AI tool to iteratively refine prompts and improve AI-generated responses. They will specify the task, generate content, ask the AI for prompt improvement suggestions, and evaluate the AI-generated improvements for clarity, accuracy, and potential biases. Adapt the learning objectives, activities, and assessments to fit my classroom context. Consider intrapersonal and interpersonal skill development along with cultural uniqueness.

Experiment Differentiation AI Prompt

Customize the following prompt to collaboratively differentiate with AI.

> How can I adjust an AI-assisted iterative improvement activity for [grade] [content] learners who [specific needs] and need [specific support]? The current activity entails learners working individually or in groups with access to a generative AI tool to iteratively refine prompts and improve AI-generated responses. They will specify the task, generate content, ask the AI for prompt improvement suggestions, and evaluate the AI-generated improvements for clarity, accuracy, and potential biases.

Integration Examples

Explore integration examples across various learning contexts.

- **English:** Learners use generative AI to draft a story or poem. After reviewing the initial output, they ask the tool, "What should I ask you to improve the plot, characters, or tone?" Each response helps them refine prompts to create a more cohesive and compelling narrative.
- **Health education:** Learners use generative AI to draft a public health message, such as the benefits of regular exercise. They engage in iterative questioning by asking the tool, "What should I ask you to make this message more engaging and relatable to teenagers?" This ensures each refinement improves the clarity and impact of the message.

- **Mathematics:** Learners use generative AI to solve and explain a mathematical problem, such as solving a quadratic equation. They improve their prompts by asking, "What should I ask you to make this explanation simpler and clearer for a beginner?" Each iteration results in better problem-solving guidance.
- **Elementary social studies:** Learners brainstorm in small groups, independent of technology, to craft a message explaining a local issue or civic concept, such as recycling or voting. The teacher then models how to use generative AI to draft the message and asks, "What should I ask you to make this clearer for fifth graders?" Each iteration shows how refining questions can improve clarity and effectiveness.
- **Professional learning:** Educators use generative AI to draft a message for parents explaining a new classroom policy. They refine their prompts by asking the tool, "What should I ask you to make this message empathetic and easy to understand for all parents?" Each iteration enhances tone and clarity.

In the following discussion, "How AI Can Enhance Skills Rather Than Replace Thinking," learners consider how AI can sharpen their skills and creativity—without replacing their own thinking.

Discussion: How AI Can Enhance Skills Rather Than Replace Thinking

Instructions: Use this protocol to plan and adapt a discussion that fits your audience, setting, and goals by reviewing the guidance and prompts prior to facilitating the discussion. This protocol serves as a flexible planning tool designed to help you frame the conversation, customize the experience, and support meaningful participation.

Big Question

How can we use AI to enhance our skills rather than replace our thinking?

Learning Goals

- Understand the distinction between enhancing skills with AI and replacing human thinking.
- Explore the role of AI in augmenting human decision-making processes.
- Investigate how to integrate AI into collaborative problem-solving scenarios.
- Examine the ways AI can enhance creative thinking and innovation.
- Analyze the importance of maintaining ethical reasoning and critical thinking when using AI.

Focus Skills

Critical Thinking	Problem Solving	Collaboration
Technological Literacy	Ethical Reasoning	Communication
Decision Making	Strategic Thinking	Evaluation and Synthesis

Discussion Customization AI Prompt

> How can I customize a discussion for my [grade] [subject] class focused on how AI can enhance our skills rather than replace our thinking?

For example:

> How can I customize a discussion for eighth-grade science learners exploring innovation who need a structured format to debate AI's role in scientific thinking?

Discussion Differentiation AI Prompt

> How can I adjust a discussion for [grade] [content] learners who [specific needs] and need support in understanding how AI can enhance our skills rather than replace our thinking?

For example:

> How can I adjust a discussion for eleventh-grade physics learners who benefit from peer teaching and need a collaborative way to break down AI concepts?

Discussion Extension AI Prompt

> How can I extend a discussion to challenge advanced [grade] [content] learners and deepen their understanding of how AI can enhance our skills rather than replace our thinking?

For example:

> How can I extend a discussion for fourth-grade computer learners who enjoy design challenges and need a chance to improve how simple AI tools work?

Reflecting and Taking Action

Every journey toward mastery begins with exploration—testing ideas, refining skills, and building confidence in new tools. In this chapter, you engaged in entry-level AI experiments, learning how to navigate practical frameworks and hands-on activities that lay the foundation for meaningful AI integration.

The tools introduced here will support your goals as an educator, helping you navigate AI's potential while developing critical strategies for its responsible use. Whether applied in classrooms, professional learning environments, or personal exploration, these skills will shape how you and your learners interact with AI thoughtfully and effectively.

To build on these foundational skills, consider the following action steps.

1. Equip yourself with foundational skills.
    a. Revisit the PROMPT Recipe, CHECK AI Framework, and BIAS Identification Framework introduced in this chapter.
    b. Reflect on how these tools can help you structure AI interactions to ensure outputs are clear, ethical, and aligned with learning objectives or professional goals.
    c. Identify opportunities to apply these frameworks in classroom instruction, professional development, or personal learning projects.
2. Engage in collaborative exploration.
    a. Use the discussions and tools in this chapter to spark dialogue with colleagues in professional learning settings or classroom discussions.
    b. Work with peers to compare different AI-generated outputs, analyze bias, and evaluate the effectiveness of various prompt strategies.
    c. Foster a culture of shared learning, encouraging discussions about ethical considerations, practical applications, and emerging trends in AI.
3. Experiment with purpose.
    a. Begin applying the frameworks from this chapter to small-scale AI experiments in your classroom, team meetings, or professional work.
    b. Use AI for brainstorming, summarization, and content refinement, testing its effectiveness in supporting lesson planning, curriculum design, or workflow optimization.
    c. Treat each experiment as a cycle of reflection and refinement, using insights gained from trials and feedback to improve AI integration strategies.
4. Pursue continued learning.
    a. Dive deeper into the resources and frameworks provided in this chapter, using them to refine your ability to prompt, evaluate, and integrate AI effectively.

   b. Explore case studies or research on AI's role in education and professional development, staying informed about best practices and ethical considerations.
   c. Encourage colleagues and learners to critically assess AI-generated content, reinforcing a mindset of skepticism, verification, and responsible use.
5. Reflect on your role as a guide.
   a. Consider how you can model intentional AI use, guiding others in ethical experimentation and critical engagement with AI-generated content.
   b. Ask yourself how you can support learners or colleagues in using AI not just as a tool, but also to enhance creativity, analysis, and innovation.
   c. Commit to leading with purpose, ensuring that AI's role in your work remains thoughtful, informed, and centered on meaningful learning.

Consider the following questions to guide your thinking.

- How can you use the CHECK AI and BIAS Identification frameworks to ensure high-quality, ethical AI interactions in your practice?
- In what ways can collaborative experimentation enhance creativity and problem solving for your learners or colleagues?
- How can foundational AI skills, like bias detection and summarization, transform your teaching, learning, or professional workflows?

By engaging in entry-level AI experiments, you've taken the first step toward deliberate and strategic AI integration. These foundational tools have helped you refine AI interactions, develop critical evaluation techniques, and build confidence in using AI effectively. But experimentation is just the beginning.

In the next chapter, we move beyond initial experimentation into real-world applications, examining how to strategically integrate AI into collaboration, problem solving, and everyday planning. You will explore AI's role in productivity, professional workflows, and creative expression while also refining your ability to balance automation with human expertise.

With each step forward, you are not only mastering AI tools—you are also shaping the ethical, creative, and purposeful use of AI in education and beyond. Let's continue this journey together, embracing AI's potential while remaining critical, intentional, and innovative in its use.

CHAPTER 4

Elevated AI Experiments

Welcome to the next step of your journey into generative AI—a space where foundational skills evolve into practical tools for solving problems and engaging with the world. In this chapter, we build on the principles introduced in the previous chapter, "Entry-Point AI Experiments," offering a range of hands-on experiments and thought-provoking discussions. Together, these activities demonstrate how AI can enhance communication, foster collaboration, and support everyday planning. By participating in these experiments, learners gain valuable practice combining foundational AI skills with subject matter expertise, recognizing that critical thinking grows from deliberate practice and task mastery.

As Mollick (2024) reminds us, "Being in the loop helps you maintain and sharpen your skills, as you actively learn from the AI and adapt to new ways of thinking and problem-solving" (p. 54). This chapter emphasizes lifelong and student-driven learning, encouraging learners to take ownership of their educational journeys. Using AI tools, they explore subjects of interest more deeply, practicing the kind of deliberate engagement that builds confidence and adaptability.

This chapter introduces AI-driven storytelling, content creation, and artistic exploration, allowing learners to experiment with AI's role as a creative partner while maintaining human originality and intent. This chapter also explores how AI can bridge linguistic and cultural gaps, engaging with experiments that examine AI-assisted translation, global collaboration, and personalized cultural exploration. These activities prompt learners to consider both the benefits and challenges of relying on AI in creative and cultural spaces, reinforcing the need for critical thinking in evaluating AI-generated content. Discussions invite learners to reflect on AI's evolving intelligence, questioning what it truly means for AI to "think" and the role humans play in shaping its applications. Ethical considerations must be at the forefront of AI integration, ensuring that learners develop not only fluency with the tools but also the discernment to question, refine, and responsibly apply AI-generated outputs. Finally, this chapter reinforces that AI is not a replacement for human intelligence but a tool for enhancing communication, organization, and creativity. Learners develop a deeper understanding of how AI can support professional and personal growth while recognizing its constraints.

Introducing the Experiments

The experiments in this chapter move beyond skill building to introduce learners to AI's role in shaping how we live and work. Discussions explore how AI can support problem solving, lifestyle improvement, and planning: all critical areas for navigating inevitable changes in the digital economy. With a focus on technology and interpersonal skills, learners also discover how tools like natural language processing enhance communication and technological fluency, helping them thrive in both collaborative and independent settings.

Through deliberate practice and reflective dialogue, this chapter equips educators and learners alike to integrate AI meaningfully into their personal and professional lives. These activities aren't just about learning technology; they're about intertwining AI with critical thinking, creativity, and ethical action, laying the foundation for lifelong growth in an AI-driven world.

At this stage of AI exploration, learners begin applying AI to enhance communication, improve decision making, and strengthen collaboration. Experiments in this chapter guide them through refining written and verbal communication, structuring ideas more effectively, and analyzing different perspectives. AI becomes a tool for organizing thoughts, reflecting on choices, and solving complex problems, reinforcing the need for subject matter expertise when evaluating AI-generated content. Collaboration plays a key role in these activities, encouraging learners to consider how AI can support teamwork and collective problem solving. Some experiments introduce AI as a tool for facilitating group interactions, streamlining workflows, and structuring shared goals, reinforcing the importance of balancing automation with human input. Others explore self-assessment and reflection, helping learners refine their work through AI-supported feedback.

As AI becomes increasingly embedded in daily routines, its role in productivity, organization, and personal management is a growing focus. Learners will explore how AI can assist in goal setting, tracking progress, and improving time management, gaining insights into how technology can support structured decision making. Experiments also introduce AI's role in financial planning, resource management, and sustainability, prompting learners to consider how AI-generated insights can aid in budgeting, wellness planning, and optimizing daily choices. These activities help learners analyze where AI enhances efficiency and where human oversight remains critical, reinforcing the theme of deliberate practice in AI integration.

Discussions challenge learners to think critically about when and how to use AI effectively, emphasizing that while AI can assist in structuring ideas and enhancing efficiency, it does not replace the judgment, creativity, and ethical considerations that define human expertise. Through the discussions, learners examine the broader implications of AI-assisted planning, raising questions about automation's impact on independence, agency, and personal responsibility.

Like any stage in a hero's journey, this chapter represents a moment of discovery and refinement. Learners encounter new challenges, including when to rely on AI, when to question its outputs, and how to integrate it thoughtfully into their workflows. These challenges are not obstacles but opportunities for deeper engagement. Let's take the next step in this journey together—experimenting, reflecting, and leading the way toward a future where AI supports, rather than replaces, the essential human skills of curiosity, collaboration, and critical thinking.

EXPERIMENT

Crafting Professional Messages

Professional communication is an essential skill, and in this experiment, learners explore how AI can act as a personal assistant in crafting clear, impactful messages. From formal emails to persuasive letters, learners will use generative AI tools to compose various forms of correspondence, specifying tone and tailoring their messages to suit specific audiences. This process sharpens their ability to adapt language to professional contexts while fostering a deeper understanding of clarity, tone, and audience.

For educators, this activity provides a valuable opportunity to model effective communication strategies while exploring how AI can enhance their own professional correspondence. Whether drafting stakeholder updates, responding to colleagues, or designing impactful communications for learners, educators can use these tools to improve precision and efficiency. By engaging in this experiment, both learners and educators gain skills in refining AI-generated outputs to ensure clarity, professionalism, and appropriateness in any context.

Learning Goals

This experiment aligns with the following learning objectives.

- Understand the role and capabilities of generative AI in professional communication.
- Develop skills in using AI tools to craft various forms of correspondence.
- Learn to use the PROMPT Recipe for effective AI interaction in creating communication.
- Apply the CHECK AI Framework to ensure the accuracy and credibility of AI-generated content.
- Identify and address biases in AI-generated content using the BIAS Identification Framework.

- Identify appropriate tones and audiences for different types of professional communication.
- Evaluate and refine AI-generated content to ensure clarity, professionalism, and appropriateness.

Focus Skills

Critical Thinking	Communication	Digital Literacy
Audience Analysis	Tone Adjustment	Ethical Reasoning
Professionalism	Writing Skills	Evaluation and Synthesis

Experiment Protocol

Use the following steps to engage with this experiment.

1. If necessary, model how to use the generative AI tool as well as the PROMPT Recipe, CHECK AI, and BIAS Identification frameworks.
2. Discuss the importance of tone, audience, and context in professional communication. Highlight examples of different types of correspondence, such as emails, letters, and memos.
3. Have learners work independently or in small groups (for example, two to four participants) based on their needs and the available resources, ensuring each participant or group has access to the generative AI tool of your choice.
4. Explain how you will evaluate learners. Share the evaluation criteria (for example, clarity, alignment with goals, creativity) and clarify whether feedback will come from peers, the educator, or both.
5. Assign each learner or group a specific communication task related to a real-world scenario. This could include responding to a business inquiry, writing a cover letter, drafting a formal complaint, or creating a thank-you note.
6. Remind learners to apply the PROMPT Recipe to ensure their prompt inputs are comprehensive and clear. Direct them to use the generative AI tool to draft their correspondence, specifying the tone and audience in their prompt, documenting the resulting outputs effectively.
7. Encourage learners to apply the CHECK AI and BIAS Identification frameworks as part of their iterative refinement process to ensure clarity, accuracy, and ethical considerations in their outputs.
8. Have groups document their findings and refine their correspondence as needed, ensuring it meets the desired standards.
9. Facilitate a discussion on the effectiveness of the AI-generated communication, addressing any challenges or improvements.

Experiment Customization AI Prompt

Customize the following prompt to collaborate with AI.

> How can I customize an AI-assisted professional communication learning experiment for my [grade] [subject] class focused on [communication type]? The learning experiment involves learners working individually or in groups with access to a generative AI tool to create various forms of correspondence. They will specify the tone and audience and evaluate the AI-generated content for clarity, appropriateness, and professionalism. Adapt the learning objectives, activities, and assessments to fit my classroom context. Consider intrapersonal and interpersonal skill development along with cultural uniqueness.

Experiment Differentiation AI Prompt

Customize the following prompt to collaboratively differentiate with AI.

> How can I adjust an AI-assisted professional communication activity for [grade] [content] learners who [specific needs] and need [specific support]? The current activity entails learners working individually or in groups with access to a generative AI tool to create various forms of correspondence. They will specify the tone and audience and evaluate the AI-generated content for clarity, appropriateness, and professionalism.

Integration Examples

Explore integration examples across various learning contexts.

- **Science:** Learners use generative AI to draft a formal email for submitting a research abstract to a scientific journal. They refine the AI-generated output to ensure professionalism, accuracy, and clarity.
- **Mathematics:** Learners use generative AI to draft a formal letter to a mathematics competition committee, requesting participation details. They refine the AI-generated output to ensure precision, politeness, and clarity.
- **World languages:** Learners use generative AI to draft a formal letter in a target language, such as inviting a cultural exchange partner to an event. They refine the AI-generated draft to ensure proper tone, grammar, and cultural sensitivity.
- **Elementary English language arts:** Learners work in small groups without technology access to draft a thank-you letter to a community helper, such as a firefighter or librarian. The teacher uses generative AI to model how to craft a professional message, and the class collaborates to revise the AI-generated draft for tone, clarity, and appropriateness.

- **Professional learning:** Educators use generative AI to draft a progress report for stakeholders, such as administrators or a school board. They refine the AI-generated draft to ensure precision, clarity, and alignment with their objectives.

EXPERIMENT

Reflecting on Choices and Decisions

Decision making is a skill we rely on every day, but how often do we take the time to think about how we make those choices? In this experiment, learners will partner with generative AI to analyze their decision-making processes, reflect on their reasoning, and explore alternative outcomes. By breaking down personal, academic, or professional scenarios with the help of AI, learners engage in metacognition—thinking about thinking—to deepen their self-awareness and critical thinking skills. This reflective practice builds a foundation for making more thoughtful, informed decisions in the future.

For educators, this activity offers a powerful tool to teach learners the importance of reflective practice while also providing a method for self-reflection in professional contexts. From supporting learners through social dilemmas to evaluating their own decision making in lesson planning or leadership roles, educators can use AI as a scaffold for deeper exploration and growth.

Learning Goals

This experiment aligns with the following learning objectives.

- Understand the role and capabilities of generative AI in reflecting on decisions.
- Develop skills in using AI tools to analyze and reflect on decision-making processes.
- Learn to use the PROMPT Recipe for effective AI interaction in decision reflection.
- Apply the CHECK AI Framework to ensure the clarity and depth of AI-generated reflections.
- Identify and address biases in AI-generated content using the BIAS Identification Framework.
- Enhance reflective thinking and decision-making skills through AI-assisted analysis.

Focus Skills

Critical Thinking	Reflective Thinking	Digital Literacy
Evaluation and Synthesis	Analytical Thinking	Decision Making
Self-Awareness	Strategic Planning	Problem Solving

Experiment Protocol

1. If necessary, model how to use the generative AI tool as well as the PROMPT Recipe, CHECK AI, and BIAS Identification frameworks.
2. Discuss the importance of reflective practice in decision making by highlighting examples of effective decision reflection and demonstrating metacognition, or thinking about thinking.
3. Have learners work independently or in small groups (for example, two to four participants) based on their needs and the available resources, ensuring each participant or group has access to the generative AI tool of your choice.
4. Explain how you will evaluate learners. Share the evaluation criteria (for example, clarity, alignment with goals, creativity) and clarify whether feedback will come from peers, the educator, or both.
5. Assign each learner or group a specific decision-making scenario to analyze using the generative AI tool. This could include personal decisions, project choices, or hypothetical situations.
6. Remind learners to apply the PROMPT Recipe to ensure their prompt inputs are comprehensive and clear. Direct them to use the generative AI tool to reflect on their decision-making processes, considering factors such as rationale, potential outcomes, and alternatives, documenting the resulting outputs effectively.
7. Encourage learners to apply the CHECK AI and BIAS Identification frameworks as part of their iterative refinement process to ensure clarity, accuracy, and ethical considerations in their outputs.
8. Have learners document their reflections and the AI feedback, making necessary adjustments to refine their decision-making processes.
9. Facilitate a discussion on the effectiveness of AI-generated reflections, addressing any challenges or improvements.

Experiment Customization AI Prompt

Customize the following prompt to collaborate with AI.

How can I customize an AI-assisted decision reflection learning experiment for my [grade] [subject] class focused on [specific decision-making scenario]? The learning experiment involves learners working individually or in groups with access to a generative AI tool to reflect on their decision-making processes. They will specify the scenario, generate reflections, and evaluate the AI-generated responses for clarity, depth, and potential biases. Adapt the learning objectives, activities, and assessments to fit my classroom context. Consider intrapersonal and interpersonal skill development along with cultural uniqueness.

Experiment Differentiation AI Prompt

Customize the following prompt to collaboratively differentiate with AI.

How can I adjust an AI-assisted decision reflection activity for [grade] [content] learners who [specific needs] and need [specific support]? The current activity entails learners working individually or in groups with access to a generative AI tool to reflect on their decision-making processes. They will specify the scenario, generate reflections, and evaluate the AI-generated responses for clarity, depth, and potential biases.

Integration Examples

Explore integration examples across various learning contexts.

- **English:** Learners use generative AI to reflect on how they chose to give peer feedback on writing assignments, analyzing whether their comments were constructive, clear, and actionable. They ask the AI for suggestions on improving their approach to provide more meaningful feedback.
- **Social studies:** Learners use generative AI to reflect on a decision to support or oppose a civic initiative, such as advocating for a local policy change. They evaluate their reasoning, explore alternative perspectives, and refine their arguments based on AI input.
- **Elementary health education:** Learners reflect in small groups—without using technology—on a recent personal choice related to health or well-being, such as choosing a snack or responding to a stressful moment. After learners share their reasoning and outcomes, the teacher uses generative AI to model additional strategies or perspectives. The class then compares their own reflections with the AI's suggestions to deepen discussion.
- **Academic counseling:** Learners use generative AI to reflect on a significant academic or career decision, such as selecting elective courses or deciding on a college major. They analyze their reasoning, explore alternative paths, and refine their planning strategies with AI input.
- **Professional learning:** Educators use generative AI to reflect on their professional growth decisions, such as pursuing additional certifications or attending conferences. They analyze their reasoning, explore potential alternatives, and refine their goals with AI support.

EXPERIMENT

Solving Problems Strategically

Problem solving is a cornerstone of success in any field, and AI can elevate this skill to new heights. In this experiment, learners collaborate with generative AI to tackle complex challenges, whether technical, real world, or hypothetical. By identifying issues, analyzing potential solutions, and refining their approaches, learners develop critical thinking, analytical skills, and systematic reasoning. This hands-on activity highlights how AI can serve as a powerful partner in breaking down problems and designing effective solutions.

For educators, this experiment offers a structured way to teach problem solving and troubleshooting while modeling how AI can support critical and strategic thinking. Whether addressing classroom challenges, planning projects, or guiding learners through real-world scenarios, educators can apply these tools to strengthen their own approaches to problem resolution. By participating in this activity, learners and educators alike gain valuable skills to navigate today's increasingly complex and technology-driven world.

Learning Goals

This experiment aligns with the following learning objectives.

- Understand the role and capabilities of generative AI in problem solving and troubleshooting.
- Develop skills in using AI tools to identify, analyze, and solve problems.
- Learn to use the PROMPT Recipe for effective AI interaction in problem resolution.
- Apply the CHECK AI Framework to ensure the accuracy and feasibility of AI-generated solutions.
- Identify and address biases in AI-generated content using the BIAS Identification Framework.
- Enhance problem-solving and troubleshooting skills through AI-assisted approaches.

Focus Skills

Critical Thinking	Problem Solving	Digital Literacy
Evaluation and Synthesis	Analytical Thinking	Reflective Thinking
Information Literacy	Strategic Planning	Systematic Reasoning

Experiment Protocol

Use the following steps to engage with this experiment.

1. If necessary, model how to use the generative AI tool as well as the PROMPT Recipe, CHECK AI, and BIAS Identification frameworks.
2. Discuss the importance of problem solving and troubleshooting in various contexts. Highlight examples of effective problem-solving strategies.
3. Have learners work independently or in small groups (for example, two to four) based on their needs and the available resources, ensuring each participant or group has access to the generative AI tool of your choice.
4. Explain how you will evaluate learners. Share the evaluation criteria (for example, clarity, alignment with goals, creativity) and clarify whether feedback will come from peers, the educator, or both.
5. Assign each learner or group a specific problem or scenario to address using the generative AI tool. This could include technical issues, real-world challenges, or hypothetical situations.
6. Remind learners to apply the PROMPT Recipe to ensure their prompt inputs are comprehensive and clear. Direct them to use the generative AI tool to identify, analyze, and propose solutions to their assigned problems. Instruct them to document the resulting outputs effectively.
7. Encourage learners to apply the CHECK AI and BIAS Identification frameworks as part of their iterative refinement process to ensure clarity, accuracy, and ethical considerations in their outputs.
8. Have learners document their problem-solving processes, solutions, and the AI feedback, making necessary adjustments to refine their approaches.
9. Facilitate a discussion on the effectiveness of AI-generated problem solving and troubleshooting, addressing any challenges or improvements.

Experiment Customization AI Prompt

Customize the following prompt to collaborate with AI.

> How can I customize an AI-assisted problem solving and troubleshooting learning experiment for my [grade] [subject] class focused on [specific problem or scenario]? The learning experiment involves learners working individually or in groups with access to a generative AI tool to identify, analyze, and solve problems. They will specify the problem, generate solutions, and evaluate the AI-generated responses for accuracy, feasibility, and potential biases. Adapt the learning objectives, activities, and assessments to fit my classroom context. Consider intrapersonal and interpersonal skill development along with cultural uniqueness.

Experiment Differentiation AI Prompt

Customize the following prompt to collaboratively differentiate with AI.

> How can I adjust an AI-assisted problem-solving and troubleshooting activity for [grade] [content] learners who [specific needs] and need [specific support]? The

current activity entails learners working individually or in groups with access to a generative AI tool to identify, analyze, and solve problems. They will specify the problem, generate solutions, and evaluate the AI-generated responses for accuracy, feasibility, and potential biases.

Integration Examples

Explore integration examples across various learning contexts.

- **Social studies:** Learners use generative AI to propose solutions for social issues, such as addressing homelessness or improving voter turnout. They refine their policy recommendations based on AI feedback to ensure feasibility and inclusivity.
- **Environmental science:** Learners use generative AI to solve an environmental issue, such as reducing urban heat islands. They evaluate the AI-generated solutions, refine their approaches, and consider the ethical and practical implications.
- **Visual art:** Learners use generative AI to address artistic challenges, such as resolving balance issues in a composition or selecting sustainable materials for a project. They refine their creative choices with AI input, ensuring alignment with their artistic goals.
- **Elementary counseling groups:** Learners collaborate in small groups to brainstorm ways to solve everyday challenges, such as resolving peer conflicts or improving teamwork, relying solely on their own ideas and discussion. Afterward, the counselor demonstrates how generative AI might approach the same problem, and the group compares solutions for inclusivity, realism, and kindness.
- **Professional learning:** Educators use generative AI to troubleshoot a classroom challenge, such as improving learner engagement during lessons. They analyze AI-generated strategies and refine their approach to meet the specific needs of their learners.

EXPERIMENT

Building Checklists

Breaking down complex tasks into manageable steps is an essential skill for navigating academic, professional, and everyday challenges. AI can make this process more efficient and precise. In this experiment, learners collaborate with generative AI to create detailed, structured checklists for multifaceted tasks, such as planning a research project or organizing an event. By specifying the components of each task and refining their outputs, learners enhance their planning, organizational, and task management skills.

For educators, this activity highlights how AI can support both learners' executive functioning and their own professional workflows. Whether streamlining lesson planning, coordinating events, or guiding learners through project management, AI-generated checklists offer a valuable tool for clarity and structure. By participating in this experiment, learners and educators alike gain a deeper appreciation for the power of structured planning in tackling complex challenges.

Learning Goals

This experiment aligns with the following learning objectives.

- Understand the role and capabilities of generative AI in creating checklists for complex tasks.
- Develop skills in using AI tools to break down complex tasks into manageable steps.
- Learn to use the PROMPT Recipe for effective AI interaction in checklist creation.
- Apply the CHECK AI Framework to ensure the clarity and effectiveness of AI-generated checklists.
- Identify and address biases in AI-generated content using the BIAS Identification Framework.
- Enhance task management and organizational skills using structured checklists.

Focus Skills

Critical Thinking	Executive Functioning	Digital Literacy
Evaluation and Synthesis	Analytical Thinking	Reflective Thinking
Problem Solving	Strategic Thinking	Task Management

Experiment Protocol

Use the following steps to engage with this experiment.

1. If necessary, model how to use the generative AI tool as well as the PROMPT Recipe, CHECK AI, and BIAS Identification frameworks.
2. Discuss the importance of breaking down complex tasks into manageable steps and using checklists in various contexts. Highlight examples of effective checklists.
3. Have learners work independently or in small groups (for example, two to four participants) based on their needs and the available resources,

ensuring each participant or group has access to the generative AI tool of your choice.

4. Explain how you will evaluate learners. Share the evaluation criteria (for example, clarity, alignment with goals, creativity) and clarify whether feedback will come from peers, the educator, or both.
5. Assign each learner or group a specific complex task related to the course content. This could include planning a research project, organizing an event, completing a lab experiment, or any other multifaceted task.
6. Remind learners to apply the PROMPT Recipe to ensure their prompt inputs are comprehensive and clear. Direct them to use the generative AI tool to create a detailed checklist for their assigned task, specifying the task components in their prompt and documenting the resulting outputs effectively.
7. Encourage learners to apply the CHECK AI and BIAS Identification frameworks as part of their iterative refinement process to ensure clarity, accuracy, and ethical considerations in their outputs.
8. Have groups document their findings and refine their checklists as needed, ensuring they meet the desired standards.
9. Facilitate a discussion on the effectiveness of the AI-generated checklists, addressing any challenges or improvements.

Experiment Customization AI Prompt

Customize the following prompt to collaborate with AI.

> How can I customize an AI-assisted task breakdown and checklist creation learning experiment for my [grade] [subject] class focused on [task]? The learning experiment involves learners working individually or in groups with access to a generative AI tool to create detailed checklists for various complex tasks. They will specify the task components and evaluate the AI-generated content for clarity, completeness, and effectiveness. Adapt the learning objectives, activities, and assessments to fit my classroom context. Consider intrapersonal and interpersonal skill development along with cultural uniqueness.

Experiment Differentiation AI Prompt

Customize the following prompt to collaboratively differentiate with AI.

> How can I adjust an AI-assisted task breakdown and checklist creation activity for [grade] [content] learners who [specific needs] and need [specific support]? The current activity entails learners working individually or in groups with access to a generative AI tool to create detailed checklists for various complex tasks. They will specify the task components and evaluate the AI-generated content for clarity, completeness, and effectiveness.

Integration Examples

Explore integration examples across various learning contexts.

- **Computer science:** Learners use generative AI to create a checklist for building a coding project, such as developing a simple app or website. Steps include defining requirements, writing code, debugging, and testing. They refine the AI-generated checklist for accuracy and usability.
- **Theater:** Learners use generative AI to create a checklist for organizing a class play or theater production. Steps include casting, set design, rehearsals, and marketing the performance. Learners evaluate the checklist for completeness and practicality.
- **Mathematics:** Learners use generative AI to create a checklist for completing a mathematics-based research project, such as analyzing statistical data or creating mathematical models. Steps include defining the problem, collecting data, and validating results. Learners refine the AI-generated checklist for accuracy and usability.
- **Elementary executive functioning:** Learners work in small groups to brainstorm the steps needed to complete a classroom task that supports organization or planning, such as preparing for a group project or managing materials for a center rotation. Without using technology, they create a checklist together. The teacher then models how generative AI might create a checklist for the same task. The class compares the two for clarity and usefulness.
- **Professional learning:** Educators use generative AI to create a checklist for designing an engaging lesson plan, including steps for setting objectives, selecting materials, and designing assessments. They refine the AI-generated checklist for clarity and alignment with curriculum goals.

EXPERIMENT

Enhancing Teamwork and Collaboration

Teamwork thrives when each team member's strengths are recognized and aligned with clear, well-defined roles. Whether working on a classroom project or navigating professional collaborations, understanding how to optimize team dynamics is essential for success. In this experiment, learners will partner with generative AI to identify team members' strengths and assign roles tailored to their unique skills. By analyzing group needs and creating structured plans, learners develop project management and organizational abilities while enhancing collaboration and strategic thinking.

For educators, this activity provides a flexible framework for teaching teamwork in classroom settings or facilitating professional development. In a classroom, learners might use AI to assign roles for a science project or a group presentation, while in a professional context, educators can explore how AI might streamline staff collaboration, event planning, or interdisciplinary initiatives. By engaging in this activity, learners and educators alike gain tools to maximize team effectiveness and navigate group work with clarity and purpose.

Learning Goals

This experiment aligns with the following learning objectives.

- Understand the role and capabilities of generative AI in defining and assigning team roles.
- Develop skills in using AI tools to allocate roles based on team members' strengths.
- Learn to use the PROMPT Recipe for effective AI interaction in role assignment.
- Apply the CHECK AI Framework to ensure the clarity and feasibility of AI-generated role assignments.
- Identify and address biases in AI-generated content using the BIAS Identification Framework.
- Enhance project management and teamwork skills through AI-assisted role assignment.

Focus Skills

Critical Thinking	Project Management	Digital Literacy
Evaluation and Synthesis	Analytical Thinking	Reflective Thinking
Collaboration	Strategic Thinking	Organizational Skills

Experiment Protocol

Use the following steps to engage with this experiment.

1. If necessary, model how to use the generative AI tool as well as the PROMPT Recipe, CHECK AI, and BIAS Identification frameworks.
2. Discuss the importance of clear role definitions and effective role assignment in team projects. Highlight examples of successful role management.
3. Have learners work independently or in small groups (for example, two to four participants) based on their needs and the available resources, ensuring each participant or group has access to the generative AI tool of your choice.

4. Explain how you will evaluate learners. Share the evaluation criteria (for example, clarity, alignment with goals, creativity) and clarify whether feedback will come from peers, the educator, or both.
5. Assign each learner or group a specific project and instruct them to use the generative AI tool to identify team members' strengths and define roles.
6. Remind learners to apply the PROMPT Recipe to ensure their prompt inputs are comprehensive and clear. Direct them to use the generative AI tool to allocate roles and responsibilities within their team, specifying the skills and strengths of each team member. Instruct them to document the resulting outputs effectively.
7. Encourage learners to apply the CHECK AI and BIAS Identification frameworks as part of their iterative refinement process to ensure clarity, accuracy, and ethical considerations in their outputs.
8. Have learners document their role assignments and the AI feedback, making necessary adjustments to refine their project plans.
9. Facilitate a discussion on the effectiveness of AI-generated role assignments, addressing any challenges or improvements.

Experiment Customization AI Prompt

Customize the following prompt to collaborate with AI.

> How can I customize an AI-assisted team role assignment learning experiment for my [grade] [subject] class focused on [specific project or activity]? The learning experiment involves learners working individually or in groups with access to a generative AI tool to analyze team member strengths and assign project roles. Learners will specify team member skills, interact with the AI tool, and evaluate the AI-generated role assignments for clarity, alignment, and effectiveness. Adapt the learning objectives, activities, and assessments to fit my classroom context. Consider intrapersonal and interpersonal skill development along with cultural uniqueness.

Experiment Differentiation AI Prompt

Customize the following prompt to collaboratively differentiate with AI.

> How can I adjust an AI-assisted team role assignment activity for my [grade] [content] learners who [specific needs] and need [specific support]? The current activity entails learners working individually or in groups with access to a generative AI tool to analyze team member strengths and assign project roles. Learners will specify team member skills, interact with the AI tool, and evaluate the AI-generated role assignments for clarity, alignment, and effectiveness.

Integration Examples

Explore integration examples across various learning contexts.

- **Science:** Learners use generative AI to assign roles for a group lab experiment, such as data collector, materials manager, and analyst, based on team members' strengths and interests. They refine the role assignments to ensure clarity and alignment with the experiment's objectives.
- **Elementary English language arts:** Learners work in small groups on a shared storytelling project. The teacher uses generative AI in advance to model how to thoughtfully assign roles, such as illustrator, narrator, and editor, based on learners' strengths. During the activity, learners collaborate without using technology, and the class refines the role assignments together to ensure everyone contributes meaningfully and understands their part.
- **Journalism:** Learners use generative AI to assign roles for creating a school newsletter, such as writer, photographer, and editor. They refine the assignments to ensure deadlines are met and content is engaging.
- **Culinary arts:** Learners use generative AI to define roles for planning a catered event, such as menu designer, prep chef, and logistics coordinator. They refine the assignments to ensure smooth execution and effective teamwork.
- **Professional learning:** Educators use generative AI to assign roles for a grade-level collaborative project, such as managing group logistics, designing rubrics, and handling peer feedback. They refine the assignments to ensure inclusivity and effectiveness.

EXPERIMENT

Creating Rubrics

Rubrics are powerful tools for guiding and evaluating performance, and AI can help learners master the art of creating them. In this experiment, learners collaborate with generative AI to design detailed rubrics for an assigned task, such as a presentation or creative writing piece. Once their rubrics are finalized, learners will use them for self-assessment, reflecting on their performance and identifying areas for improvement. This hands-on activity fosters critical thinking, self-assessment, and collaborative skills while emphasizing the importance of clear assessment criteria in achieving meaningful growth.

For educators, this activity offers a dual advantage: It provides a structured way to teach learners about assessment and self-reflection while also showcasing how AI can streamline rubric development in professional settings. From evaluating learner work to setting standards for team projects, AI-generated rubrics offer educators an efficient and effective tool for creating transparent, actionable criteria. By engaging in this experiment, both learners and educators deepen their understanding of assessment as a key to continuous improvement.

Learning Goals

This experiment aligns with the following learning objectives.

- Understand the components and purpose of a rubric.
- Develop skills in creating effective assessment criteria using generative AI.
- Learn to use the PROMPT Recipe for effective AI interaction.
- Apply the CHECK AI Framework to review and refine AI-generated content.
- Identify and address biases in AI using the BIAS Identification Framework.
- Learn to use a rubric for self-assessment and reflection.
- Enhance critical thinking and self-evaluation skills.

Focus Skills

Critical Thinking	Self-Assessment	Collaboration
Communication	Reflective Thinking	Analytical Thinking
Strategic Planning	Technical Proficiency	Decision Making

Experiment Protocol

Use the following steps to engage with this experiment.

1. If necessary, model how to use the generative AI tool as well as the PROMPT Recipe, CHECK AI, and BIAS Identification frameworks.
2. Explain the purpose and components of a rubric, including criteria, levels of performance, and descriptors.
3. Have learners work independently or in small groups (for example, two to four participants) based on their needs and the available resources, ensuring each participant or group has access to the generative AI tool of your choice.
4. Explain how you will evaluate learners. Share the evaluation criteria (for example, clarity, alignment with goals, creativity) and clarify whether feedback will come from peers, the educator, or both.
5. Assign a common task or project that the learners will be working on, such as a short presentation, a creative writing piece, or a science experiment. The groups should discuss.

6. Remind learners to apply the PROMPT Recipe to ensure their prompt inputs are comprehensive and clear. Direct them to use the generative AI tool to brainstorm and list the key elements that should be assessed for the assigned task and to document the resulting outputs effectively.
7. Guide learners to categorize these elements into criteria (for example, creativity, organization, clarity, technical skills), to define levels of performance for each criterion (for example, leading, advancing, implementing, learning), and to write descriptors for each level of performance—utilizing AI.
8. Encourage learners to apply the CHECK AI and BIAS Identification frameworks as part of their iterative refinement process to ensure clarity, accuracy, and ethical considerations in their outputs.
9. Have groups exchange their AI-generated rubrics with other groups for feedback and suggestions for improvement, revising their rubrics as a result.
10. Ask learners to complete the initial assigned task, using the rubric as a guide. After completing the task, learners use their rubric to assess their own performance, writing a brief reflection on what they learned from the self-assessment process and how they can improve.
11. Facilitate a discussion on the experience of creating and using rubrics for self-assessment. Discuss the benefits and challenges encountered.

Experiment Customization AI Prompt

Customize the following prompt to collaborate with AI.

> How can I customize a learning experiment where learners create a rubric using generative AI and use it for self-assessment in my [grade] [subject] class focused on [specific project or task]? The learning experiment involves learners working in small groups to develop rubrics with the help of AI, complete an assigned task, and use the rubric for self-assessment. Groups will also participate in peer reviews and class discussions to reflect on the process. Adapt the learning objectives, activities, and assessments to fit my classroom context. Consider intrapersonal and interpersonal skill development along with cultural uniqueness.

Experiment Differentiation AI Prompt

Customize the following prompt to collaboratively differentiate with AI.

> How can I adjust a learning experiment where learners create a rubric using generative AI and use it for self-assessment for [grade] [content] learners who [specific needs] and need [specific support]? The current activity entails learners working in small groups to develop rubrics with the help of AI, complete an assigned task, and use the rubric for self-assessment. The current process includes peer reviews and class discussions to reflect on the process.

Integration Examples

Explore integration examples across various learning contexts.

- **Mathematics:** Learners use generative AI to create a rubric for assessing a mathematics-based project or problem set. Criteria might include logical reasoning, accuracy, and presentation. After completing their problems, learners use the rubric to evaluate their approaches and identify strategies for improvement.
- **Health education:** Learners use generative AI to create a rubric for a personal wellness plan. Criteria might include practicality, inclusivity, and goal alignment. After drafting their plans, learners use the rubric to evaluate its feasibility and make adjustments.
- **Business:** Learners use generative AI to develop a rubric for assessing a business pitch, focusing on innovation, persuasiveness, and clarity of communication. After delivering their pitches, learners use the rubric to reflect on the effectiveness of their presentation and refine their approach.
- **Elementary music:** Learners rehearse a group performance, such as a class song or rhythm routine. Together with the teacher, who models the use of generative AI, they codevelop a simple rubric with criteria like participation, rhythm, and teamwork. Learners then use the collaboratively created rubric (without using technology themselves) to reflect on their performance and set goals for improvement.
- **Professional learning:** Educators use generative AI to design a rubric for evaluating the effectiveness of their lesson plans, focusing on alignment with objectives, engagement strategies, and assessment methods. They apply the rubric to reflect on their planning process and improve future lessons.

The following discussion, "Generative AI—Exploring Capabilities and Constraints," invites learners to explore the strengths and limitations of generative AI and how these capabilities shape its real-world use.

Discussion: Generative AI—Exploring Capabilities and Constraints

Instructions: Use this protocol to plan and adapt a discussion that fits your audience, setting, and goals by reviewing the guidance and prompts prior to facilitating the discussion. This protocol serves as a flexible planning tool designed to help you frame the conversation, customize the experience, and support meaningful participation.

Big Question

What are the current abilities and limitations of generative AI, and how do they impact various fields and industries?

Learning Goals

- Understand the key functions and capabilities of generative AI models.
- Explore the applications of generative AI in fields such as art, entertainment, healthcare, and education.
- Analyze the limitations and challenges generative AI faces in terms of creativity, accuracy, and reliability.
- Evaluate the ethical implications and potential biases in generative AI outputs.
- Investigate the impact of generative AI on jobs and the creative industries.
- Discuss the potential risks and misuse of generative AI, including misinformation and deepfakes.
- Develop critical thinking about the future advancements and regulatory needs for generative AI.
- Promote awareness of the skills necessary to work with and develop generative AI systems.

Focus Skills

Critical Thinking	Ethical Reasoning	Evaluation and Synthesis
Technological Literacy	Information Literacy	Decision Making
Communication	Strategic Thinking	Problem Solving

Discussion Customization AI Prompt

> How can I customize a discussion for my [grade] [subject] class focused on the current abilities and limitations of generative AI?

For example:

> How can I customize a discussion for twelfth-grade journalism learners exploring media evolution by analyzing how generative AI contributes to misinformation?

Discussion Differentiation AI Prompt

> How can I adjust a discussion for [grade] [content] learners who [specific needs] and need [specific support] to understand the current abilities and limitations of generative AI?

For example:

> How can I adjust a discussion for eighth-grade mathematics learners who benefit from visuals and need support understanding how AI handles patterns and problem solving?

Discussion Extension AI Prompt

> How can I extend a discussion to challenge advanced [grade] [content] learners and deepen their understanding of the current abilities and limitations of generative AI?

For example:

> How can I extend a discussion for sixth-grade humanities learners who enjoy debate and need a space to ask whether AI creates or just mimics?

EXPERIMENT

Creating Customized Roles for Tasks

An AI persona is a customized role or character designed to help accomplish specific tasks. For example, learners might prompt the AI by saying, "Take on the role of a marine biologist analyzing ocean pollution data," or "Take on the role of a historian researching ancient civilizations." By specifying the role, learners give the AI essential context, tailoring its responses to align with the task at hand. In this experiment, learners use generative AI tools to create and customize personas for tasks like research, creative writing, or data analysis. This hands-on activity sharpens critical thinking, creativity, and digital literacy while showcasing how AI can adapt to diverse applications. These early skills in role customization also lay the groundwork for agentic AI, where AI systems act more autonomously, take on complex roles, and carry out tasks with minimal direct input from the user while still aligning with human goals.

For educators, this activity highlights the versatility of AI in enhancing both learning and professional workflows. Learners might create personas to support group projects or tackle challenging assignments, while educators can explore task-specific AI tools for lesson planning, staff collaboration, or classroom innovation. By participating in this experiment, learners and educators alike gain valuable skills in customizing AI interactions and leveraging AI's potential as a collaborative partner.

Learning Goals

This experiment aligns with the following learning objectives.

- Understand the role and capabilities of generative AI in creating task-specific personas.
- Develop skills in customizing AI personas for different tasks such as research, creative writing, and data analysis.
- Learn to use the PROMPT Recipe for effective AI interaction in persona creation.
- Apply the CHECK AI Framework to ensure the accuracy and relevance of AI-generated personas.
- Identify and address biases in AI-generated content using the BIAS Identification Framework.
- Enhance digital literacy and creativity through the creation of AI personas.

Focus Skills

Critical Thinking	Creativity	Digital Literacy
Information Literacy	Analytical Thinking	Reflective Thinking
Problem Solving	Evaluation and Synthesis	Ethical Reasoning

Experiment Protocol

Use the following steps to engage with this experiment.

1. If necessary, model how to use the generative AI tool as well as the PROMPT Recipe, CHECK AI, and BIAS Identification frameworks.
2. Discuss the importance of creating personas for different tasks and the role of customization in enhancing AI interaction. Highlight examples of task-specific personas in various fields.
3. Have learners work independently or in small groups (for example, two to four participants) based on their needs and the available resources, ensuring each participant or group has access to the generative AI tool of your choice.
4. Explain how you will evaluate learners. Share the evaluation criteria (for example, clarity, alignment with goals, creativity) and clarify whether feedback will come from peers, the educator, or both.
5. Assign each learner or group a specific task for which they will create an AI persona, such as research, creative writing, or data analysis.
6. Remind learners to apply the PROMPT Recipe to ensure their prompt inputs are comprehensive and clear. Direct them to use the generative AI tool to create and customize personas tailored to their assigned tasks and to document the resulting outputs effectively. If desired, guide learners to prompt the AI by saying, "Take on the role of [persona]," to provide clear context for the task.
7. Encourage learners to apply the CHECK AI and BIAS Identification frameworks as part of their iterative refinement process to ensure clarity, accuracy, and ethical considerations in their outputs.
8. Have learners document their original task requirements, AI-generated personas, and any revisions made based on the evaluation.
9. Facilitate a discussion on the effectiveness of AI-generated personas, addressing any challenges or improvements.

Experiment Customization AI Prompt

Customize the following prompt to collaborate with AI.

> How can I customize an AI-powered persona-creation learning experiment for my [grade] [subject] class focused on [specific task]? The learning experiment involves learners working individually or in groups with access to a generative AI tool to create and customize AI personas tailored for specific tasks. They will specify the task, generate AI personas, and evaluate the AI-generated personas for accuracy, relevance, and potential biases. Adapt the learning objectives, activities, and assessments to fit my classroom context. Consider intrapersonal and interpersonal skill development along with cultural uniqueness.

Experiment Differentiation AI Prompt

Customize the following prompt to collaboratively differentiate with AI.

> How can I adjust an AI-powered persona-creation activity for [grade] [content] learners who [specific needs] and need [specific support]? The current activity entails learners working individually or in groups with access to a generative AI tool to create and customize AI personas tailored for specific tasks. They will specify the task, generate AI personas, and evaluate the AI-generated personas for accuracy, relevance, and potential biases.

Integration Examples

Explore integration examples across various learning contexts.

- **History:** Learners prompt the AI to become a historian specializing in ancient civilizations, guiding them in researching the cultural, political, and economic aspects of a chosen civilization. The persona helps frame responses with relevant sources and balanced perspectives.
- **English:** Learners create a persona as a creative writing coach to guide them in crafting compelling narratives. The AI offers advice on character development, plot twists, and tone. Learners evaluate and refine the persona's suggestions to align with their story goals.
- **Elementary social studies:** The teacher models the use of an AI tool to create a persona as a cultural guide who introduces aspects of daily life in a selected country. Learners engage with the information the teacher shares—such as local customs, holidays, and foods—through classroom discussion, reflection, and related activities. The class evaluates and expands on these ideas together without the learners directly using AI.
- **Science:** Learners prompt the AI to take on the role of a marine biologist to analyze ocean pollution data. The persona offers insights into trends, impacts on marine life, and potential solutions. Learners refine the persona's output to ensure accuracy and depth.
- **Professional learning:** Educators use an AI persona as a collaboration mentor to guide them in planning interdisciplinary projects with colleagues. The persona offers strategies for assigning roles, setting goals, and tracking progress.

EXPERIMENT

Streamlining Goals and Progress Tracking

Goal setting is a powerful skill for personal and academic growth, and AI can help learners refine and achieve their objectives with greater precision. In this experiment, learners partner with generative AI to set, refine, and track their goals, receiving interactive feedback and coaching to ensure their goals are SMART (strategic and specific, measurable, attainable, results-oriented, and time bound). By leveraging AI tools, learners sharpen their self-regulation, critical thinking, and goal-setting skills while gaining insight into the value of continuous improvement. Learners should avoid entering private or personally identifying information into AI tools unless specifically authorized to do so, as information shared with AI may not be fully private.

For educators, this activity offers a structured way to teach learners the principles of effective goal setting while introducing AI's potential as a personal development coach. Educators can also apply these strategies to their own professional growth, using AI to plan, refine, and track their goals. By participating in this experiment, learners and educators alike enhance their ability to turn aspirations into actionable plans, fostering success in both academic and professional contexts.

Learning Goals

This experiment aligns with the following learning objectives.

- Understand the role and capabilities of generative AI in goal setting.
- Develop skills in using AI tools to set, refine, and track goals.
- Learn to use the PROMPT Recipe for effective AI interaction in goal setting.
- Apply the CHECK AI Framework to ensure the clarity and effectiveness of AI-generated goals.
- Identify and address biases in AI-generated content using the BIAS Identification Framework.
- Enhance self-regulation and continuous improvement through interactive goal setting.

Focus Skills

Critical Thinking	Goal Setting	Digital Literacy
Self-Regulation	Analytical Thinking	Reflective Thinking
Problem Solving	Evaluation and Synthesis	Self-Evaluation

Experiment Protocol

Use the following steps to engage with this experiment.

1. If necessary, model how to use the generative AI tool as well as the PROMPT Recipe, CHECK AI, and BIAS Identification frameworks.
2. Discuss the importance of goal setting in personal and academic development. Highlight examples of effective goal-setting strategies. Introduce SMART goals if needed.
3. Have learners work independently or in small groups (for example, two to four participants) based on their needs and the available resources, ensuring each participant or group has access to the generative AI tool of your choice.
4. Explain how you will evaluate learners. Share the evaluation criteria (for example, clarity, alignment with goals, creativity) and clarify whether feedback will come from peers, the educator, or both.
5. Assign each learner the task of setting specific personal or academic goals using the generative AI tool, specifying the components of their goals in their prompt.
6. Remind learners to apply the PROMPT Recipe to ensure their prompt inputs are comprehensive and clear. Direct them to use the generative AI tool to receive feedback and coaching on their goals, ensuring the goals are SMART. Instruct them to document the resulting outputs effectively.
7. Encourage learners to apply the CHECK AI and BIAS Identification frameworks as part of their iterative refinement process to ensure clarity, accuracy, and ethical considerations in their outputs.
8. Have learners document their goals and the AI feedback, making necessary adjustments to refine their goals.
9. Facilitate a discussion on the effectiveness of AI-generated goal setting, addressing any challenges or improvements.

Experiment Customization AI Prompt

Customize the following prompt to collaborate with AI.

> How can I customize an AI-assisted goal-setting learning experiment for my [grade] [subject] class focused on [type of goals]? The learning experiment involves learners working individually with access to a generative AI tool to set and refine personal or academic goals. They will specify the components of their goals and evaluate the AI-generated goals for clarity, feasibility, and alignment with their objectives. Adapt the learning objectives, activities, and assessments to fit my classroom context. Consider intrapersonal and interpersonal skill development along with cultural uniqueness.

Experiment Differentiation AI Prompt

Customize the following prompt to collaboratively differentiate with AI.

> How can I adjust an AI-assisted goal-setting activity for [grade] [content] learners who [specific needs] and need [specific support]? The current activity entails learners working individually with access to a generative AI tool to set and refine personal or academic goals. They will specify the components of their goals and evaluate the AI-generated goals for clarity, feasibility, and alignment with their objectives.

Integration Examples

Explore integration examples across various learning contexts.

- **Elementary classroom routines:** Learners brainstorm classroom goals such as improving transition times or keeping materials organized. The teacher models how to transform these into SMART goals using generative AI, while learners observe and contribute ideas. Together, they track progress using visual tools and classroom routines, without direct learner use of AI.
- **Mathematics:** Learners use generative AI to establish SMART goals for mastering specific mathematics skills, such as solving quadratic equations or improving test accuracy. They refine these goals based on AI feedback and create a plan for daily practice.
- **Automotive technology:** Learners set SMART goals for diagnosing and repairing a vehicle issue, such as mastering diagnostic tools or completing the repair within a set time frame. They use AI to refine their goals and plan the steps to accomplish the task effectively.
- **College and career readiness:** Learners set SMART goals for preparing a college application or building a professional résumé, such as completing drafts by specific deadlines or practicing interview skills. They use AI to refine their goals and receive coaching on steps to improve their applications and preparation strategies.
- **Professional learning:** Educators use generative AI to set SMART goals for professional development, such as integrating technology into lessons or improving classroom management techniques. The AI provides feedback on making the goals actionable and measurable, supporting continuous improvement.

EXPERIMENT

Using AI Tools for Time Management and Productivity

Managing time effectively is an essential skill, but it's often easier said than done. In this experiment, learners harness the power of AI to simplify scheduling and planning, creating detailed calendars, timetables, and task lists for their projects or events. By refining their schedules with AI feedback, learners enhance their organizational skills and develop a deeper appreciation for structured time management.

For educators, this activity offers a way to teach time management in a hands-on, interactive format while exploring how AI tools can optimize planning. From organizing lesson plans to coordinating meetings, AI can support educators in balancing their professional responsibilities. By participating in this experiment, learners and educators alike gain practical tools to tackle tasks and timelines with confidence and efficiency.

Learning Goals

This experiment aligns with the following learning objectives.

- Understand the role and capabilities of generative AI in creating schedules, calendars, and timetables.
- Develop skills in using AI tools to plan and organize tasks and events.
- Learn to use the PROMPT Recipe for effective AI interaction in scheduling.
- Apply the CHECK AI Framework to ensure the clarity and feasibility of AI-generated schedules.
- Identify and address biases in AI-generated content using the BIAS Identification Framework.
- Enhance organizational and time management skills using AI-generated schedules.

Focus Skills

Critical Thinking	Time Management	Digital Literacy
Organizational Skills	Analytical Thinking	Reflective Thinking
Strategic Planning	Evaluation and Synthesis	Task Management

Experiment Protocol

Use the following steps to engage with this experiment.

1. If necessary, model how to use the generative AI tool as well as the PROMPT Recipe, CHECK AI, and BIAS Identification frameworks.

2. Discuss the importance of effective scheduling and time management in personal and academic success. Highlight examples of effective schedules and timetables.
3. Have learners work independently or in small groups (for example, two to four participants) based on their needs and the available resources, ensuring each participant or group has access to the generative AI tool of your choice.
4. Explain how you will evaluate learners. Share the evaluation criteria (for example, clarity, alignment with goals, creativity) and clarify whether feedback will come from peers, the educator, or both.
5. Assign each learner or group a specific task or event to plan using the generative AI tool. This could include planning a study schedule, creating a calendar for a project, or organizing a timetable for an event.
6. Remind learners to apply the PROMPT Recipe to ensure their prompt inputs are comprehensive and clear. Direct them to use the generative AI tool to create detailed schedules, specifying the components of their schedules in their prompt and documenting the resulting outputs effectively.
7. Encourage learners to apply the CHECK AI and BIAS Identification frameworks as part of their iterative refinement process to ensure clarity, accuracy, and ethical considerations in their outputs.
8. Have learners document their schedules and the AI feedback, making necessary adjustments to refine their plans.
9. Facilitate a discussion on the effectiveness of AI-generated scheduling, addressing any challenges or improvements.

Experiment Customization AI Prompt

Customize the following prompt to collaborate with AI.

> How can I customize an AI-assisted scheduling and planning learning experiment for my [grade] [subject] class focused on [task or event]? The learning experiment involves learners working individually or in groups with access to a generative AI tool to create and refine schedules, calendars, and timetables for various tasks and events. They will specify the components of their schedules and evaluate the AI-generated plans for clarity, feasibility, and alignment with their objectives. Adapt the learning objectives, activities, and assessments to fit my classroom context. Consider intrapersonal and interpersonal skill development along with cultural uniqueness.

Experiment Differentiation AI Prompt

Customize the following prompt to collaboratively differentiate with AI.

How can I adjust an AI-assisted scheduling and planning activity for [grade] [content] learners who [specific needs] and need [specific support]? The current activity entails learners working individually with access to a generative AI tool to create and refine schedules, calendars, and timetables for various tasks and events. They will specify the components of their schedules and evaluate the AI-generated plans for clarity, feasibility, and alignment with their objectives.

Integration Examples

Explore integration examples across various learning contexts.

- **Science:** Learners use generative AI to create a detailed schedule for completing a long-term lab project, including milestones for data collection, analysis, and reporting. They refine their plans based on AI feedback.
- **World languages:** Learners use generative AI to plan a weekly language practice schedule, including time for vocabulary, grammar, speaking, and cultural exploration. They refine their schedule to balance skill areas effectively.
- **Elementary physical education (PE):** Learners discuss goals for improving skills like coordination or teamwork in upcoming PE units. The teacher models how to use generative AI to design a practice schedule supporting these goals, while learners observe and give input. Together, the class adjusts their routine using the AI-informed schedule, without learners directly using technology.
- **Theater:** Learners use generative AI to organize a production timeline for a play, including casting, set design, rehearsals, and marketing. They evaluate the AI-generated schedule for feasibility and coverage of key tasks.
- **Professional learning:** Educators use generative AI to create a schedule for conducting classroom observations or learning walks, including pre-observation planning, observation days, and follow-up meetings. They refine the timeline to ensure equitable coverage and timely feedback.

EXPERIMENT

Budgeting Made Easy With AI Assistance

Budgeting is a vital skill for managing financial resources effectively, whether for personal use, projects, or organizational goals. In this experiment, learners will collaborate with AI tools to create detailed, accurate budgets tailored to their specific needs. From planning personal expenses to allocating project resources, learners strengthen their financial literacy and strategic planning abilities through hands-on interaction with AI. This activity underscores the importance of resource management and demonstrates how AI can streamline and enhance the budgeting process.

For educators, this activity offers an opportunity to integrate financial literacy into the classroom while leveraging AI for practical applications. Learners might use AI to develop budgets for real-world scenarios, while educators can explore similar tools to manage class resources, school projects, or even their own personal financial goals. By engaging with this experiment, learners and educators alike build essential skills for planning and managing resources effectively in a technology-driven landscape.

Learning Goals

This experiment aligns with the following learning objectives.

- Understand the role and capabilities of generative AI in creating budgets.
- Develop skills in using AI tools to plan and organize financial resources.
- Learn to use the PROMPT Recipe for effective AI interaction in budgeting.
- Apply the CHECK AI Framework to ensure the clarity and accuracy of AI-generated budgets.
- Identify and address biases in AI-generated content using the BIAS Identification Framework.
- Enhance financial literacy and resource management skills using AI-generated budgets.

Focus Skills

Critical Thinking	Financial Literacy	Digital Literacy
Organizational Skills	Analytical Thinking	Reflective Thinking
Strategic Planning	Evaluation and Synthesis	Resource Management

Experiment Protocol

Use the following steps to engage with this experiment.

1. If necessary, model how to use the generative AI tool as well as the PROMPT Recipe, CHECK AI, and BIAS Identification frameworks.
2. Discuss the importance of budgeting and financial planning in personal and organizational success. Highlight examples of effective budgets.
3. Have learners work independently or in small groups (for example, two to four participants) based on their needs and the available resources, ensuring each participant or group has access to the generative AI tool of your choice.

4. Explain how you will evaluate learners. Share the evaluation criteria (for example, clarity, alignment with goals, creativity) and clarify whether feedback will come from peers, the educator, or both.
5. Assign each learner or group a specific type of budget to create using the generative AI tool, reinforcing that they should not include identifying information. This could include a personal budget, project budget, or organizational budget.
6. Remind learners to apply the PROMPT Recipe to ensure their prompt inputs are comprehensive and clear. Direct them to use the generative AI tool to create detailed budgets, specifying the components of their budgets in their prompt and documenting the resulting outputs effectively.
7. Encourage learners to apply the CHECK AI and BIAS Identification frameworks as part of their iterative refinement process to ensure clarity, accuracy, and ethical considerations in their outputs.
8. Have learners document their budgets and the AI feedback, making necessary adjustments to refine their plans.
9. Facilitate a discussion on the effectiveness of AI-generated budgeting, addressing any challenges or improvements.

Experiment Customization AI Prompt

Customize the following prompt to collaborate with AI.

> How can I customize an AI-assisted budgeting learning experiment for my [grade] [subject] class focused on [type of budget]? The learning experiment involves learners working individually with access to a generative AI tool to create and refine various types of budgets. They will specify the components of their budgets and evaluate the AI-generated plans for clarity, accuracy, and feasibility. Adapt the learning objectives, activities, and assessments to fit my classroom context. Consider intrapersonal and interpersonal skill development along with cultural uniqueness.

Experiment Differentiation AI Prompt

Customize the following prompt to collaboratively differentiate with AI.

> How can I adjust an AI-assisted budgeting activity for [grade] [content] learners who [specific needs] and need [specific support]? The current activity entails learners working individually with access to a generative AI tool to create and refine various types of budgets. They will specify the components of their budgets and evaluate the AI-generated plans for clarity, accuracy, and feasibility.

Integration Examples

Explore integration examples across various learning contexts.

- **Family and consumer science:** Learners use generative AI to draft a family budget, considering costs for groceries, utilities, entertainment, and savings. They refine their plans based on AI-generated suggestions for prioritizing essentials.
- **Business:** Learners use generative AI to create a budget for launching a small business, allocating resources for marketing, inventory, and operations. They evaluate the AI-generated budget for practicality and alignment with business objectives.
- **Social studies:** Learners use generative AI to develop a government budget for addressing a social issue, such as homelessness or education reform. They evaluate their budgets for feasibility and impact, refining based on peer and AI feedback.
- **Elementary mathematics:** Learners explore needs and wants by planning a classroom event, estimating costs for items like decorations, snacks, and supplies. The teacher models how generative AI can suggest sample budgets, while learners compare and discuss priorities. Together, they revise their event plan without direct learner use of technology.
- **Professional learning:** Educators use generative AI to create a budget for a grant proposal, allocating funds for specific goals such as technology upgrades, staff training, or learner programs. They adjust their budgets based on AI-generated insights for clarity and feasibility.

EXPERIMENT

Enhancing Fitness and Wellness Planning

Physical activity isn't just about fitness—it's a cornerstone of mental health, cognitive performance, and overall well-being. In this experiment, learners will use generative AI tools to create personalized workout routines and wellness plans tailored to their goals, abilities, and preferences. These plans may include exercise schedules and balanced meal suggestions that support sustained energy, focus, and recovery. By exploring the connection between regular movement, nutrition, and improved emotional resilience, learners gain a deeper understanding of how daily habits shape long-term health. This hands-on activity also demonstrates how AI can assist in planning and problem solving across various domains.

For educators, this experiment offers a versatile framework for exploring themes like discipline, goal setting, and the science of well-being. Whether discussing the impact of fitness and nutrition on focus and learning, examining wellness in leadership and teamwork, or connecting habits to environmental sustainability, this activity integrates easily into any content area. By participating, learners and educators alike gain valuable insights into the importance of balanced living and the potential of AI as a planning tool.

Learning Goals

This experiment aligns with the following learning objectives.

- Understand the role and capabilities of generative AI in creating personalized fitness and wellness plans.
- Develop skills in using AI tools to plan and organize exercise routines and healthy meal suggestions.
- Learn to use the PROMPT Recipe for effective AI interaction in wellness planning.
- Apply the CHECK AI Framework to ensure the clarity and effectiveness of AI-generated wellness content.
- Identify and address biases in AI-generated content using the BIAS Identification Framework.
- Enhance knowledge of fitness, nutrition, and planning strategies using AI-generated routines.

Focus Skills

Critical Thinking	Fitness Literacy	Nutritional Literacy
Organizational Skills	Analytical Thinking	Reflective Thinking
Strategic Planning	Evaluation and Synthesis	Exercise Implementation

Experiment Protocol

Use the following steps to engage with this experiment.

1. If necessary, model how to use the generative AI tool as well as the PROMPT Recipe, CHECK AI, and BIAS Identification frameworks.
2. Discuss the significance of regular physical activity, nutrition, and personalized planning in promoting overall wellness. Provide examples of balanced workout routines and meal plans to illustrate these benefits.
3. Have learners work independently or in small groups (for example, two to four participants) based on their needs and the available resources, ensuring each participant or group has access to the generative AI tool of your choice.
4. Explain how you will evaluate learners. Share the evaluation criteria (for example, clarity, alignment with goals, creativity) and clarify whether feedback will come from peers, the educator, or both.
5. Assign each learner or group the task of creating a personalized wellness plan using the generative AI tool, specifying both fitness and nutrition goals in their prompt.

6. Remind learners to apply the PROMPT Recipe to ensure their prompt inputs are comprehensive and clear. Direct them to use the generative AI tool to generate exercise plans and meal ideas tailored to their needs, including a variety of routines and food options. Instruct them to document the resulting outputs effectively.
7. Encourage learners to apply the CHECK AI and BIAS Identification frameworks as part of their iterative refinement process to ensure clarity, accuracy, and ethical considerations in their outputs.
8. Have learners document their final wellness plans, including workout routines, meals, and supporting details, making any necessary refinements.
9. Facilitate a discussion on the effectiveness of AI-generated wellness planning, addressing any challenges, adjustments, or improvements.

Experiment Customization AI Prompt

Customize the following prompt to collaborate with AI.

> How can I customize an AI-assisted fitness and wellness planning learning experiment for my [grade] [subject] class focused on [specific wellness, nutrition, or fitness goals]? The learning experiment involves learners working individually with access to a generative AI tool to create and refine personalized workout routines and meal plans. They will also explore the broader connections between physical activity, nutrition, mental health, and productivity. Adapt the learning objectives, activities, and assessments to fit my classroom context. Consider intrapersonal and interpersonal skill development along with cultural uniqueness.

Experiment Differentiation AI Prompt

Customize the following prompt to collaboratively differentiate with AI.

> How can I adjust an AI-assisted fitness and wellness planning activity for [grade] [content] learners who [specific needs] and need [specific support]? The activity entails learners working individually with access to a generative AI tool to create and refine personalized exercise routines and nutritional plans. They will also examine how physical activity and food choices impact focus, mental well-being, and overall productivity, tailoring the experiment to suit their needs.

Integration Examples

Explore integration examples across various learning contexts.

- **Elementary physical education:** Learners brainstorm examples of healthy meals and daily physical activities that support their well-being. Without using technology themselves, they observe the teacher modeling how AI can generate sample wellness plans. Using these examples for inspiration, learners create their own simple wellness plans that combine nutritious food choices and regular movement, developing an understanding of balanced, healthy habits.

- **Psychology:** Learners use generative AI to develop fitness and nutrition routines that support mental health, such as reducing anxiety or enhancing focus. They assess the AI's suggestions for feasibility, inclusivity, and emotional well-being.
- **Science:** Learners use generative AI to create fitness and nutrition plans that illustrate principles of biomechanics and human physiology. They evaluate how physical activity and dietary choices affect muscle function, energy, and overall health.
- **Mathematics:** Learners use generative AI to calculate caloric expenditure and nutritional intake as part of a wellness plan. They analyze data to understand the relationship between effort, energy, and health outcomes.
- **Professional learning:** Educators use generative AI to design collaborative wellness plans for staff, combining fitness activities and healthy meal ideas. They reflect on how shared routines support staff well-being, morale, and balance.

EXPERIMENT

Designing Travel Itineraries

Travel planning is about more than choosing destinations: It's an opportunity to explore cultural, historical, and logistical aspects of a location. In this experiment, learners use generative AI tools to design personalized travel itineraries tailored to specific interests, whether exploring distant places or discovering new experiences within their own city or community. By crafting schedules that account for user preferences, local attractions, and travel logistics, learners develop skills in research, problem solving, and creative thinking. This activity goes beyond itinerary planning to encourage learners to think critically about how travel, at any scale, impacts personal growth, cultural awareness, and environmental sustainability.

For educators, this experiment integrates easily into a range of content areas. Learners in geography might explore the physical landscape of their destination, while history classes could focus on local heritage. Environmental science learners might evaluate the sustainability of travel choices, and economics learners could analyze travel costs and budgeting. By engaging with this experiment, learners and educators alike discover how AI can enhance planning while fostering a deeper appreciation for the interconnectedness of travel and global awareness.

Learning Goals

This experiment aligns with the following learning objectives.

- Understand the role and capabilities of generative AI in planning personalized itineraries and exploring global cultures.
- Develop skills in using AI tools to create custom vacation schedules while considering cultural, historical, and logistical factors.
- Learn to use the PROMPT Recipe for effective AI interaction in itinerary planning.
- Apply the CHECK AI Framework to ensure the accuracy, cultural sensitivity, and relevance of AI-generated itineraries.
- Identify and address biases in AI-generated content using the BIAS Identification Framework.
- Enhance research, cultural awareness, and planning skills through AI-assisted itinerary creation.
- Explore the environmental and economic impacts of travel choices.

Focus Skills

Critical Thinking	Digital Literacy	Problem Solving
Information Literacy	Analytical Thinking	Reflective Thinking
Strategic Planning	Evaluation and Synthesis	Creativity

Experiment Protocol

Use the following steps to engage with this experiment.

1. If necessary, model how to use the generative AI tool as well as the PROMPT Recipe, CHECK AI, and BIAS Identification frameworks.
2. Discuss the importance of personalized travel planning to explore global cultures, historical significance, and logistical problem solving. Highlight examples of itineraries that consider these aspects.
3. Have learners work independently or in small groups (for example, two to four participants) based on their needs and the available resources, ensuring each participant or group has access to the generative AI tool of your choice.
4. Explain how you will evaluate learners. Share the evaluation criteria (for example, clarity, alignment with goals, creativity) and clarify whether feedback will come from peers, the educator, or both.
5. Assign each learner or group a specific location and user interests to research and create an AI-generated itinerary. Include cultural, historical, and environmental considerations alongside travel logistics. Learners

should request hyperlinks and specific preferences and verify the suggested locations on the itinerary.

6. Remind learners to apply the PROMPT Recipe to ensure their prompt inputs are comprehensive and clear. Direct them to use the generative AI tool to create and customize itineraries based on the assigned user interests and location. Instruct them to document the resulting outputs effectively.
7. Encourage learners to apply the CHECK AI and BIAS Identification frameworks as part of their iterative refinement process to ensure clarity, accuracy, and ethical considerations in their outputs.
8. Have learners document their original AI prompt request, AI-generated itineraries, and any revisions made based on the evaluation.
9. Facilitate a discussion on the effectiveness of AI-generated itineraries, addressing any challenges or improvements.

Experiment Customization AI Prompt

Customize the following prompt to collaborate with AI.

> How can I customize an AI-generated itinerary planning learning experiment for my [grade] [subject] class focused on [specific location or theme, such as cultural exploration or environmental sustainability]? The learning experiment involves learners working individually or in groups with access to a generative AI tool to create personalized travel schedules based on user interests and specific locations. They will specify the location and user preferences, request hyperlinks, verify the suggested locations, explore cultural and historical relevance, and evaluate the AI-generated itineraries for accuracy, relevance, and potential biases. Adapt the learning objectives, activities, and assessments to fit my classroom context. Consider intrapersonal and interpersonal skill development along with cultural uniqueness.

Experiment Differentiation AI Prompt

Customize the following prompt to collaboratively differentiate with AI.

> How can I adjust an AI-generated itinerary planning activity for [grade] [content] learners who [specific needs] and need [specific support]? The current activity entails learners working individually or in groups with access to a generative AI tool to create personalized travel schedules based on user interests and specific locations. They will specify the location and user preferences, request hyperlinks, verify suggested locations, and evaluate the AI-generated itineraries for clarity, cultural relevance, and accessibility. The modified activity should address individual needs while maintaining a focus on cultural exploration and practical planning skills.

Integration Examples

Explore integration examples across various learning contexts.

- **World languages:** Learners use generative AI to design itineraries for a foreign country where the target language is spoken. They include language immersion activities, cultural festivals, and interactions with locals to enhance their language and cultural skills.
- **Elementary social studies:** Learners brainstorm how families or communities plan trips to destinations near or far. They do not use AI directly; instead, the teacher models how generative AI can assist in creating a sample itinerary based on budget, transportation, and activities. Learners review the example and discuss how personal choices impact travel decisions.
- **Geography:** Learners use generative AI to explore the physical geography of a destination, designing itineraries that highlight natural features like mountains, rivers, and deserts, alongside cultural landmarks.
- **Environmental science:** Learners use generative AI to create eco-conscious travel itineraries, incorporating sustainable transportation options, eco-friendly accommodations, and activities that promote environmental conservation.
- **Professional learning:** Teachers use generative AI to design comprehensive field trip itineraries for learners, including educational activities, travel logistics, and cultural exploration. They evaluate AI outputs for safety, feasibility, and alignment with curriculum objectives.

EXPERIMENT

Bridging Languages and Cultures

Language translation is more than converting words—it's a gateway to understanding cultural nuances, historical contexts, and diverse perspectives. In this experiment, learners use generative AI tools to translate texts between languages, ensuring accuracy and contextual appropriateness by following best practices and incorporating native speaker feedback whenever possible. This hands-on activity enhances learners' translation skills, deepens their linguistic and cultural understanding, and emphasizes the critical role of human oversight in interpreting meaning.

For educators, this experiment offers opportunities to integrate language translation into various subjects. Social studies classes might translate historical documents, while science learners could work with international research papers. Literature classes could explore texts in their original languages to uncover cultural nuances. By participating, learners and educators alike develop a greater appreciation for global communication and the potential of AI tools to bridge linguistic divides.

Learning Goals

This experiment aligns with the following learning objectives.

- Understand the role and capabilities of generative AI in language translation.
- Develop skills in using AI tools to translate text between languages.
- Learn best practices for ensuring translation accuracy, including the PROMPT Recipe and CHECK AI Framework.
- Identify and address biases and contextual inaccuracies in AI-generated translations using the BIAS Identification Framework.
- Enhance linguistic and cultural understanding through AI-assisted translation and human review.

Focus Skills

Critical Thinking	Digital Literacy	Problem Solving
Information Literacy	Analytical Thinking	Reflective Thinking
Language Proficiency	Evaluation and Synthesis	Cross-Cultural Communication

Experiment Protocol

Use the following steps to engage with this experiment.

1. If necessary, model how to use the generative AI tool as well as the PROMPT Recipe, CHECK AI, and BIAS Identification frameworks.
2. Discuss the broader impact of language translation on global understanding, cultural appreciation, and interdisciplinary studies. Highlight examples of translation in literature, history, and science.
3. Have learners work independently or in small groups (for example, two to four participants) based on their needs and the available resources, ensuring each participant or group has access to the generative AI tool of your choice.
4. Explain how you will evaluate learners. Share the evaluation criteria (for example, clarity, alignment with goals, creativity) and clarify whether feedback will come from peers, the educator, or both.
5. Assign each learner or group an interdisciplinary task, such as translating excerpts from historical texts, scientific research, or literary works, based on the subject area.
6. Remind learners to apply the PROMPT Recipe to ensure their prompt inputs are comprehensive and clear. Direct them to use the generative AI tool to translate the assigned text, ensuring they request the AI to translate sentence by sentence so they can verify translations. Instruct them to document the resulting outputs effectively.

7. Encourage learners to apply the CHECK AI and BIAS Identification frameworks as part of their iterative refinement process to ensure clarity, accuracy, and ethical considerations in their outputs.
8. Have learners document their original text, AI-generated translations, and any revisions made based on the evaluation. Encourage learners to seek native speaker review and provide feedback to the AI to improve the process.
9. Facilitate a discussion on the effectiveness of AI-generated translations and the importance of human oversight, addressing any challenges or improvements.

Experiment Customization AI Prompt

Customize the following prompt to collaborate with AI.

> How can I customize an AI-enhanced language translation learning experiment for my [grade] [subject] class focused on [specific text or theme, such as cultural exchange or historical analysis]? The learning experiment involves learners working individually or in groups with access to a generative AI tool to translate text between languages. They will specify the target language; request sentence-by-sentence translations; and verify the accuracy, cultural appropriateness, and context of the outputs. They will then document their findings. Learners will also incorporate native speaker review whenever possible to ensure appropriateness and contextual accuracy and provide feedback to improve AI performance. Adapt the learning objectives, activities, and assessments to fit my classroom context. Consider intrapersonal and interpersonal skill development along with cultural uniqueness.

Experiment Differentiation AI Prompt

Customize the following prompt to collaboratively differentiate with AI.

> How can I adjust an AI-enhanced language translation activity for [grade] [content] learners who [specific needs] and need [specific support]? The current activity entails learners working individually or in groups with access to a generative AI tool to translate text between languages. They will specify the target language; request sentence-by-sentence translations; and verify the accuracy, cultural appropriateness, and context of the outputs. They will then document their findings. Adaptations should include strategies to ensure accessibility and inclusivity while maintaining a focus on cross-cultural understanding and practical communication skills.

Integration Examples

Explore integration examples across various learning contexts.

- **World languages:** Learners translate excerpts from novels, poems, or articles in the target language, ensuring accuracy while analyzing cultural nuances. They evaluate AI translations for tone, idiomatic expressions, and contextual appropriateness.
- **Social studies:** Learners translate sections of historical documents, treaties, or speeches into different languages. They evaluate the AI's ability to capture historical context and provide culturally sensitive translations.
- **Mathematics:** Learners translate mathematical word problems into different languages, ensuring the AI captures both language and mathematical accuracy.
- **Elementary music:** Learners explore simple songs from different cultures and languages, discussing the meaning and cultural significance of the lyrics. They do not use AI directly; instead, the teacher models how generative AI can translate and adapt song lyrics while preserving rhythm, tone, and cultural meaning. Learners compare the translations and discuss how language influences musical expression.
- **Professional learning:** Educators use generative AI to create multilingual classroom resources or announcements, ensuring accessibility for linguistically diverse learners and families.

EXPERIMENT

Storytelling and Scriptwriting

Storytelling has the power to bring ideas, events, and characters to life, making it a cornerstone of effective communication and engagement. In this experiment, learners collaborate with AI tools to create immersive skits or video scripts featuring historical, literary, or famous individuals. By drafting, refining, and personalizing their scripts, learners deepen their creative writing skills while exploring the rich contexts of history and literature. This hands-on activity also demonstrates how storytelling can connect audiences to complex ideas through engaging narratives and vivid characters.

For educators, this experiment offers an opportunity to integrate storytelling into various subjects, from history and literature to social studies and even STEM. Learners might use AI to script a dramatic retelling of a historical event, reimagine a scene from a novel, or even create dialogues for scientific discoveries. By participating, learners and educators alike discover the potential of AI as a tool for crafting meaningful and creative narratives.

Learning Goals

This experiment aligns with the following learning objectives.

- Understand the role and capabilities of generative AI in scriptwriting and storytelling.
- Develop skills in using AI tools to create immersive skits and video scripts.
- Learn to use the PROMPT Recipe for effective AI interaction in creative writing tasks.
- Apply the CHECK AI Framework to ensure the accuracy and relevance of AI-generated scripts.
- Identify and address biases and contextual inaccuracies in AI-generated content using the BIAS Identification Framework.
- Enhance creative writing, historical understanding, and narrative skills through AI-assisted scriptwriting.

Focus Skills

Critical Thinking	Digital Literacy	Historical and Literary Analysis
Information Literacy	Analytical Thinking	Reflective Thinking
Creativity	Evaluation and Synthesis	Cross-Cultural Communication

Experiment Protocol

Use the following steps to engage with this experiment.

1. If necessary, model how to use the generative AI tool as well as the PROMPT Recipe, CHECK AI, and BIAS Identification frameworks.
2. Discuss the importance of storytelling as a universal skill that enhances communication across contexts, including media, leadership, and advocacy, while also reflecting historical and literary accuracy.
3. Have learners work independently or in small groups (for example, two to four participants) based on their needs and the available resources, ensuring each participant or group has access to the generative AI tool of your choice.
4. Explain how you will evaluate learners. Share the evaluation criteria (for example, clarity, alignment with goals, creativity) and clarify whether feedback will come from peers, the educator, or both.
5. Assign each learner or group a specific scenario, figure, or theme to include in their script, such as historical events, literary scenes, or contemporary topics like climate change or technological innovations, depending on the subject focus.

6. Remind learners to apply the PROMPT Recipe to ensure their prompt inputs are comprehensive and clear. Direct them to use the generative AI tool to draft scripts, incorporating engaging dialogue and accurate details, with the option to present their work through multimedia formats such as videos, animations, or live performances.
7. Encourage learners to apply the CHECK AI and BIAS Identification frameworks as part of their iterative refinement process to ensure clarity, accuracy, and ethical considerations in their outputs.
8. Have learners document their original script drafts, AI-generated content, and any revisions made based on the evaluation. Encourage learners to provide feedback to the AI to improve the process.
9. Facilitate a discussion on the effectiveness of AI-generated scripts and the importance of historical and literary accuracy, addressing any challenges or improvements.

Experiment Customization AI Prompt

Customize the following prompt to collaborate with AI.

> How can I customize an AI-enhanced scriptwriting learning experiment for my [grade] [subject] class focused on [specific scenario or figure]? The learning experiment involves learners working individually or in groups with access to a generative AI tool to create immersive skits or video scripts featuring historical, literary, or famous individuals. They will specify the scenario, request step-by-step assistance in creating engaging dialogue and accurate details, verify the content for accuracy and context, and document their findings. Learners will incorporate the best practice of providing feedback to the AI to improve the process. Adapt the learning objectives, activities, and assessments to fit my classroom context. Consider intrapersonal and interpersonal skill development along with cultural uniqueness.

Experiment Differentiation AI Prompt

Customize the following prompt to collaboratively differentiate with AI.

> How can I adjust an AI-enhanced scriptwriting activity for [grade] [content] learners who [specific needs] and need [specific support]? The current activity entails learners working individually or in groups with access to a generative AI tool to create immersive skits or video scripts featuring historical, literary, or famous individuals. They will specify the scenario, request step-by-step assistance in creating engaging dialogue and accurate details, verify the content for accuracy and context, and document their findings. Learners will incorporate the best practice of providing feedback to the AI to improve the process.

Integration Examples

Explore integration examples across various learning contexts.

- **English:** Learners collaborate with AI to rewrite a classic scene from a Shakespeare play in a modern setting. They analyze how to adapt dialogue, tone, and themes while retaining the original message.
- **History:** Students use AI to create a dramatic script retelling a significant historical event, such as the signing of the Declaration of Independence. The skit includes dialogue that highlights the differing perspectives of key figures.
- **Theater:** Learners work with AI to draft a short original play or reimagine a classic scene. They focus on creating compelling character arcs, stage directions, and dramatic tension.
- **Elementary library studies:** Learners explore how to adapt stories for different audiences and media formats, such as picture books or audio stories. The teacher uses AI to model possible dialogue or setting adjustments based on audience needs. Learners do not interact with AI directly but apply the modeled examples to guide their own retellings.
- **Professional learning:** Educators use AI to cocreate professional development role-plays that simulate challenging classroom scenarios, such as managing difficult parent-teacher conferences or incorporating learner feedback into lesson planning.

In the following discussion, "Generative AI Intelligence" (page 160), learners explore how the Turing Test offers one way to evaluate generative AI's capabilities compared to human intelligence. The Turing Test, first proposed by Alan Turing in 1950, is a way to evaluate a machine's ability to exhibit intelligent behavior indistinguishable from that of a human. In the test, a human evaluator engages in a conversation with both a person and a machine without knowing which is which. If the evaluator cannot reliably tell them apart, the machine is said to have "passed" the Turing Test.

Discussion: Generative AI Intelligence

Instructions: Use this protocol to plan and adapt a discussion that fits your audience, setting, and goals by reviewing the guidance and prompts prior to facilitating the discussion. This protocol serves as a flexible planning tool designed to help you frame the conversation, customize the experience, and support meaningful participation.

Big Question

What is the Turing Test, and how do modern generative AI systems measure up to this standard?

Learning Goals

- Understand the concept and historical context of the Turing Test.
- Explore the criteria and objectives of the Turing Test.
- Analyze the evolution of AI from early computing to modern generative AI.
- Evaluate the capabilities and limitations of generative AI in passing the Turing Test.
- Discuss examples of AI that have attempted to pass the Turing Test.
- Investigate the ethical implications and societal impact of AI systems passing the Turing Test.
- Develop critical thinking about the future of AI and its potential to pass more sophisticated versions of the Turing Test.
- Promote awareness of the differences between human intelligence and machine intelligence.

Focus Skills

Critical Thinking	Ethical Reasoning	Evaluation and Synthesis
Technological Literacy	Information Literacy	Decision Making
Communication	Strategic Thinking	Problem Solving

Discussion Customization AI Prompt

> How can I customize a discussion for my [grade] [subject] class focused on the Turing Test and generative AI?

For example:

> How can I customize a discussion for high school computer science learners focusing on the Turing Test and algorithms behind generative AI?

Discussion Differentiation AI Prompt

> How can I adjust a discussion for [grade] [content] learners who [specific needs] and need [specific support] to understand the Turing Test and generative AI?

For example:

> How can I adjust a discussion for fifth-grade technology learners who benefit from structure and need clear examples to understand the Turing Test and generative AI?

Discussion Extension AI Prompt

> How can I extend a discussion to challenge advanced [grade] [content] learners and deepen their understanding of the Turing Test and generative AI?

For example:

> How can I extend a discussion for twelfth-grade philosophy learners who enjoy debate and need a challenge to question the Turing Test and generative AI?

Reflecting and Taking Action

At this stage of your AI journey, you have moved beyond exploration. Now, you are actively applying AI to enhance collaboration, decision making, and productivity in real-world contexts. The experiments in this chapter challenged you to refine AI's role in communication, workflow optimization, and problem solving, reinforcing the importance of balancing automation with human expertise.

These activities pushed you to think critically about where AI adds value, when human oversight is essential, and how AI can support both individual and collective goals. Now, as you reflect on these experiences, it is time to turn insights into action. Use the following steps to continue refining your strategic AI integration, ensuring that you use AI with purpose, adaptability, and ethical awareness in your professional and educational settings.

1. Equip yourself with strategic AI skills.
   a. Revisit the AI-supported communication, planning, and collaboration techniques explored in this chapter.
   b. Identify which AI tools best align with your teaching practices, professional responsibilities, or organizational goals.
   c. Reflect on how AI-driven time management, productivity, and teamwork strategies can improve efficiency while maintaining human-centered decision making.
2. Engage in collaborative exploration.
   a. Lead discussions with colleagues or learners about best practices for integrating AI into team-based projects and problem-solving activities.
   b. Compare AI-generated recommendations or written content with human-led strategies, analyzing when AI is helpful and when human intuition is irreplaceable.
   c. Work with peers or learners to experiment with AI-supported feedback and self-assessment tools, evaluating their impact on learning and professional growth.
3. Experiment with purpose.
   a. Apply AI to real-world planning and productivity tasks, such as meeting agendas, progress tracking, or task management, to refine your AI-enhanced workflows.
   b. Explore AI's potential for reflection and self-improvement using AI-generated insights to analyze choices, refine decision making, or develop strategic plans.
   c. Test AI tools for bridging communication gaps, whether through language translation, collaborative writing, or structured brainstorming sessions.
4. Pursue ongoing learning.

   a. Stay informed about new AI applications for organization, productivity, and communication, ensuring your AI strategies remain relevant and effective.
   b. Deepen your understanding of how AI can support diverse learning and working styles, making AI-driven tools accessible to a wider range of users.
   c. Continue practicing AI evaluation techniques, ensuring that the AI-generated content you rely on remains accurate, unbiased, and contextually appropriate.
5. Reflect on your role as a guide.
   a. Consider how you can model thoughtful AI use, helping others navigate when and how to integrate AI into their workflows.
   b. Reflect on the balance between automation and human input, ensuring AI enhances productivity while still allowing for creative, ethical, and independent thinking.
   c. Commit to leading with intentionality, helping your learning community approach AI with confidence, curiosity, and responsibility.

Consider the following questions to guide your thinking.

- How can AI enhance collaboration and communication in your professional or instructional settings?
- In what ways can AI tools help streamline productivity and planning? Where is human oversight still necessary?
- How can you use AI responsibly to support decision making, organization, and creativity without replacing essential human skills?

With a deeper understanding of AI's role in productivity, collaboration, and workflow efficiency, the next phase of your journey moves beyond organizing and optimizing tasks to creating, analyzing, and interpreting information. AI is no longer just a tool for streamlining work—it is evolving into a collaborative partner in research, writing, and ethical inquiry.

In the next chapter, you will explore how AI can assist in source analysis, citation management, and writing refinement, deepening its integration into knowledge production and creative expression. You'll also examine AI's role in media ethics, bias detection, and misinformation, grappling with the challenges posed by AI-generated content and deepfake technology. Discussions prompt you to reflect on which skills remain uniquely human in a workforce shaped by AI and how to use AI to enhance rather than replace critical thinking.

As we move forward, we focus on using AI effectively with discernment, ethical awareness, and strategic intent. Let's take this next step together, preparing to engage with AI as a research assistant, a writing collaborator, and a tool for innovation, while also ensuring that human expertise remains at the core of every interaction.

CHAPTER 5

Experienced AI Experiments

The role of AI in education, creativity, and the workforce is evolving at an unprecedented pace. As with every major technological advancement in history, some jobs will disappear while new opportunities emerge, reshaping the skills learners need to thrive. This chapter explores AI as a strategic tool for research, writing, critical analysis, and innovation, offering experiments and discussions that prepare learners for a future where AI is deeply embedded in their professional and creative lives.

Building on previous explorations of AI integration, this chapter shifts toward advanced cognitive tasks, examining how AI can assist in source analysis, citation management, writing refinement, and information synthesis. Learners will experiment with AI's ability to coedit writing, simulate expert critiques, and provide structured feedback, positioning AI not as a replacement for human intellect but as a collaborative partner in knowledge creation. As Andy Nguyen, Yvonne Hong, Belle Dang, and Xiaoshan Huang (2024) note, "By efficiently offloading certain cognitive tasks to AI, writers can free up cognitive resources, allowing for a more focused and meaningful engagement in the creative aspects of the writing process" (p. 860). The experiments in this chapter encourage learners to strategically integrate AI into their writing process, reinforcing the idea that AI can enhance—but not replace—critical thinking and original insight.

This chapter introduces AI's role in evaluating information, detecting bias in image generation, and engaging with complex ethical considerations. Where we explored bias in AI-generated text in earlier experiments, this chapter extends that inquiry into the visual domain, prompting learners to critically analyze how AI systems create, distort, or reinforce representations in art and media. Discussions challenge learners to examine the implications of deepfakes, AI-generated art, and evolving copyright concerns, deepening their understanding of how AI shapes digital culture and media landscapes. As AI's influence grows, developing AI literacy becomes just as essential as learning how to use the tools themselves.

Introducing the Experiments

To further explore the risks posed by AI-generated media, this chapter includes a deeper dive into deepfake technology and misinformation. Learners engage with the Is It REAL or AI? Framework, a structured method for critically evaluating digital content. This framework guides learners through analyzing intent, verifying sources, and assessing credibility, equipping them with essential media literacy and critical thinking skills. By applying this framework to real-world examples, learners develop strategies to identify manipulated content, assess its potential impact, and build awareness campaigns that promote responsible engagement with AI-generated media.

At the same time, AI is reshaping the workforce, raising critical questions about which skills remain uniquely human and which may be augmented, or even replaced, by AI. While automation has historically impacted lower-paid, lower-skilled jobs, emerging AI capabilities suggest that higher-skilled roles, particularly those relying on intellectual abilities such as comprehension and conceptualization, may also be affected (Taylor, Nelson, O'Donnell, Davies, & Hillary, 2022). This evolving reality underscores the importance of adaptability, critical thinking, and social intelligence, all skills that remain irreplaceable even as AI takes on increasingly complex cognitive tasks. The experiments in this chapter encourage learners to explore how to leverage AI to enhance human expertise rather than diminish it, equipping them with the strategies needed to navigate an AI-augmented professional landscape.

As AI's creative capabilities expand, so do its applications in media, design, leadership, and strategic planning. Experiments encourage learners to examine AI's role in artistic creation, innovation, and social media strategy, exploring both the benefits and ethical dilemmas that accompany AI-generated content. AI-assisted inquiry and prototyping activities will introduce strategic leadership and decision-making frameworks, prompting learners to consider how AI can drive innovation while reinforcing the human skills that remain essential. Discussions extend these themes into the future of work, encouraging educators and learners to reflect on applying AI responsibly and effectively in evolving professional landscapes.

The goal of this chapter is not just to develop AI fluency but also to cultivate a strategic, reflective, and ethical approach to AI integration. As learners engage in these experiments, they will consider how to reap the benefits of AI while proactively mitigating risks, ensuring that AI enhances their capabilities rather than diminishes their autonomy. Like any pivotal moment in a hero's journey, this stage requires discernment, adaptability, and forward-thinking leadership.

By the end of this chapter, learners will have explored AI's role in shaping the writing process, knowledge production, media ethics, and strategic decision making, equipping them with both technical proficiency and critical awareness. As we navigate this ever-evolving landscape, the challenge is not just to use AI effectively, but to also do so with purpose, creativity, and integrity. Let's step into this next phase of experimentation, equipping ourselves and our learners to lead with confidence in the AI-driven world ahead.

EXPERIMENT

Analyzing Primary Sources

Primary sources provide a direct window into historical events, literary movements, and scientific discoveries, but interpreting them requires careful analysis, contextual understanding, and critical reflection. In this experiment, learners use AI tools to examine and interpret text-based primary sources, uncovering themes, historical contexts, rhetorical devices, and implicit biases. By combining AI-generated insights with their own analytical reasoning, learners refine their ability to engage deeply with primary documents and develop nuanced interpretations. This activity highlights the collaborative potential of AI in enriching textual analysis while emphasizing the importance of human oversight in ensuring ethical and contextual accuracy.

For educators, this experiment offers an interdisciplinary framework that integrates analytical rigor into a variety of subjects. History classes might analyze primary sources such as letters or treaties, literature classes could explore classic texts or manuscripts, and science learners might examine groundbreaking research papers. By participating, learners and educators alike deepen their understanding of how AI can enhance complex textual analysis while fostering skills in critical thinking and ethical reasoning.

Learning Goals

This experiment aligns with the following learning objectives.

- Understand the role and capabilities of generative AI in analyzing text-based primary sources.
- Develop advanced skills in using AI tools to uncover themes, contexts, rhetorical devices, and implicit biases in primary documents.
- Learn to use the PROMPT Recipe for effective AI interaction in analyzing texts.
- Apply the CHECK AI Framework to ensure the accuracy and depth of AI-generated analyses.
- Identify and address biases, contextual inaccuracies, and limitations in AI-generated content using the BIAS Identification Framework.
- Enhance interpretive, analytical, and reflective skills through AI-assisted textual exploration.

Focus Skills

Critical Thinking	Textual Analysis	Digital Literacy
Historical Contextualization	Analytical Thinking	Reflective Thinking
Information Literacy	Evaluation and Synthesis	Argument Evaluation

Experiment Protocol

Use the following steps to engage with this experiment.

1. If necessary, model how to use the generative AI tool as well as the PROMPT Recipe, CHECK AI, and BIAS Identification frameworks.
2. Discuss the importance of contextualizing and critically examining primary sources, including identifying rhetorical strategies, implicit assumptions, and cultural biases.
3. Have learners work independently or in small groups (for example, two to four participants) based on their needs and the available resources, ensuring each participant or group has access to the generative AI tool of your choice.
4. Explain how you will evaluate learners. Share the evaluation criteria (for example, clarity, alignment with goals, creativity) and clarify whether feedback will come from peers, the educator, or both.
5. Assign each learner or group a specific primary source document to analyze using the generative AI tool. This could include historical letters, literary texts, scientific papers, or other primary documents. Ask learners to identify not only explicit themes but also rhetorical techniques, underlying assumptions, and potential biases.
6. Remind learners to apply the PROMPT Recipe to ensure their prompt inputs are comprehensive and clear. Direct them to use the generative AI tool to generate analyses of their assigned texts, specifying the aspects they wish to examine (for example, themes, historical context, rhetorical devices). Instruct them to document the resulting outputs effectively.
7. Encourage learners to apply the CHECK AI and BIAS Identification frameworks as part of their iterative refinement process to ensure clarity, accuracy, and ethical considerations in their outputs.
8. Have learners document their analyses and the AI feedback, making necessary adjustments to refine their interpretations.
9. Facilitate a discussion on the effectiveness of AI-generated text analyses, addressing any challenges or improvements.

Experiment Customization AI Prompt

Customize the following prompt to collaborate with AI.

How can I customize an AI-assisted text analysis learning experiment for my [grade] [subject] class focused on [specific primary source]? The learning experiment involves learners working individually with access to a generative AI tool to analyze and interpret primary source documents. They will specify the aspects of the text they wish to examine and evaluate the AI-generated analyses for accuracy, depth, and interpretive insight. Adapt the learning objectives, activities, and assessments to fit my classroom context. Consider intrapersonal and interpersonal skill development along with cultural uniqueness.

Experiment Differentiation AI Prompt

Customize the following prompt to collaboratively differentiate with AI.

How can I adjust an AI-assisted text analysis activity for [grade] [content] learners who [specific needs] and need [specific support]? The current activity entails learners working individually with access to a generative AI tool to analyze and interpret primary source documents. They will specify the aspects of the text they wish to examine and evaluate the AI-generated analyses for accuracy, depth, and interpretive insight.

Integration Examples

Explore integration examples across various learning contexts.

- **Elementary social studies:** Learners examine age-appropriate primary sources such as historical photographs, simple letters, or community artifacts. The teacher uses AI to model generating questions to explore context, purpose, and point of view. Learners do not use AI directly but apply the modeled questions to guide their own analysis and discussion.
- **Science:** Learners interpret seminal works like Rachel Carson's *Silent Spring* (1962) or Darwin's *On the Origin of Species* (1859). They identify the scientific context, rhetorical techniques, and societal implications of the text.
- **World language:** Students translate and analyze primary sources from the target language, like excerpts from Victor Hugo's *Les Misérables* (1862) or Miguel de Cervantes's letters. They explore linguistic nuances, historical context, and cultural meaning.
- **Visual art:** Learners analyze artists' manifestos or critical essays, such as Salvador Dalí's writings or Bauhaus declarations. They explore the cultural and historical contexts driving artistic movements.
- **Professional learning:** Educators from different subject areas collaborate using AI tools to analyze a shared primary source. For instance, a history teacher, literature teacher, and science teacher could collectively examine writings from the Enlightenment period. AI helps uncover themes and contextual relevance across disciplines, fostering new interdisciplinary project ideas for the classroom.

EXPERIMENT

Mastering Citation Skills

Referencing and citing sources accurately is an essential practice in academic and professional communication. In this experiment, learners use generative AI tools to create citations and references in styles like APA and MLA, generate proper in-text citations, and hyperlink sources appropriately. By engaging with AI, learners refine their understanding of citation conventions, sharpen their academic writing skills, and explore the importance of precise referencing in supporting arguments and maintaining academic integrity. This hands-on activity demonstrates how AI can streamline the citation process while fostering ethical research habits.

For educators, this experiment provides opportunities to integrate citation skills into diverse disciplines. History classes might focus on sourcing primary materials, science learners could practice citing research articles, and literature learners might refine their use of textual references. Additionally, these skills extend beyond academics to professional contexts, where accurate referencing is critical in publishing, reporting, and collaboration.

Learning Goals

This experiment aligns with the following learning objectives.

- Understand the role and capabilities of generative AI in creating citations and references.
- Develop skills in using AI tools to generate citations in various styles.
- Learn to use the PROMPT Recipe for effective AI interaction in citation generation.
- Apply the CHECK AI Framework to ensure the accuracy and completeness of AI-generated citations.
- Identify and address biases in AI-generated content using the BIAS Identification Framework.
- Enhance academic writing and organizational skills by integrating the use of AI-generated references.

Focus Skills

Critical Thinking	Academic Integrity	Digital Literacy
Organizational Skills	Analytical Thinking	Reflective Thinking
Information Literacy	Evaluation and Synthesis	Ethical Reasoning

Experiment Protocol

Use the following steps to engage with this experiment.

1. If necessary, model how to use the generative AI tool as well as the PROMPT Recipe, CHECK AI, and BIAS Identification frameworks.
2. Discuss the importance of proper citation and referencing in academic and professional contexts. Highlight how accurate citations support ethical practices, strengthen arguments, and build credibility in research. Provide examples of APA, MLA, and other citation styles.
3. Have learners work independently or in small groups (for example, two to four participants) based on their needs and the available resources, ensuring each participant or group has access to the generative AI tool of your choice.
4. Explain how you will evaluate learners. Share the evaluation criteria (for example, clarity, alignment with goals, creativity) and clarify whether feedback will come from peers, the educator, or both.
5. Assign each learner or group the task of creating a reference list using the generative AI tool, specifying the citation style they need to use.
6. Remind learners to apply the PROMPT Recipe to ensure their prompt inputs are comprehensive and clear. Direct them to use the generative AI tool to generate proper in-text citations for their work and document the resulting outputs effectively.
7. Encourage learners to apply the CHECK AI and BIAS Identification frameworks as part of their iterative refinement process to ensure clarity, accuracy, and ethical considerations in their outputs.
8. Have learners document their citations and the AI feedback, making necessary adjustments to refine their references.
9. Facilitate a discussion on the effectiveness of AI-generated citations, addressing any challenges or improvements.

Experiment Customization AI Prompt

Customize the following prompt to collaborate with AI.

> How can I customize an AI-assisted citation and referencing learning experiment for my [grade] [subject] class focused on [specific citation style]? The learning experiment involves learners working individually with access to a generative AI tool to create citations and references in various styles. They will specify the citation style, generate proper in-text citations, and hyperlink sources appropriately. Adapt the learning objectives, activities, and assessments to fit my classroom context. Consider intrapersonal and interpersonal skill development along with cultural uniqueness.

Experiment Differentiation AI Prompt

Customize the following prompt to collaboratively differentiate with AI.

How can I adjust an AI-assisted citation and referencing activity for [grade] [content] learners who [specific needs] and need [specific support]? The current activity entails learners working individually with access to a generative AI tool to create citations and references in various styles. They will specify the citation style, generate proper in-text citations, and hyperlink sources appropriately.

Integration Examples

Explore integration examples across various learning contexts.

- **English:** Learners use generative AI to cite textual evidence from novels, essays, or literary critiques in a research paper. They verify the AI-generated citations against an MLA style guide and refine any errors to meet academic standards.
- **Psychology:** Learners create APA-style references for studies and theoretical papers used in a psychological research project. They assess the AI's ability to correctly handle nuanced source types like meta-analyses and systematic reviews.
- **Elementary English:** Learners gather sources for a research paper and practice creating citations. The teacher demonstrates how to generate properly formatted citations using generative AI, while learners apply the modeled examples to cite their own sources accurately without using AI themselves.
- **Science:** Learners cite journal articles and research papers for a lab report or research project using AI-generated APA references. They also verify the citation's completeness (for example, DOI, publication year) and ensure consistency across multiple sources.
- **Professional learning:** Educators use generative AI to create citations for curriculum development research. They ensure that references for educational theories, instructional strategies, and assessment frameworks are accurate and formatted for reports or presentations to stakeholders.

EXPERIMENT

Coediting for Stronger Writing

Editing is a critical step in the writing process, turning rough drafts into polished, impactful work. In this experiment, learners collaborate with AI tools as coeditors, using generative AI to review, critique, and refine their written work. By engaging with AI as a partner, learners enhance their writing and editing skills while exploring the value of iterative improvement in crafting effective communication.

This activity also demonstrates how AI can act as a powerful tool in the writing process, offering constructive feedback and alternative perspectives.

For educators, this experiment supports diverse writing tasks, from essays and research reports to creative projects. Learners in science might use AI to refine lab reports, history learners could improve analytical essays, and literature classes might focus on short stories or poetry. By participating, learners and educators alike gain valuable insights into the collaborative potential of AI in improving written communication across disciplines.

Learning Goals

This experiment aligns with the following learning objectives.

- Understand the role and collaborative potential of generative AI in reviewing and editing written work.
- Develop skills in using AI tools to review and critique writing.
- Learn to use the PROMPT Recipe for effective AI interaction in editing tasks.
- Apply the CHECK AI Framework to ensure the clarity and accuracy of AI-generated editing suggestions.
- Identify and address biases in AI-generated content using the BIAS Identification Framework.
- Enhance writing and editing skills through AI-assisted collaboration.

Focus Skills

Critical Thinking	Writing and Editing	Digital Literacy
Problem Solving	Analytical Thinking	Reflective Thinking
Information Literacy	Evaluation and Synthesis	Ethical Reasoning

Experiment Protocol

Use the following steps to engage with this experiment.

1. If necessary, model how to use the generative AI tool as well as the PROMPT Recipe, CHECK AI, and BIAS Identification frameworks.
2. Discuss the importance of collaboration in the writing process and the role of editing. Highlight examples of how coediting improves writing in academic, creative, and professional contexts.
3. Have learners work independently or in small groups (for example, two to four participants) based on their needs and the available resources, ensuring each participant or group has access to the generative AI tool of your choice.

4. Explain how you will evaluate learners. Share the evaluation criteria (for example, clarity, alignment with goals, creativity) and clarify whether feedback will come from peers, the educator, or both.
5. Assign each learner or group a specific writing task (for example, essays, lab reports, or creative pieces) tailored to their subject area, emphasizing the iterative nature of editing for effective communication.
6. Remind learners to apply the PROMPT Recipe to ensure their prompt inputs are comprehensive and clear. Direct them to use the generative AI tool to review and critique their writing, treating the AI as a coeditor.
7. Encourage learners to apply the CHECK AI and BIAS Identification frameworks as part of their iterative refinement process to ensure clarity, accuracy, and ethical considerations in their outputs.
8. Have learners document their original drafts, AI editing suggestions, and the revised drafts, making necessary adjustments to refine their work.
9. Facilitate a discussion on the effectiveness of AI as a coeditor, addressing any challenges or improvements.

Experiment Customization AI Prompt

Customize the following prompt to collaborate with AI.

> How can I customize an AI-assisted coediting learning experiment for my [grade] [subject] class focused on [specific writing task]? The learning experiment involves learners working individually or in groups with access to a generative AI tool to review, critique, and improve their writing. They will specify the writing task, generate content, use the AI as a coeditor, and evaluate the AI-generated editing suggestions for clarity, accuracy, and potential biases. Adapt the learning objectives, activities, and assessments to fit my classroom context. Consider intrapersonal and interpersonal skill development along with cultural uniqueness.

Experiment Differentiation AI Prompt

Customize the following prompt to collaboratively differentiate with AI.

> How can I adjust an AI-assisted coediting activity for [grade] [content] learners who [specific needs] and need [specific support]? The current activity entails learners working individually or in groups with access to a generative AI tool to review, critique, and improve their writing. They will specify the writing task, generate content, use the AI as a coeditor, and evaluate the AI-generated editing suggestions for clarity, accuracy, and potential biases.

Integration Examples

Explore integration examples across various learning contexts.

- **Journalism:** Learners write news articles or opinion pieces and use generative AI to refine their headlines, grammar, and overall flow. The AI critiques tone and readability, ensuring adherence to journalistic standards.
- **Elementary library studies:** Learners write short book reviews or summaries of library books they've read. The teacher uses AI as a modeling tool to demonstrate how to refine language for clarity, tone, and audience. Learners observe and discuss the teacher-modeled AI revisions, analyzing how word choices affect meaning and reader engagement.
- **Graphic design:** Learners write artist statements or project proposals explaining their design processes and use AI to refine the clarity and tone. The AI offers suggestions to make the language more engaging and professional.
- **Engineering:** Learners draft technical reports or project proposals and use AI to enhance clarity and technical accuracy. The AI provides feedback on structure and terminology, helping learners communicate complex ideas effectively.
- **Professional learning:** Educators collaborate with AI to refine newsletters or emails to parents, ensuring the tone is professional, engaging, and inclusive.

EXPERIMENT

Simulating Expert Critiques

Feedback from experts and historical figures can provide transformative insights into learning and skill development. In this experiment, learners collaborate with AI tools to simulate feedback from renowned experts or historical figures in their respective fields. By engaging with generative AI, learners gain new perspectives on their work, refine their critical thinking and analytical skills, and appreciate the value of diverse viewpoints in the learning process.

For educators, this experiment highlights how to use AI to introduce interdisciplinary perspectives into feedback. Learners might receive constructive critiques on essays from literary icons, feedback on scientific hypotheses from leading scientists, or analysis of historical interpretations from political figures. By participating, learners and educators explore the power of AI to simulate diverse and meaningful perspectives that enrich learning.

Learning Goals

This experiment aligns with the following learning objectives.

- Understand the role and potential of generative AI in simulating expert feedback.
- Develop skills in using AI tools to receive and interpret feedback from renowned experts or historical figures.
- Learn to use the PROMPT Recipe for effective AI interaction in obtaining expert feedback.
- Apply the CHECK AI Framework to ensure the accuracy and relevance of AI-generated feedback.
- Identify and address biases in AI-generated content using the BIAS Identification Framework.
- Enhance critical thinking, perspective taking, and analytical skills through AI-assisted expert feedback.

Focus Skills

Critical Thinking	Perspective Taking	Digital Literacy
Historical Contextualization	Analytical Thinking	Reflective Thinking
Information Literacy	Evaluation and Synthesis	Ethical Reasoning

Experiment Protocol

Use the following steps to engage with this experiment.

1. If necessary, model how to use the generative AI tool as well as the PROMPT Recipe, CHECK AI, and BIAS Identification frameworks.
2. Discuss the value of diverse perspectives in feedback and how expert viewpoints can shape learning. Highlight historical or modern examples of expert critiques.
3. Have learners work independently or in small groups (for example, two to four participants) based on their needs and the available resources, ensuring each participant or group has access to the generative AI tool of your choice.
4. Explain how you will evaluate learners. Share the evaluation criteria (for example, clarity, alignment with goals, creativity) and clarify whether feedback will come from peers, the educator, or both.
5. Assign each learner or group a specific task, such as writing an essay, creating a project, or conducting an analysis.
6. Remind learners to apply the PROMPT Recipe to ensure their prompt inputs are comprehensive and clear. Direct them to use the generative AI tool to generate feedback on their work, specifying that the feedback

should be from the perspective of a famous expert or historical figure. Instruct them to document the resulting outputs effectively.

7. Encourage learners to apply the CHECK AI and BIAS Identification frameworks as part of their iterative refinement process to ensure clarity, accuracy, and ethical considerations in their outputs.
8. Have learners document their original work, AI-generated expert feedback, and any revisions made based on the feedback.
9. Facilitate a discussion on the effectiveness of AI-generated expert feedback, addressing any challenges or improvements.

Experiment Customization AI Prompt

Customize the following prompt to collaborate with AI.

> How can I customize an AI-assisted expert feedback learning experiment for my [grade] [subject] class focused on [specific task]? The learning experiment involves learners working individually or in groups with access to a generative AI tool to receive feedback from the perspective of a famous expert or historical figure. They will specify the task, generate content, use the AI to provide expert feedback, and evaluate the AI-generated responses for accuracy, relevance, and potential biases. Adapt the learning objectives, activities, and assessments to fit my classroom context. Consider intrapersonal and interpersonal skill development along with cultural uniqueness.

Experiment Differentiation AI Prompt

Customize the following prompt to collaboratively differentiate with AI.

> How can I adjust an AI-assisted expert feedback activity for [grade] [content] learners who [specific needs] and need [specific support]? The current activity entails learners working individually or in groups with access to a generative AI tool to receive feedback from the perspective of a famous expert or historical figure. They will specify the task, generate content, use the AI to provide expert feedback, and evaluate the AI-generated responses for accuracy, relevance, and potential biases.

Integration Examples

Explore integration examples across various learning contexts.

- **History:** Learners submit analyses of historical events and receive critiques from AI simulating historical figures like Winston Churchill or Frederick Douglass. Feedback focuses on the depth of historical understanding and critical interpretation.
- **Elementary visual art:** Learners create simple art pieces inspired by studied techniques (for example, color mixing or symmetry). The teacher

uploads anonymous learner artwork into the AI tool to simulate feedback from famous artists (such as Claude Monet or Faith Ringgold). Learners observe the modeled feedback and reflect on how it relates to their creative choices without directly interacting with AI themselves.

- **Creative writing:** Learners submit poems, short stories, or scripts and receive feedback from AI representing literary icons like Maya Angelou or George Orwell. Feedback highlights narrative techniques, tone, and character development.
- **Business:** Learners present mock business plans or marketing campaigns, receiving feedback from AI personas like Steve Jobs or Warren Buffett. Feedback focuses on strategy, innovation, and market understanding.
- **Professional learning:** Teams of educators propose cross-curricular projects, receiving feedback from AI representing subject matter experts. Feedback highlights integration, innovation, and practical implementation.

EXPERIMENT

Synthesizing and Analyzing Sources

Analyzing and synthesizing information from multiple sources is a vital skill for both academic and professional contexts. In this experiment, learners use AI tools to upload and analyze one or more source documents, requesting the AI to summarize, compare, synthesize key insights, and generate new content when appropriate. Learners also refine AI-generated citations to ensure academic integrity. Through this process, learners develop critical thinking, research, writing, and synthesis skills while exploring how AI can streamline complex research tasks and support creating original, well-cited content. Learners should avoid uploading private or confidential files and should only use public domain, open-access, or properly authorized materials when working with AI tools.

For educators, this experiment supports a range of research-based assignments across disciplines. Whether learners are summarizing scientific studies, comparing historical accounts, analyzing policy documents, or drafting original essays, they gain hands-on experience conducting research, evaluating sources, and organizing information. The experiment also emphasizes ethical research practices, including accurate citation, source evaluation, and awareness of potential biases in AI-generated content.

Learning Goals

This experiment aligns with the following learning objectives.

- Understand the role and capabilities of generative AI in analyzing, synthesizing, and generating content from uploaded documents.
- Develop skills in using AI tools to summarize, compare, and synthesize multiple sources while creating content with proper citations.
- Learn to use the PROMPT Recipe for effective AI interaction in research and writing tasks.
- Apply the CHECK AI Framework to ensure the accuracy, completeness, and relevance of AI-generated summaries, comparisons, and citations.
- Identify and address biases in AI-generated content using the BIAS Identification Framework.
- Enhance research, writing, synthesis, and academic integrity skills through AI-assisted multisource analysis.

Focus Skills

Critical Thinking	Research	Digital Literacy
Synthesis	Analytical Thinking	Reflective Thinking
Information Literacy	Comparative Analysis	Academic Integrity

Experiment Protocol

Use the following steps to engage with this experiment.

1. If necessary, model how to use the generative AI tool as well as the PROMPT Recipe, CHECK AI, and BIAS Identification frameworks.
2. Discuss the importance of analyzing, comparing, and synthesizing multiple sources to develop deeper understanding and original content. Highlight examples from various fields, such as historical analysis, scientific research, literary studies, or policy evaluations, where synthesis and proper citation are critical for academic integrity.
3. Have learners work independently or in small groups (for example, two to four participants) based on their needs and the available resources, ensuring each participant or group has access to the generative AI tool of your choice.
4. Explain how you will evaluate learners. Share the evaluation criteria (for example, clarity, alignment with goals, creativity) and clarify whether feedback will come from peers, the educator, or both.
5. Assign each learner or group a specific topic or research question to explore. Instruct learners how to gather and upload one or more source documents related to their topic (for example, articles, books, reports, or datasets).

Learners may use these sources to generate summaries, comparisons, synthesized content, or new written material with proper citations.

6. Remind learners to apply the PROMPT Recipe to ensure their prompt inputs are comprehensive and clear. Direct them to use the generative AI tool to analyze, summarize, compare, and synthesize the uploaded sources. Learners may also generate new written content with proper in-text citations and reference lists based on the synthesized material. Instruct them to document the resulting outputs effectively.
7. Guide learners through the process of refining their research questions, analyses, and written content based on the initial AI-generated output and feedback.
8. Encourage learners to apply the CHECK AI and BIAS Identification frameworks as part of their iterative refinement process to ensure clarity, accuracy, completeness, and ethical considerations in their analyses, synthesis, and citations.
9. Have learners document their original sources, AI-generated summaries, comparisons, synthesized content, citations, and reflections on the analysis process. Instruct learners on how to present their findings, incorporating the synthesized information, comparisons, and properly cited materials.
10. Facilitate a discussion on the effectiveness of AI in analyzing, synthesizing, and generating content from multiple sources, addressing any challenges or improvements.

Experiment Customization AI Prompt

Customize the following prompt to collaborate with AI.

How can I customize an AI-driven document analysis and synthesis learning experiment for my [grade] [subject] class focused on [specific topic]? The learning experiment involves learners working individually or in groups with access to a generative AI tool to analyze, summarize, compare, synthesize, and generate written content from one or more uploaded sources. Learners will review AI-generated content, ensure proper citations, and evaluate the outputs for accuracy, completeness, and academic integrity. Adapt the learning objectives, activities, and assessments to fit my classroom context. Consider intrapersonal and interpersonal skill development along with cultural uniqueness.

Experiment Differentiation AI Prompt

Customize the following prompt to collaboratively differentiate with AI.

How can I adjust an AI-driven document analysis and synthesis activity for my [grade] [content] learners who [specific needs] and need [specific support]? The current activity entails learners working individually or in groups with access to a generative AI tool to analyze, summarize, compare, synthesize, and generate written content from one or more uploaded sources. Learners will review AI-generated content, ensure proper citations, and evaluate the outputs for accuracy, completeness, and academic integrity.

Integration Examples

Explore integration examples across various learning contexts.

- **Media studies:** Learners analyze open-source articles, public reports, and instructor-provided summaries on a contemporary issue. Using AI, they summarize and compare narratives across sources, evaluate media biases, and assess the accuracy of AI-generated insights.
- **Engineering:** Learners analyze open-access technical research papers, public patent records, and authorized case studies to design solutions for engineering challenges. Using AI, they summarize key points, compare methodologies, synthesize findings, and create drafts of technical proposals.
- **Environmental science:** Learners upload open-access climate research papers, public policy documents, and authorized case studies to synthesize reports on global sustainability. AI assists in identifying recurring themes, comparing regional strategies, generating new written content, and ensuring proper citations.
- **Elementary social studies:** Learners explore texts and teacher-selected resources on cultural traditions and daily life from different communities. The teacher uses AI to analyze a small set of sources, generating summaries learners review together to discuss key details and similarities, building foundational analysis and reflection skills. Learners do not interact directly with AI tools.
- **Professional learning:** Educators analyze lesson plans, curriculum standards, and open-access academic research across multiple disciplines. With AI assistance, they synthesize information, generate interdisciplinary written content, ensure citations are accurate, and refine proposals that promote critical thinking and real-world application.

The following discussion, "Generative AI and Copyright—Navigating New Frontiers" (page 180), invites learners to explore the complex legal and ethical questions emerging as generative AI reshapes ideas of authorship, ownership, and creative rights.

Discussion: Generative AI and Copyright—Navigating New Frontiers

Instructions: Use this protocol to plan and adapt a discussion that fits your audience, setting, and goals by reviewing the guidance and prompts prior to facilitating the discussion. This protocol serves as a flexible planning tool designed to help you frame the conversation, customize the experience, and support meaningful participation.

Big Question

What are the current conversations around generative AI and copyright, and how do they impact policy at local, national, and international levels?

Learning Goals

- Understand the challenges and complexities of applying copyright law to generative AI.
- Explore how local, national, and international policies address the use of generative AI in content creation.
- Analyze the implications of generative AI on traditional views of creativity, authorship, and ownership.
- Evaluate the ethical and legal considerations in using copyrighted material to train AI models.
- Investigate case studies and current events that illustrate the ongoing debates about generative AI and copyright.
- Develop critical thinking about the balance between innovation and the protection of intellectual property rights.

Focus Skills

Critical Thinking	Ethical Reasoning	Decision Making
Technological Literacy	Information Literacy	Evaluation and Synthesis
Communication	Strategic Thinking	Policy Analysis

Discussion Customization AI Prompt

> How can I customize a discussion for my [grade] [subject] class focused on generative AI and copyright issues?

For example:

> How can I customize a discussion for tenth-grade English learners using case studies to explore the use of copyrighted content in generative AI training?

Discussion Differentiation AI Prompt

> How can I adjust a discussion for [grade] [content] learners who [specific needs] and need [specific support] to understand generative AI and copyright issues?

For example:

> How can I adjust a discussion for eighth-grade English language arts learners with dyslexia who need audio access and text-to-speech tools to understand generative AI and copyright issues?

Discussion Extension AI Prompt

> How can I extend a discussion to challenge advanced [grade] [content] learners and deepen their understanding of generative AI and copyright issues?

For example:

> How can I extend a discussion for eleventh-grade political science learners who enjoy research and need a challenge linking legal trends to generative AI and copyright?

EXPERIMENT

Exploring Bias in Generative AI Art

AI is transforming the way we create and evaluate art, but it also raises critical questions about bias and ethical responsibility. In this experiment, learners use generative AI tools to create artwork, including depictions of people, and critically analyze the results for potential biases. Through this process, learners deepen their understanding of AI's creative potential while recognizing the limitations and ethical challenges inherent in AI-generated outputs. This hands-on activity enhances creative skills, critical thinking, and ethical reasoning, equipping learners to engage thoughtfully with emerging technologies.

For educators, this experiment goes beyond learner engagement—it's a chance to use AI tools to infuse their own lessons with creativity. Teachers can experiment with AI to create visuals for classroom materials, design interactive projects, or illustrate abstract concepts through dynamic, tailored artwork. This also provides an opportunity to model creative and critical thinking, encouraging learners to reflect on both the possibilities and challenges of AI. By incorporating AI-generated art into their work, educators can spark curiosity, enhance lesson delivery, and foster richer discussions about ethics, representation, and technology.

Learning Goals

This experiment aligns with the following learning objectives.

- Understand the role and capabilities of generative AI in creating and evaluating art.
- Develop skills in using AI tools to generate and refine artwork, including depictions of people.
- Learn to use the PROMPT Recipe for effective AI interaction in art-creation tasks.
- Apply the CHECK AI Framework to critically analyze AI-generated art.
- Identify and address biases in AI-generated images using the BIAS Identification Framework.
- Enhance creativity, critical thinking, and ethical reasoning through AI-assisted art creation and analysis.

Focus Skills

Critical Thinking	Creativity	Digital Literacy
Visual Literacy	Analytical Thinking	Reflective Thinking
Information Literacy	Evaluation and Synthesis	Ethical Reasoning

Experiment Protocol

Use the following steps to engage with this experiment.

1. If necessary, model how to use the generative AI tool as well as the PROMPT Recipe, CHECK AI, and BIAS Identification frameworks.
2. Discuss the transformative potential of AI in art creation while highlighting ethical challenges, such as reinforcing stereotypes or excluding diverse perspectives. Use real-world examples of AI-generated art to frame the discussion.
3. Have learners work independently or in small groups (for example, two to four participants) based on their needs and the available resources, ensuring each participant or group has access to the generative AI tool of your choice. Note that not all generative AI tools create images.
4. Explain how you will evaluate learners. Share the evaluation criteria (for example, clarity, alignment with goals, creativity) and clarify whether feedback will come from peers, the educator, or both.
5. Assign each learner or group tasks tailored to their interests, such as creating AI-generated portraits, landscapes, or abstract art that reflects specific themes or cultural contexts. Guide learners to analyze depictions of people critically for representation and fairness.
6. Remind learners to apply the PROMPT Recipe to ensure their prompt inputs are comprehensive and clear. Direct them to use the generative AI tool to generate their artwork. Instruct them to document the resulting outputs effectively.
7. Encourage learners to apply the CHECK AI and BIAS Identification frameworks as part of their iterative refinement process to ensure clarity, accuracy, and ethical considerations in their outputs.
8. Have learners document their original prompts, AI-generated artwork, and any revisions made based on their evaluation. Encourage learners to provide feedback to the AI to improve the process.
9. Facilitate a discussion on the effectiveness of AI-generated art and the importance of ethical considerations, addressing any challenges or improvements.

Experiment Customization AI Prompt

Customize the following prompt to collaborate with AI.

> How can I customize an AI-generated art creation and analysis learning experiment for my [grade] [subject] class focused on [specific art project]? The learning experiment involves learners working individually or in groups with access to a generative AI tool to create and critically analyze artwork, including depictions of people. They will specify the art project, verify the content for accuracy and context, and document

their findings. Learners will incorporate the best practice of providing feedback to the AI to improve the process. Learners will be reminded to use the following BIAS Identification Framework.

- **Be aware:** Understand and recognize different types of bias, including gender, racial, and confirmation bias.
- **Identify:** Spot potential biases in AI responses, such as biased language, unfair treatment of certain groups, or exclusion of important perspectives.
- **Analyze:** Critically examine AI outputs by asking who benefits or is harmed by this output and whether it reinforces any stereotypes.
- **Seek solutions:** Revise AI prompts, use inclusive data, and consider diverse viewpoints to improve fairness and inclusivity.

Adapt the learning objectives, activities, and assessments to fit my classroom context. Consider intrapersonal and interpersonal skill development along with cultural uniqueness.

Experiment Differentiation AI Prompt

Customize the following prompt to collaboratively differentiate with AI.

How can I adjust an AI-generated art creation and analysis activity for [grade] [content] learners who [specific needs] and need [specific support]? The current activity entails learners working individually or in groups with access to a generative AI tool to create and critically analyze artwork, including depictions of people. They will specify the art project, verify the content for accuracy and context, and document their findings. Learners will incorporate the best practice of providing feedback to the AI to improve the process. Learners will be reminded to use the following BIAS Identification Framework.

- **Be aware:** Understand and recognize different types of bias, including gender, racial, and confirmation bias.
- **Identify:** Spot potential biases in AI responses, such as biased language, unfair treatment of certain groups, or exclusion of important perspectives.
- **Analyze:** Critically examine AI outputs by asking who benefits or is harmed by this output and whether it reinforces any stereotypes.
- **Seek solutions:** Revise AI prompts, use inclusive data, and consider diverse viewpoints to improve fairness and inclusivity.

Integration Examples

Explore integration examples across various learning contexts.

- **English:** Learners generate book cover designs for literary works using AI, evaluating whether the visuals align with the book's themes and accurately represent its characters and settings. They critique how bias in AI could affect the interpretation of a narrative.
- **Elementary social studies:** Learners explore teacher-selected images of historical figures or community events. The teacher uses AI to generate additional images for comparison. As a class, learners discuss how some images may leave out details, give the wrong impression, or show unfair ideas, introducing the concept of bias in how information is shown. Learners do not use AI directly.
- **Forensic science:** Learners generate AI images depicting crime scene reconstructions or forensic evidence. They analyze how accurately the AI reflects diverse contexts and whether biases in visualizations might affect interpretations or outcomes in legal scenarios.
- **Health education:** Students generate imagery promoting health initiatives such as nutrition or mental health awareness using AI and evaluate whether the artwork is inclusive and avoids stigmatization. They refine their output to ensure sensitivity and appropriateness.
- **Professional learning:** Educators use AI to create visual aids for lessons, such as depictions of historical events, science concepts, or cultural themes. They critically evaluate the AI outputs for inclusivity and representation, ensuring accuracy in teaching materials.

EXPERIMENT

Discerning Whether It's REAL or AI

AI has introduced unprecedented opportunities and challenges in the digital age, with deepfakes representing one of the most pressing issues. These AI-generated manipulations of images, videos, and text can spread misinformation, cause emotional harm, and disrupt trust in media and society. In this experiment, learners will design a deepfake awareness campaign using the Is It REAL or AI? Framework to critically evaluate and address the dangers posed by deepfakes. By creating materials like posters, videos, and presentations, learners gain valuable skills in media literacy, critical thinking, and ethical reasoning while raising awareness about the importance of verifying digital content.

The Is It REAL or AI? Framework is a powerful tool designed to guide learners in assessing the authenticity of online content. This framework offers a structured, step-by-step process for identifying misinformation, analyzing intent, and verifying sources. The following overview of the framework's key steps, the basis of the REAL acronym, shows the processes learners will apply throughout this experiment.

- **Reflect:** Take a moment to consider the content. Consider the source of the information, the context in which it appears, and any immediate reactions you have. Ask yourself if the content aligns with known facts or if it evokes an unusually strong emotional response, which can be a red flag.
- **Evaluate:** Evaluate the details within the content. Look for signs of credibility such as proper grammar, citations, and the presence of verifiable data. Check for inconsistencies or anomalies in the information presented. Cross-reference the content with trusted sources to see whether they corroborate the information.
- **Analyze:** Analyze the intentions behind the content. Consider why this content was created and who benefits from its dissemination. Determine whether there are any biases or agendas that could influence the portrayal of information. Use tools and resources to check for AI-generated elements, such as image inconsistencies or unnatural language patterns.
- **Look for evidence:** Look for evidence supporting the content's claims. Verify facts with reputable sources and check if other credible outlets report the same information. Use reverse image searches to confirm the origin of images. Seek out expert opinions or fact-checking websites.

Learning Goals

This experiment aligns with the following learning objectives.

- Understand the concept of deepfakes and their impact on misinformation.
- Develop skills in using the Is It REAL or AI? Framework to assess digital content.
- Learn to design and implement an awareness campaign.
- Enhance critical thinking and media literacy skills.
- Promote ethical reasoning and digital citizenship.
- Apply the CHECK AI and BIAS Identification Framework to ensure fair and unbiased evaluation.

Focus Skills

Critical Thinking	Media Literacy	Digital Literacy
Project Management	Analytical Thinking	Reflective Thinking
Information Literacy	Communication	Ethical Reasoning

Experiment Protocol

Use the following steps to engage with this experiment.

1. If necessary, model how to use the generative AI tool as well as the PROMPT Recipe, CHECK AI, and BIAS Identification frameworks. Introduce the Is It REAL or AI? Framework to critically assess examples of deepfakes and other AI-generated content.
2. Discuss the importance of understanding and identifying deepfakes and misinformation. Highlight examples of deepfakes and their potential impact. Explain to learners that the data that generative AI tools utilize comes from the internet, which is inherently biased and does not equitably represent diverse perspectives and viewpoints.
3. Have learners work independently or in small groups (for example, two to four participants) based on their needs and the available resources, ensuring each participant or group has access to the generative AI tool of your choice.
4. Explain how you will evaluate learners. Share the evaluation criteria (for example, clarity, alignment with goals, creativity) and clarify whether feedback will come from peers, the educator, or both.
5. Assign each group the task of researching deepfakes, including the issues of misinformation, emotional harm, and other related perils.
6. Remind learners to apply the PROMPT Recipe to ensure their prompt inputs are comprehensive and clear. Direct them to use the generative AI tool to develop materials for the deepfake awareness campaign, including posters, videos, social media posts, and presentations. Instruct them to document the resulting outputs effectively.
7. Encourage learners to apply the CHECK AI and BIAS Identification frameworks as part of their iterative refinement process to ensure clarity, accuracy, and ethical considerations in their outputs.
8. Facilitate a group discussion where each group presents their campaign materials and receives feedback from their peers. Encourage learners to provide constructive feedback and suggest improvements.
9. Consolidate the group work into a unified deepfake awareness campaign. Develop a plan for implementing the deepfake awareness campaign, including timelines for the creation, submission, display, and distribution of the materials. Ensure all groups have input in the final version.
10. Facilitate a reflection session after the campaign, discussing what worked well, what could be improved, and the importance of ethical considerations in digital content creation.

Experiment Customization AI Prompt

Customize the following prompt to collaborate with AI.

How can I customize a deepfake awareness campaign learning experiment for my [grade] [subject] class focused on [specific theme]? The learning experiment involves learners working collaboratively in groups to develop a deepfake awareness campaign. They will research deepfakes, request step-by-step assistance in creating campaign materials, verify the content for accuracy and context, and document their findings. Learners will use the following Is It REAL or AI? Framework.

- **Reflect:** Take a moment to consider the content. Consider the source of the information, the context in which it appears, and any immediate reactions you have. Ask yourself if the content aligns with known facts or if it evokes an unusually strong emotional response, which can be a red flag.
- **Evaluate:** Evaluate the details within the content. Look for signs of credibility such as proper grammar, citations, and the presence of verifiable data. Check for inconsistencies or anomalies in the information presented. Cross-reference the content with trusted sources to see whether they corroborate the information.
- **Analyze:** Analyze the intentions behind the content. Consider why this content was created and who benefits from its dissemination. Determine whether there are any biases or agendas that could influence the portrayal of information. Use tools and resources to check for AI-generated elements, such as image inconsistencies or unnatural language patterns.
- **Look for evidence:** Look for evidence supporting the content's claims. Verify facts with reputable sources and check if other credible outlets report the same information. Use reverse image searches to confirm the origin of images. Seek out expert opinions or fact-checking websites.

Experiment Differentiation AI Prompt

Customize the following prompt to collaboratively differentiate with AI.

How can I adjust a deepfake awareness campaign design activity for [grade] [content] learners who [specific needs] and need [specific support]? The current activity entails learners working collaboratively in groups to develop a deepfake awareness campaign. They will research deepfakes, request step-by-step assistance in creating campaign materials, verify the content for accuracy and context, and document their findings. Learners will use the following Is It REAL or AI? Framework.

- **Reflect:** Take a moment to consider the content. Consider the source of the information, the context in which it appears, and any immediate reactions you have. Ask yourself if the content aligns with known facts or if it evokes an unusually strong emotional response, which can be a red flag.

- **Evaluate:** Evaluate the details within the content. Look for signs of credibility such as proper grammar, citations, and the presence of verifiable data. Check for inconsistencies or anomalies in the information presented. Cross-reference the content with trusted sources to see whether they corroborate the information.
- **Analyze:** Analyze the intentions behind the content. Consider why this content was created and who benefits from its dissemination. Determine whether there are any biases or agendas that could influence the portrayal of information. Use tools and resources to check for AI-generated elements, such as image inconsistencies or unnatural language patterns.
- **Look for evidence:** Look for evidence supporting the content's claims. Verify facts with reputable sources and check if other credible outlets report the same information. Use reverse image searches to confirm the origin of images. Seek out expert opinions or fact-checking websites.

Integration Examples

Explore integration examples across various learning contexts.

- **Media studies:** Learners investigate the role of deepfakes in influencing public opinion by analyzing case studies of viral misinformation campaigns. Using the Is It REAL or AI? Framework, they assess the authenticity of digital content and create a social media infographic to educate others on how to identify manipulated media. This activity develops critical thinking and media literacy skills while emphasizing ethical digital practices.
- **Elementary visual art:** Learners examine teacher-selected examples of both AI-generated and authentic images. The teacher uses the Is It REAL or AI? Framework to model how to spot clues that reveal whether the images are real or manipulated (such as extra fingers, inconsistent shadows, or distorted text). Learners analyze these examples through guided discussion and then create simple classroom posters that share tips for recognizing image authenticity, building early media literacy skills without using AI tools directly.
- **Psychology:** Learners examine the psychological impact of deepfakes on trust and emotional well-being, using real-world examples to analyze the role of manipulated content in shaping perceptions. Guided by the Is It REAL or AI? Framework, they design campaign materials focused on

protecting mental health in the digital age, incorporating insights into how misinformation influences cognitive biases and emotional responses.

- **History:** Students investigate historical events, speeches, or video recordings that have been manipulated through deepfakes. Using the Is It REAL or AI? Framework, they create campaign materials highlighting the dangers of altering societal and historical narratives, proposing strategies to protect the integrity of historical records.
- **Professional learning:** Educators analyze examples of deepfake media, applying the Is It REAL or AI? Framework to identify indicators of manipulation. They develop lesson plans that incorporate awareness campaigns into their subject areas, enhancing their ability to teach critical evaluation skills in digital contexts.

The following discussion, "Deepfakes—Ethics, Impact, and Psychological Harm" (page 190), guides learners in examining how deepfakes create ethical, psychological, and social challenges across educational and everyday contexts.

Discussion: Deepfakes—Ethics, Impact, and Psychological Harm

Instructions: Use this protocol to plan and adapt a discussion that fits your audience, setting, and goals by reviewing the guidance and prompts prior to facilitating the discussion. This protocol serves as a flexible planning tool designed to help you frame the conversation, customize the experience, and support meaningful participation.

Big Question

How can we understand and address the challenges and psychological harm posed by deepfakes in both educational settings and our everyday lives?

Learning Goals

- Understand what deepfakes are and how they are created.
- Identify the potential risks of deepfakes in various contexts.
- Explore the impact of deepfakes on learning, teacher practices, and daily activities.
- Discuss the ethical implications of creating and using deepfakes.
- Analyze case studies of deepfakes in education and everyday life.
- Investigate the role of consent, data privacy, and protection against deepfake-related crimes.
- Develop strategies for detecting and responding to deepfakes in educational and personal contexts.
- Examine the psychological impact of deepfakes on individuals and communities.
- Explore the legal and societal responses to deepfakes.

Focus Skills

Critical Thinking	Decision Making	Research Skills
Technological Literacy	Evaluation and Synthesis	Ethical Reasoning
Communication	Strategic Thinking	Problem Solving

Discussion Customization AI Prompt

> How can I customize a discussion for my [grade] [subject] class focused on understanding and addressing the challenges and psychological harm posed by deepfakes in both educational settings and our everyday lives?

For example:

> How can I customize a discussion for second-grade media studies learners who need simple examples to understand how videos can trick our feelings?

Discussion Differentiation AI Prompt

> How can I adjust a discussion for [grade] [content] learners who [specific needs] and need support in understanding and addressing the challenges and psychological harm posed by deepfakes in both educational settings and our everyday lives?

For example:

> How can I adjust a discussion for seventh-grade English language arts learners who need simplified language and examples to understand deepfakes and their effects?

Discussion Extension AI Prompt

> How can I extend a discussion to challenge advanced [grade] [content] learners and deepen their understanding of and ability to address the challenges and psychological harm posed by deepfakes in both educational settings and our everyday lives?

For example:

> How can I extend a discussion for twelfth-grade AP psychology learners through a debate on the ethical and psychological impact of deepfakes in school and life?

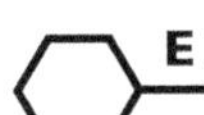

EXPERIMENT

Driving Innovation and Prototyping

AI is revolutionizing the product development process, opening limitless possibilities for creativity and problem solving. In this experiment, learners use generative AI tools to brainstorm, refine, prototype, and pitch innovative product ideas. This immersive approach cultivates creative thinking, enhances problem-solving skills, and strengthens presentation abilities while showcasing AI's transformative role in the product development cycle.

For educators, this experiment provides an adaptable framework for integrating design thinking and entrepreneurial skills into their classrooms. By leveraging AI tools, teachers can create interactive teaching aids, refine lesson plans, and design creative problem-solving challenges tailored to their learners' needs. Additionally, educators can apply these methods professionally to prototype new instructional strategies or classroom innovations, modeling creative and iterative thinking for their learners. This dual purpose allows educators to grow as innovators while empowering their learners.

Learning Goals

This experiment aligns with the following learning objectives.

- Understand the role and capabilities of generative AI in the product development cycle.
- Develop skills in using AI tools to brainstorm, refine, and prototype product concepts.
- Learn to use the PROMPT Recipe for effective AI interaction in generating and refining product ideas.
- Apply the CHECK AI Framework to ensure the feasibility and relevance of AI-generated product concepts.
- Identify and address biases in AI-generated ideas using the BIAS Identification Framework.
- Enhance creative thinking, problem solving, prototyping, and presentation skills through AI-assisted product development.

Focus Skills

Critical Thinking	Innovation	Digital Literacy
Creativity	Prototyping	Strategic Planning
Problem Solving	Presentation Skills	Ethical Reasoning

Experiment Protocol

Use the following steps to engage with this experiment.

1. If necessary, model how to use the generative AI tool as well as the PROMPT Recipe, CHECK AI, and BIAS Identification frameworks.
2. Discuss the importance of product ideation and the role of innovative thinking in driving progress. Highlight examples of successful products developed through creative ideation.
3. Have learners work independently or in small groups (for example, two to four participants) based on their needs and the available resources, ensuring each participant or group has access to the generative AI tool of your choice.
4. Explain how you will evaluate learners. Share the evaluation criteria (for example, clarity, alignment with goals, creativity) and clarify whether feedback will come from peers, the educator, or both.
5. Remind learners to apply the PROMPT Recipe to ensure their prompt inputs are comprehensive and clear. Direct them to use the generative AI tool to generate ideas for new products, specifying the features, target audience, and potential benefits. Instruct them to document the resulting outputs effectively.
6. Encourage learners to apply the CHECK AI and BIAS Identification frameworks as part of their iterative refinement process to ensure clarity, accuracy, and ethical considerations in their outputs.
7. Guide learners through the process of refining their product ideas using AI tools and making adjustments based on feasibility and market research. Support the creation of prototypes for the refined product ideas using available materials and tools.
8. Instruct learners on how to pitch their product ideas, considering key aspects such as market need, target audience, and unique selling points.
9. Have learners document their original ideas, AI-generated product concepts, refinements, prototypes, and the rationale behind each iteration.
10. Facilitate a class discussion on the experience of product innovation, prototyping, and pitching. Discuss the benefits and challenges encountered.

Experiment Customization AI Prompt

Customize the following prompt to collaborate with AI.

> How can I customize an AI-driven product ideation, refining, prototyping, and pitching learning experiment for my [grade] [subject] class focused on [specific task]? The learning experiment involves learners working individually or in groups with access

to a generative AI tool to brainstorm, refine, prototype, and pitch product ideas. They will specify the task, generate concepts, use the AI to enhance their ideas, create prototypes, and evaluate the AI-generated responses for feasibility, relevance, and potential biases. Learners will also pitch their product ideas, considering market need, target audience, and unique selling points. Adapt the learning objectives, activities, and assessments to fit my classroom context. Consider intrapersonal and interpersonal skill development along with cultural uniqueness.

Experiment Differentiation AI Prompt

Customize the following prompt to collaboratively differentiate with AI.

How can I adjust an AI-driven product ideation, refining, prototyping, and pitching activity for [grade] [content] learners who [specific needs] and need [specific support]? The current activity entails learners working individually or in groups with access to a generative AI tool to brainstorm, refine, prototype, and pitch product ideas. They will specify the task, generate concepts, use the AI to enhance their ideas, create prototypes, and evaluate the AI-generated responses for feasibility, relevance, and potential biases. Learners will also pitch their product ideas, considering market need, target audience, and unique selling points.

Integration Examples

Explore integration examples across various learning contexts.

- **Science:** Learners design a product that addresses a real-world scientific challenge, such as reducing carbon emissions or improving water purification. AI tools guide learners in brainstorming solutions, refining their prototypes, and evaluating environmental impacts, fostering critical thinking and ethical reasoning.
- **Mathematics:** Learners use AI to develop a product concept that incorporates mathematical principles, such as optimizing geometric shapes for packaging or calculating cost efficiencies. This activity builds analytical thinking and problem solving by linking abstract concepts to tangible outcomes.
- **English:** Students create a product concept inspired by literary works, such as a tool to assist fictional characters in overcoming their challenges. AI supports the process by refining creative ideas and crafting compelling pitches, enhancing creativity and communication skills.
- **Psychology:** Learners create a product that supports mental health, such as an app for mindfulness or stress management. AI guides them in refining their ideas and addressing ethical considerations, building critical thinking, empathy, and innovation skills.

- **Professional learning:** Educators prototype new methods to inspire curiosity and creativity in learners. AI supports brainstorming interactive projects and inquiry-based activities, enhancing problem solving and classroom engagement.

EXPERIMENT

Using AI for Action Planning

AI has revolutionized strategic planning, offering new tools to streamline project management and enhance leadership effectiveness. In this experiment, learners will utilize generative AI tools to develop action plans, coordinate tasks, and lead initiatives. Through this hands-on process, learners will cultivate strategic thinking, leadership, and problem-solving skills while experiencing the value of AI in managing complex projects.

For educators, this experiment provides a practical framework for embedding leadership and strategic planning into classroom activities. Beyond teaching, educators can use AI tools to refine professional goals, design impactful initiatives, and coordinate school projects. Whether tackling classroom challenges, organizing community events, or enhancing professional collaboration, educators will find opportunities to model leadership and showcase innovative uses of AI in managing real-world tasks.

Learning Goals

This experiment aligns with the following learning objectives.

- Understand the role and applications of generative AI in action planning and initiative management.
- Develop skills in using AI tools to create detailed action plans and coordinate initiatives.
- Learn to use the PROMPT Recipe for effective AI interaction in planning tasks.
- Apply the CHECK AI Framework to ensure the feasibility and relevance of AI-generated action plans.
- Identify and address biases in AI-generated plans using the BIAS Identification Framework.
- Strengthen strategic thinking, leadership, and collaborative project management skills through AI-assisted activities.

Focus Skills

Critical Thinking	Leadership	Digital Literacy
Communication	Project Management	Strategic Planning
Problem Solving	Collaboration	Ethical Reasoning

Experiment Protocol

Use the following steps to engage with this experiment.

1. If necessary, model how to use the generative AI tool as well as the PROMPT Recipe, CHECK AI, and BIAS Identification frameworks.
2. Discuss the importance of action planning and leadership in driving successful initiatives. Highlight examples of effective leadership and planning from various fields.
3. Have learners work independently or in small groups (for example, two to four participants) based on their needs and the available resources, ensuring each participant or group has access to the generative AI tool of your choice.
4. Explain how you will evaluate learners. Share the evaluation criteria (for example, clarity, alignment with goals, creativity) and clarify whether feedback will come from peers, the educator, or both.
5. Assign each learner or group a specific initiative or project to plan and lead.
6. Remind learners to apply the PROMPT Recipe to ensure their prompt inputs are comprehensive and clear. Direct them to use the generative AI tool to develop detailed action plans, specifying the goals, resources, timelines, and key activities. Instruct them to document the resulting outputs effectively.
7. Guide learners through the process of refining their action plans using AI tools, making adjustments based on feasibility and stakeholder feedback. Instruct learners on how to present their initiatives, considering key aspects such as impact, stakeholder engagement, and sustainability.
8. Encourage learners to apply the CHECK AI and BIAS Identification frameworks as part of their iterative refinement process to ensure clarity, accuracy, and ethical considerations in their outputs.
9. If feasible, facilitate the coordination and execution of the initiatives, ensuring that learners follow their action plans and adapt as necessary.
10. Have learners document their original action plans, AI-generated enhancements, refinements, execution steps, and outcomes.
11. Facilitate a class discussion on the experience of strategic planning and leading initiatives. Discuss the benefits and challenges encountered.

Experiment Customization AI Prompt

Customize the following prompt to collaborate with AI.

> How can I customize an AI-driven action planning and initiative leadership learning experiment for my [grade] [subject] class focused on [specific task]? The learning experiment involves learners working individually or in groups with access to a generative AI tool to develop detailed action plans and lead initiatives. They will specify the task, generate plans, use the AI to enhance their strategies, execute the initiatives, and evaluate the AI-generated responses for feasibility, relevance, and potential biases. Learners will also present their initiatives, considering impact, stakeholder engagement, and sustainability. Adapt the learning objectives, activities, and assessments to fit my classroom context. Consider intrapersonal and interpersonal skill development along with cultural uniqueness.

Experiment Differentiation AI Prompt

Customize the following prompt to collaboratively differentiate with AI.

> How can I adjust an AI-driven action planning and initiative leadership activity for [grade] [content] learners who [specific needs] and need [specific support]? The current activity entails learners working individually or in groups with access to a generative AI tool to develop detailed action plans and lead initiatives. They will specify the task, generate plans, use the AI to enhance their strategies, execute the initiatives, and evaluate the AI-generated responses for feasibility, relevance, and potential biases. Learners will also present their initiatives, considering impact, stakeholder engagement, and sustainability.

Integration Examples

Explore integration examples across various learning contexts.

- **Civics:** Learners plan and lead a mock community initiative addressing a local issue, such as public safety or environmental awareness. Using AI tools, learners create action plans, assign roles, and evaluate potential challenges, fostering leadership and civic engagement.
- **English:** Learners lead a book drive or literacy campaign, with AI helping them design promotional strategies, track donations, and set milestones. This highlights communication, organizational skills, and community impact.
- **Science:** Learners develop a project plan for an environmental conservation initiative, such as reducing plastic waste in their school. AI assists with goal setting, resource allocation, and timeline creation, emphasizing problem solving and strategic thinking.

- **Culinary arts:** Learners plan and execute a themed schoolwide food event, such as an international food fair. AI assists in menu planning, task delegation, and budgeting, reinforcing teamwork, creativity, and project management.
- **Professional learning:** Educators use AI tools to develop and execute plans for schoolwide initiatives, such as professional development days or fundraising events. AI supports strategic planning, stakeholder engagement, and logistics management.

EXPERIMENT

Designing a Social Media Strategy

Generative AI is reshaping the way we strategize, create, and execute social media campaigns, offering powerful tools to streamline the process and maximize impact. In this experiment, learners leverage AI tools to design, implement, and evaluate comprehensive social media campaigns. From crafting engaging content to analyzing campaign metrics, this hands-on activity fosters essential skills in content creation, marketing, and strategic planning.

For educators, this experiment serves as a platform to integrate digital marketing concepts into the classroom. Teachers can use AI tools to design lesson-specific campaigns, engage learners with interactive activities, or even promote schoolwide initiatives. By experiencing the potential of AI in social media strategizing, educators can explore creative ways to enhance engagement and communication within their learning communities.

Learning Goals

This experiment aligns with the following learning objectives.

- Understand the role and applications of generative AI in designing and managing social media campaigns.
- Develop skills in using AI tools for creating, refining, and evaluating social media content.
- Learn to use the PROMPT Recipe for effective AI interaction in generating and refining campaign content.
- Apply the CHECK AI Framework to ensure the effectiveness and relevance of AI-generated social media posts.
- Identify and address biases in AI-generated content using the BIAS Identification Framework.
- Strengthen content creation, marketing, and analytical skills through AI-assisted campaign management.

Focus Skills

Critical Thinking	Content Creation	Digital Literacy
Marketing	Project Management	Strategic Planning
Collaboration	Creativity	Ethical Reasoning

Experiment Protocol

Use the following steps to engage with this experiment.

1. If necessary, model how to use the generative AI tool as well as the PROMPT Recipe, CHECK AI, and BIAS Identification frameworks.
2. Discuss the role of social media in achieving marketing goals and highlight examples of successful campaigns. Emphasize the importance of content relevance and ethical considerations.
3. Have learners work independently or in small groups (for example, two to four participants) based on their needs and the available resources, ensuring each participant or group has access to the generative AI tool of your choice.
4. Explain how you will evaluate learners. Share the evaluation criteria (for example, clarity, alignment with goals, creativity) and clarify whether feedback will come from peers, the educator, or both.
5. Assign each learner or group a specific campaign goal (for example, brand awareness, advocacy, community engagement), platform, and duration. Instruct them to align their campaigns with target audience needs.
6. Remind learners to apply the PROMPT Recipe to ensure their prompt inputs are comprehensive and clear. Direct them to use the generative AI tool to create ideas for various types of social media posts, including text, images, videos, and interactive content. Instruct them to document the resulting outputs effectively.
7. Encourage learners to apply the CHECK AI and BIAS Identification frameworks as part of their iterative refinement process to ensure clarity, accuracy, and ethical considerations in their outputs.
8. Guide learners in refining their campaign posts based on target audience engagement strategies and stakeholder feedback. Instruct learners on how to use analytics tools (if feasible) to track metrics such as engagement, reach, and conversion rates.
9. If aligned with school or district policy, facilitate the scheduling and publishing of the social media posts according to the campaign plan.
10. Have learners document their original ideas, AI-generated content, refinements, posts, and analytics results.
11. Facilitate a class discussion on the experience of creating and refining a social media campaign for marketing goals. Discuss the benefits and challenges encountered.

Experiment Customization AI Prompt

Customize the following prompt to collaborate with AI.

How can I customize an AI-driven social media campaign experiment for my [grade] [subject] class focused on [specific task]? The learning experiment involves learners working individually or in groups with access to a generative AI tool to create, manage, and evaluate a social media campaign. They will specify the purpose of the campaign, the desired platform, and the length of the campaign. Learners will generate and refine various types of social media posts, track engagement metrics, and evaluate the success of their campaign. Adapt the learning objectives, activities, and assessments to fit my classroom context. Consider intrapersonal and interpersonal skill development along with cultural uniqueness.

Experiment Differentiation AI Prompt

Customize the following prompt to collaboratively differentiate with AI.

How can I adjust an AI-driven social media campaign activity for [grade] [content] learners who [specific needs] and need [specific support]? The current activity entails learners working individually or in groups with access to a generative AI tool to create, manage, and evaluate a social media campaign. They will specify the purpose of the campaign, the desired platform, and the length of the campaign. Learners will generate and refine various types of social media posts, track engagement metrics, and evaluate the success of their campaign.

Integration Examples

Explore integration examples across various learning contexts.

- **Business:** Learners create a social media campaign to promote a mock product launch, using AI to design visually engaging content and optimize posts for maximum reach. Learners analyze campaign performance metrics, building marketing, project management, and analytical skills.
- **History:** Learners create a campaign to commemorate a historical event, using AI to draft visually appealing posts and infographics. The activity emphasizes historical research, creativity, and digital literacy while fostering an understanding of public memory.
- **Visual art:** Learners design a campaign promoting local art exhibitions, using AI to generate compelling visuals, artist profiles, and event details. This emphasizes creativity, audience engagement, and project management.
- **Physical education:** Learners create a fitness campaign using AI to generate motivational content, exercise tips, and tracking tools for a community challenge. The project integrates strategic planning, collaboration, and health promotion skills.

- **Professional learning:** Educators develop campaigns to engage parents and community members in school events, using AI to create informative and visually appealing content. This supports communication, organizational skills, and stakeholder engagement.

EXPERIMENT

Analyzing and Managing Risk

AI is revolutionizing strategic planning by enabling more precise analysis and proactive risk management. In this experiment, learners use generative AI tools to evaluate existing plans, goals, or initiatives, identifying potential areas of failure and proposing solutions to mitigate risks. This hands-on approach cultivates critical thinking, strengthens strategic planning skills, and demonstrates the value of AI in improving the likelihood of success in any endeavor.

For educators, this experiment offers practical methods to integrate risk assessment and strategic review into classroom instruction or administrative planning. Teachers can apply these AI tools to evaluate their lesson plans, curricula, or school initiatives, refining strategies and addressing potential challenges before implementation. This process not only models effective planning for learners but also enriches educators' approaches to achieving their goals with precision and foresight.

Learning Goals

This experiment aligns with the following learning objectives.

- Understand the role and capabilities of generative AI in risk assessment and strategic planning.
- Develop skills in using AI tools to identify weaknesses and propose remedies in plans and initiatives.
- Learn to use the PROMPT Recipe for effective AI interaction in plan review tasks.
- Apply the CHECK AI Framework to ensure the accuracy and relevance of AI-generated analysis and suggestions.
- Identify and address biases in AI-generated content using the BIAS Identification Framework.
- Enhance critical thinking, strategic planning, and problem-solving skills through AI-assisted review processes.

Focus Skills

Critical Thinking	Risk Assessment	Digital Literacy
Strategic Planning	Analytical Thinking	Reflective Thinking
Problem Solving	Evaluation and Synthesis	Information Literacy

Experiment Protocol

Use the following steps to engage with this experiment.

1. If necessary, model how to use the generative AI tool as well as the PROMPT Recipe, CHECK AI, and BIAS Identification frameworks.
2. Discuss the importance of reviewing plans, goals, and initiatives to identify potential weaknesses and promote success. Highlight examples of successful plan reviews and improvements.
3. Have learners work independently or in small groups (for example, two to four participants) based on their needs and the available resources, ensuring each participant or group has access to the generative AI tool of your choice.
4. Explain how you will evaluate learners. Share the evaluation criteria (for example, clarity, alignment with goals, creativity) and clarify whether feedback will come from peers, the educator, or both.
5. Assign each learner or group a specific plan, goal, or initiative, which could be created with or without AI, to review using the AI tool.
6. Remind learners to apply the PROMPT Recipe to ensure their prompt inputs are comprehensive and clear. Direct them to use the generative AI tool to review their assigned document, incorporating the request for the AI to identify potential areas of failure, predict weaknesses, and suggest remedies. Instruct learners to document the resulting outputs effectively.
7. Encourage learners to apply the CHECK AI and BIAS Identification frameworks as part of their iterative refinement process to ensure clarity, accuracy, and ethical considerations in their outputs.
8. Have learners document their original plan, AI-generated analysis, suggested remedies, and any revisions made based on the evaluation. Encourage learners to provide feedback to the AI to improve the process.
9. Facilitate a discussion on the effectiveness of AI-generated review and risk analysis, addressing any challenges or improvements.

Experiment Customization AI Prompt

Customize the following prompt to collaborate with AI.

> How can I customize an AI-mediated plan review learning experiment for my [grade] [subject] class focused on [specific plan, goal, or initiative]? The learning experiment involves learners working individually or in groups with access to a generative AI tool to review existing plans, goals, or initiatives. They will specify the document, request step-by-step analysis to identify potential areas of failure, predict weaknesses, suggest remedies, and document their findings. Learners will incorporate the best practice of providing feedback to the AI to improve the process. Adapt the learning objectives, activities, and assessments to fit my classroom context. Consider intrapersonal and interpersonal skill development along with cultural uniqueness.

Experiment Differentiation AI Prompt

Customize the following prompt to collaboratively differentiate with AI.

> How can I adjust an AI-mediated plan review activity for [grade] [content] learners who [specific needs] and need [specific support]? The current activity entails learners working individually or in groups with access to a generative AI tool to review existing plans, goals, or initiatives. They will specify the document, request step-by-step analysis to identify potential areas of failure, predict weaknesses, suggest remedies, and document their findings. Learners will incorporate the best practice of providing feedback to the AI to improve the process.

Integration Examples

Explore integration examples across various learning contexts.

- **Economics:** Learners use AI tools to analyze business proposals or investment plans, identifying potential risks such as financial instability or market challenges. They propose strategic solutions to mitigate risks, building risk assessment, analytical thinking, and decision-making skills.
- **History:** Learners review historical military or political strategies with AI, identifying risks that contributed to their failure and proposing alternative actions. This fosters strategic thinking, historical contextualization, and ethical reasoning.
- **Engineering:** Learners analyze engineering project blueprints using AI, identifying risks such as design flaws or material inefficiencies. They suggest modifications to improve functionality, honing technical reasoning, strategic planning, and innovation skills.
- **Environmental science:** Learners evaluate environmental conservation plans using AI, identifying risks such as resource depletion or ineffective strategies. They develop solutions to enhance sustainability, integrating critical thinking, problem solving, and ecological awareness.
- **Professional learning:** Educators review their professional growth plans with AI, identifying potential barriers like time constraints or resource gaps. They create actionable steps to overcome challenges, fostering goal setting, strategic planning, and self-assessment.

The following discussion, "AI and the Future of Work" (page 204), invites learners to explore how AI is reshaping careers and industries, and how individuals can prepare for these evolving opportunities and challenges.

Discussion: AI and the Future of Work

Instructions: Use this protocol to plan and adapt a discussion that fits your audience, setting, and goals by reviewing the guidance and prompts prior to facilitating the discussion. This protocol serves as a flexible planning tool designed to help you frame the conversation, customize the experience, and support meaningful participation.

Big Question

How might AI impact careers across different industries, and what can individuals do to adapt to these changes?

Learning Goals

- Understand the various ways AI is transforming different industries and job roles.
- Explore the potential for AI to create new career opportunities while also displacing certain jobs.
- Analyze the skills that will be in demand in an AI-driven job market.
- Evaluate the ethical and economic implications of AI on employment.
- Investigate strategies for workforce adaptation and continuous learning in response to AI advancements.
- Discuss the role of education and training in preparing individuals for AI-integrated careers.
- Develop critical thinking about the long-term societal and economic effects of AI on careers.
- Promote awareness of the importance of adaptability and lifelong learning in an evolving job market.

Focus Skills

Critical Thinking	Decision Making	Collaboration
Technological Literacy	Emotional Intelligence	Future Planning
Communication	Strategic Thinking	Problem Solving

Discussion Customization AI Prompt

> How can I customize a discussion for my [grade] [subject] class focused on how AI might impact careers?

For example:

> How can I customize a discussion for middle school computer science learners exploring how AI is changing the skills needed for tech careers?

Discussion Differentiation AI Prompt

> How can I adjust a discussion for [grade] [content] learners who [specific needs] and need [specific support] to understand how AI might impact careers?

For example:

> How can I adjust a discussion for tenth-grade career studies learners with ADHD and varied gender identities to explore how AI is shaping future jobs?

Discussion Extension AI Prompt

> How can I extend a discussion to challenge advanced [grade] [content] learners and deepen their understanding of how AI might impact careers?

For example:

> How can I extend a discussion as a high school career counselor for eleventh-grade learners interested in emerging tech to explore how AI is reshaping future careers?

Reflecting and Taking Action

At this stage in your AI journey, you have moved beyond organization and efficiency. Now, you are leveraging AI as a research assistant, a writing collaborator, and a critical thinking partner. The experiments in this chapter challenged you to engage AI in source analysis, citation management, writing refinement, and ethical inquiry, positioning AI not just as a tool for automation but as a cocreator in knowledge production.

These activities pushed you to think critically about bias in AI-generated content, deepfake technology, and misinformation, reinforcing the importance of ethical literacy alongside AI fluency. As AI's role in media, education, and the workforce expands, your ability to evaluate, refine, and challenge AI outputs will become an essential skill in ensuring AI supports—not replaces—human expertise.

As you reflect on these experiences, consider how to continue refining your approach to AI-assisted research, writing, and ethical engagement.

1. Equip yourself with advanced AI research and writing skills.
    a. Revisit the AI-supported source analysis, citation management, and writing refinement techniques explored in this chapter.
    b. Identify how AI can assist in structuring ideas, enhancing clarity, and refining written communication without compromising critical thinking and originality.
    c. Reflect on how AI-assisted editing, summarization, and content generation can streamline your writing workflow while maintaining academic and professional integrity.
2. Engage in ethical and collaborative inquiry.
    a. Lead discussions with colleagues or learners about the impact of AI-generated media, bias in image and text generation, and misinformation in digital content.
    b. Compare AI-generated analyses with human interpretation, assessing when AI is helpful and when human judgment remains irreplaceable.
    c. Apply the Is It REAL or AI? Framework to assess AI-generated images, media, and written content, strengthening media literacy and critical evaluation skills.
3. Experiment with purpose.
    a. Test AI's role in academic and professional writing, refining prompting strategies for content structure, idea development, and clarity improvement.
    b. Apply AI to fact-checking and credibility assessment, using AI-generated insights to verify accuracy, bias, and ethical considerations in research.

   c. Explore AI-assisted tools for knowledge synthesis, experimenting with AI-generated summaries, argument structure, and conceptual organization.
4. Pursue continued learning and AI literacy.
   a. Stay informed about new AI tools for research, writing, and media ethics, ensuring that your AI strategies remain aligned with best practices.
   b. Deepen your understanding of AI's evolving role in journalism, academia, and content creation, making informed decisions about how to integrate AI responsibly.
   c. Continue refining AI evaluation techniques, ensuring that AI-generated content meets ethical, factual, and contextual standards.
5. Reflect on your role as a guide and ethical AI leader.
   a. Consider how you can model thoughtful AI-assisted research and writing, helping others develop AI literacy alongside critical thinking.
   b. Reflect on the balance between AI automation and human judgment, ensuring that AI enhances content creation, ethical inquiry, and responsible knowledge production.
   c. Commit to leading with intentionality, helping your learning community critically engage with AI in ways that prioritize accuracy, integrity, and ethical awareness.

Consider the following questions to guide your thinking.

- How can AI assist in research, writing, and knowledge synthesis, and where is human expertise still necessary?
- In what ways can AI tools support fact-checking, bias detection, and credibility assessment in your work?
- How can you ensure that AI is used responsibly in content creation, maintaining academic and ethical integrity?

As AI's role in research and writing deepens, the next challenge is to move from knowledge creation to innovation and design. The next chapter explores how to use AI not just to assist in content creation but to build, customize, and innovate new solutions.

You will experiment with AI's role in business planning, coaching, and interactive simulations, developing skills that prepare you to lead AI-driven advancements rather than simply adapt to them. These next steps will push the boundaries of AI fluency, positioning you as a creator, innovator, and ethical AI leader. It's time to move beyond using AI as an analytical tool to working with AI as a platform for strategic thinking, innovation, and leadership.

CHAPTER 6

Expert AI Experiments

For learners, educators, and professionals alike, the challenge is no longer just understanding how AI works but mastering how to direct it effectively, turning AI into a strategic partner for problem solving, teaching, and innovation. The experiments in this chapter focus on the next level of AI fluency, where creation, innovation, and design take center stage. Learners will not only refine AI's capabilities but also explore new ways to develop, customize, and build with AI, laying the foundation for future leaders who will shape AI's evolution.

This chapter begins with experiments that encourage AI-powered creation, helping learners explore how AI can assist in business planning, website development, personalized coaching, and interactive simulations. These activities challenge learners to push the boundaries of AI's potential, thinking beyond traditional applications and into the realm of innovation and design. The text emphasizes advanced prompting techniques, allowing learners to generate more refined, precise AI outputs. However, the chapter still retains structured scaffolds, including sample prompts, to support educators and ensure effective AI integration in classrooms and professional settings. As the chapter progresses, the focus shifts toward data-driven decision making, where AI assists in information analysis, visualization, and forecasting. Learners gain hands-on experience with AI's ability to process and interpret large-scale data, preparing them for high-level analytical roles in AI-enhanced fields. These are not just technical skills—they are foundational for navigating an AI-powered future where data literacy, strategic insights, and analytical precision drive innovation. The chapter concludes with AI-assisted coding and game development, where learners explore AI's ability to generate interactive content, refine programming logic, and enhance creative storytelling.

Introducing the Experiments

The experiments in this chapter challenge learners to design, build, and innovate, using AI as both a cocreator and an interactive tool for problem solving. By working through these projects, learners will deepen their understanding of AI-driven design thinking, interactivity, and user experience development.

However, with increased AI capabilities comes a greater responsibility for strategic decision making and ethical considerations. The discussion "AI—The Double-Edged Sword of Human Advancement" (page 225) challenges learners to critically examine the balance between AI's benefits and its potential risks. As AI becomes more deeply embedded in professional and educational landscapes, learners must consider whether they are shaping AI or whether AI is shaping them.

This chapter's final experiments introduce data visualization, forecasting, and predictive modeling, pushing AI into its most advanced applications yet. In these activities, learners refine their ability to harness AI as a forward-thinking tool, transforming raw information into actionable insights. Simultaneously, discussions explore the delicate balance between innovation and regulation, prompting learners to reflect on how AI can drive progress without sacrificing ethical integrity.

Like any pivotal moment in a hero's journey, this stage represents the transition from skilled practitioner to strategic leader. AI is no longer just a tool: It is a collaborative force that, when used with precision, can expand human capabilities. The future AI leaders trained in this chapter will not just work with AI—they will design, build, and innovate with it, shaping the next wave of AI-driven advancements.

By engaging with these experiments, you are not just refining your technical fluency—you are preparing to lead in an AI-driven world. The ability to harness AI for strategic insights, real-time collaboration, and interactive learning will set you apart as an innovator, whether in the classroom or the workplace. Let's take this next step together, transforming AI from a tool into a true professional and educational partner.

EXPERIMENT

Developing a Business Plan

Developing a business plan demands strategic thinking, creativity, and attention to detail, making it a fundamental exercise in entrepreneurial skill building. This experiment immerses learners in the business planning process with the help of generative AI tools, enabling them to create detailed plans that include market research, financial projections, and marketing strategies. Through this hands-on approach, learners gain practical experience while understanding the key elements of successful ventures.

For educators, this experiment serves as an opportunity to bring entrepreneurship into the classroom in a tangible and engaging way. Teachers can leverage AI to demonstrate business planning processes, create real-world examples for learner analysis, or even develop innovative plans for their educational programs. This integration of AI fosters creative problem solving and connects theoretical concepts to real-world applications.

Learning Goals

This experiment aligns with the following learning objectives.

- Understand the role and capabilities of generative AI in business planning.
- Develop skills in using AI tools to write comprehensive business plans.
- Learn to use the PROMPT Recipe for effective AI interaction in generating business content.
- Apply the CHECK AI Framework to ensure the accuracy and relevance of AI-generated business plans.
- Identify and address biases in AI-generated business content using the BIAS Identification Framework.
- Enhance strategic thinking, market analysis, financial planning, and business writing skills through AI-assisted business plan development.

Focus Skills

Critical Thinking	Market Analysis	Digital Literacy
Strategic Planning	Analytical Thinking	Ethical Reasoning
Financial Planning	Business Writing	Communication

Experiment Protocol

Use the following steps to engage with this experiment.

1. If necessary, model how to use the generative AI tool as well as the PROMPT Recipe, CHECK AI, and BIAS Identification frameworks.
2. Discuss the importance of business planning and the key components of a successful business plan. Highlight examples of well-written business plans, including how learners should best present their business plans. Ensure learners consider key aspects such as market need, target audience, unique selling points, and financial viability.
3. Have learners work independently or in small groups (for example, two to four participants) based on their needs and the available resources, ensuring each participant or group has access to the generative AI tool of your choice.
4. Explain how you will evaluate learners. Share the evaluation criteria (for example, clarity, alignment with goals, creativity) and clarify whether feedback will come from peers, the educator, or both.
5. Assign each learner or group a specific business idea or venture to develop a business plan for.
6. Remind learners to apply the PROMPT Recipe to ensure their prompt inputs are comprehensive and clear. Direct them to use the generative

AI tool to write various sections of the business plan, including market research, competitive analysis, marketing strategy, operations plan, and financial projections. Instruct them to document the resulting outputs effectively.

7. Encourage learners to apply the CHECK AI and BIAS Identification frameworks as part of their iterative refinement process to ensure clarity, accuracy, and ethical considerations in their outputs.
8. Have learners document their original ideas, AI-generated content, refinements, and final business plans.
9. Facilitate a class discussion on the effectiveness of AI in business planning, addressing any challenges or improvements.

Experiment Customization AI Prompt

Customize the following prompt to collaborate with AI.

> How can I customize an AI-driven business plan writing learning experiment for my [grade] [subject] class focused on [specific business idea]? The learning experiment involves learners working individually or in groups with access to a generative AI tool to create comprehensive business plans. They will specify the business idea, generate content for each section of the business plan, and evaluate AI-generated content for accuracy and relevance. Adapt the learning objectives, activities, and assessments to fit my classroom context. Consider intrapersonal and interpersonal skill development along with cultural uniqueness.

Experiment Differentiation AI Prompt

Customize the following prompt to collaboratively differentiate with AI.

> How can I adjust an AI-driven business plan writing activity for [grade] [content] learners who [specific needs] and need [specific support]? The current activity involves learners working individually or in groups with access to a generative AI tool to create comprehensive business plans. They will specify the business idea, generate content for each section of the business plan, and evaluate AI-generated content for accuracy and relevance.

Integration Examples

Explore integration examples across various learning contexts.

- **English:** Learners create persuasive and professional narratives for their business plans, including mission statements and investor presentations. AI refines their communication skills by offering feedback on tone, style, and clarity, emphasizing the importance of storytelling in business.

- **Economics:** Learners analyze consumer behavior trends, supply-demand dynamics, and market shifts to guide the business planning process. Using AI, they refine these insights into actionable market research, strengthening their understanding of data-driven decision making and economic principles.
- **Mathematics:** Learners apply financial modeling techniques to calculate revenue projections, profit margins, and break-even analyses. AI tools assist in creating detailed visual representations of financial data, fostering both analytical thinking and strategic planning skills.
- **Environmental science:** Learners design eco-conscious business ideas, integrating sustainable practices into their operational plans. AI tools help analyze environmental impact, ensuring their proposals align with global sustainability goals while enhancing critical thinking and ethical reasoning.
- **Professional learning:** Educators collaborate with AI to design a schoolwide entrepreneurship program, outlining funding strategies, partnerships, and measurable success criteria. This application highlights the importance of leadership and community engagement.

EXPERIMENT

Working With AI as a Personalized Coach

Imagine having a personal coach available at your fingertips, ready to provide real-time feedback and tailored guidance. In this experiment, learners use generative AI tools to identify areas for growth and receive personalized coaching in a dynamic, back-and-forth format. Whether refining public speaking, enhancing writing skills, or tackling problem-solving challenges, learners experience how AI can act as a supportive mentor, fostering skill improvement and self-awareness.

For educators, this experiment highlights the potential of AI to enhance personalized learning experiences. Teachers can use AI tools to simulate coaching interactions, develop targeted feedback strategies, and support diverse learner needs. Beyond the classroom, educators can leverage AI for their professional growth, such as refining lesson delivery, improving communication skills, or preparing for presentations. This experiment also empowers educators to model a growth mindset and personalize development approaches for their learners.

Learning Goals

This experiment aligns with the following learning objectives.

- Understand the role and capabilities of generative AI in personalized coaching and feedback.
- Develop skills in using AI tools to receive constructive feedback and improve performance.
- Learn to use the PROMPT Recipe for effective AI interaction in obtaining feedback.
- Apply the CHECK AI Framework to ensure the accuracy and relevance of AI-generated feedback.
- Identify and address biases in AI-generated content using the BIAS Identification Framework.
- Enhance self-awareness, critical thinking, and personal development skills through AI-assisted coaching.

Focus Skills

Critical Thinking	Self-Awareness	Problem Solving
Reflective Thinking	Digital Marketing	Digital Literacy
Analytical Thinking	Ethical Reasoning	Information Literacy

Experiment Protocol

Use the following steps to engage with this experiment.

1. If necessary, model how to use the generative AI tool as well as the PROMPT Recipe, CHECK AI, and BIAS Identification frameworks.
2. Discuss the values of personalized coaching and feedback in personal development. Highlight examples of effective coaching scenarios. Encourage the use of text, voice, or visual review capabilities if supported by the AI tool. Instruct learners to identify specific areas where they need coaching (for example, public speaking, writing, problem solving, and so on). Reinforce that they should never enter confidential or identifying information into AI tools.
3. Have learners work independently or in small groups (for example, two to four participants) based on their needs and the available resources, ensuring each participant or group has access to the generative AI tool of your choice.
4. Explain how you will evaluate learners. Share the evaluation criteria (for example, clarity, alignment with goals, creativity) and clarify whether feedback will come from peers, the educator, or both.
5. Remind learners to apply the PROMPT Recipe to ensure their prompt inputs are comprehensive and clear. Direct them to interact with the AI tool to refine their skills, receiving and responding to feedback in a

back-and-forth manner. Instruct them to document the resulting outputs effectively.

6. If needed, provide learners with sample prompts to use with the AI tool to initiate the coaching interaction. Sample prompts include the following.
    a. "I need coaching in [specific area]. Please provide feedback on my performance and suggest improvements."
    b. "Can you help me improve my [skill]? Here is what I have done so far: [description or upload]."
    c. "Listen to my [recording or speech] and provide feedback on how I can improve."
    d. "Review this visual of my [task or performance] and give me constructive feedback."

   The learner may also create their own prompt to increase cognitive demand.
7. Encourage learners to apply the CHECK AI and BIAS Identification frameworks as part of their iterative refinement process to ensure clarity, accuracy, and ethical considerations in their outputs.
8. Have learners document their original performance, AI-generated feedback, and any improvements made based on the feedback.
9. Facilitate discussions on the effectiveness of AI in personalized coaching, addressing any challenges or improvements.

Experiment Customization AI Prompt

Customize the following prompt to collaborate with AI.

> How can I customize an AI-driven coaching and feedback learning experiment for my [grade] [subject] class focused on [specific area of development]? The learning experiment involves learners working individually or in groups with access to a generative AI tool to receive personalized coaching and feedback. They will identify specific areas for coaching, interact with the AI tool, receive and respond to feedback, and evaluate the AI-generated content for accuracy and relevance. Adapt the learning objectives, activities, and assessments to fit my classroom context. Consider intrapersonal and interpersonal skill development along with cultural uniqueness.
>
> Sample learner prompt: "I need coaching in [specific area]. Please provide feedback on my performance and suggest improvements."

Experiment Differentiation AI Prompt

Customize the following prompt to collaboratively differentiate with AI.

> How can I adjust an AI-driven coaching and feedback activity for [grade] [content] learners who [specific needs] and need [specific support]? The current activity entails learners working individually or in groups with access to a generative AI tool to receive personalized coaching and feedback. They will identify specific areas for coaching, interact with the AI tool, receive and respond to feedback, and evaluate the AI-generated content for accuracy and relevance.
>
> Sample learner prompt: "I need coaching in [specific area]. Please provide feedback on my performance and suggest improvements."

Integration Examples

Explore integration examples across various learning contexts.

- **English:** Learners use AI coaching to refine their persuasive essays, focusing on improving argument structure, audience engagement, and tone. This iterative process enhances writing skills while fostering critical thinking and self-awareness through personalized feedback.
- **Visual art:** Learners submit visual projects, receiving AI feedback on composition, color balance, and innovation. By iterating their designs, they enhance creativity, visual literacy, and critical thinking, connecting art with broader problem-solving strategies.
- **Science:** Learners design experiments or analyze lab reports, receiving AI guidance on improving clarity, accuracy, and logical flow. This iterative coaching cultivates information literacy, analytical thinking, and strategic planning skills essential for scientific inquiry.
- **Physical education:** Learners create fitness plans or submit recordings of sports techniques for AI feedback on form and performance. This approach emphasizes personal development, collaboration, and self-awareness while integrating health science concepts.
- **Professional learning:** Educators practice delivering professional presentations or speeches, using AI for tone, pacing, and structure feedback. This process enhances confidence, ethical reasoning, and the ability to engage diverse audiences effectively.

EXPERIMENT

Developing Negotiation Skills

In this experiment, learners interact with generative AI tools to simulate negotiation scenarios, allowing them to practice key tactics and strategies in a dynamic, risk-free environment. As many AI tools now support voice input, students can either type or speak their responses, enabling more natural, conversational practice.

Through real-time feedback and iterative improvement, learners refine their communication and problem-solving skills while gaining confidence in negotiation.

For educators, this experiment offers an innovative way to integrate negotiation skills into their curriculum. AI tools can generate realistic negotiation scenarios, provide instant feedback on learner performance, and suggest tailored strategies for improvement. Teachers can use these tools to model effective negotiation techniques, analyze learner progress, and foster a deeper understanding of negotiation principles in a collaborative classroom environment.

Learning Goals

This experiment aligns with the following learning objectives.

- Understand the fundamentals of negotiation and the importance of negotiation in various contexts.
- Develop skills in using AI tools to practice negotiation tactics and strategies.
- Learn to use the PROMPT Recipe for effective AI interaction during negotiations.
- Apply the CHECK AI Framework to review and refine AI-generated negotiation feedback.
- Identify and address biases in AI-generated content using the BIAS Identification Framework.
- Enhance critical thinking, communication, and problem-solving skills through AI-assisted negotiation practice.

Focus Skills

Critical Thinking	Negotiation	Communication
Reflective Thinking	Problem Solving	Digital Literacy
Analytical Thinking	Ethical Reasoning	Collaboration

Experiment Protocol

Use the following steps to engage with this experiment.

1. If necessary, model how to use the generative AI tool as well as the PROMPT Recipe, CHECK AI, and BIAS Identification frameworks.
2. Discuss the importance of negotiation skills in personal and professional contexts, highlighting key negotiation principles such as engaging in negotiation scenarios and receiving feedback on learners' tactics and strategies. Encourage the use of voice capabilities if supported by the AI tool.

3. Have learners work independently or in small groups (for example, two to four participants) based on their needs and the available resources, ensuring each participant or group has access to the generative AI tool of your choice.
4. Explain how you will evaluate learners. Share the evaluation criteria (for example, clarity, alignment with goals, creativity) and clarify whether feedback will come from peers, the educator, or both.
5. Remind learners to apply the PROMPT Recipe to ensure their prompt inputs are comprehensive and clear. Direct them to use the generative AI tool to identify specific areas or scenarios for negotiation practice (for example, salary negotiations, conflict resolution, business deals) and to document the resulting outputs effectively.
6. If needed, provide sample prompts, such as the following, to use with the AI tool to initiate negotiation scenarios.

    > Engage in a simulated negotiation with me regarding [topic of negotiation]. I will play the role of [your role], and you (the AI) will play the role of [other party's role]. The negotiation will include the following elements, with each side taking turns to respond: I will start by stating my request and providing initial reasons. You will then respond with potential concerns or objections. I will provide further justification for my request, emphasizing [key justification]. You will then ask about potential solutions to mitigate any negative impacts. I will propose specific solutions to address those concerns. You will mention any relevant policies or constraints. I will suggest potential compromises or flexible arrangements. Finally, you will conclude by summarizing the discussion and providing a decision or next steps. Please wait for my response after each of your points before proceeding to the next one. Let's begin the negotiation.

    The learner may also create their own prompt to increase cognitive demand.
7. Encourage learners to apply the CHECK AI and BIAS Identification frameworks as part of their iterative refinement process to ensure clarity, accuracy, and ethical considerations in their outputs.
8. Have learners document their negotiation strategies, AI-generated feedback, and improvements made based on the feedback.
9. Facilitate discussions on the effectiveness of AI in negotiation training, addressing any challenges or improvements.

Experiment Customization AI Prompt

Customize the following prompt to collaborate with AI.

How can I customize an AI-driven negotiation skills training experiment for my [grade] [subject] class focused on [specific negotiation scenario]? The training experiment involves learners working individually or in groups with access to a generative AI tool to practice negotiation skills. They will engage in negotiation scenarios, receive and respond to feedback, and evaluate the AI-generated content for accuracy and relevance. Adapt the learning objectives, activities, and assessments to fit my classroom context. Consider intrapersonal and interpersonal skill development along with cultural uniqueness.

Experiment Differentiation AI Prompt

Customize the following prompt to collaboratively differentiate with AI.

How can I adjust an AI-driven negotiation skills training activity for [grade] [content] learners who [specific needs] and need [specific support]? The current activity entails learners working individually or in groups with access to a generative AI tool to practice negotiation skills. They will engage in negotiation scenarios, receive and respond to feedback, and evaluate the AI-generated content for accuracy and relevance.

Integration Examples

Explore integration examples across various learning contexts.

- **Agriculture:** Learners simulate negotiations over land use or crop distribution with AI acting as stakeholders such as farmers or policymakers. This fosters strategic planning, ethical reasoning, and an understanding of agricultural sustainability.
- **Mathematics:** Learners use AI to simulate budget negotiations for a school event or community project. They apply their mathematics skills to justify financial proposals, interpret constraints, and adjust their strategies based on numerical data provided by the AI.
- **Healthcare:** Learners simulate healthcare negotiations, such as coordinating patient care plans or resolving conflicts between providers. The exercise emphasizes collaborative problem solving and ethical reasoning in medical contexts.
- **Psychology:** Learners explore the psychology behind negotiation by practicing conflict resolution scenarios using AI-generated prompts. They analyze how emotions, biases, and communication styles impact outcomes and propose strategies to improve negotiation dynamics.
- **Professional learning:** Educators use AI to simulate difficult conversations or workplace negotiations, receiving feedback on their strategies. This helps them develop conflict resolution skills applicable to classroom management and peer collaboration.

Mastering Interview Skills

AI is changing the way we prepare for important milestones like job or admissions interviews. In this experiment, learners use generative AI tools to simulate interview scenarios and practice structured responses using the STAR method (situation, task, action, result), a widely used behavioral interviewing framework developed by Development Dimensions International (DDI, n.d.). As many AI tools now include voice functionality, students can either type or speak their responses, enabling more realistic, conversational practice. This hands-on approach builds learners' communication, self-presentation, and critical thinking skills in a supportive environment.

For educators, this experiment offers a structured way to integrate career readiness into the curriculum while also refining their own interviewing and communication skills. Teachers can use AI to generate realistic interview questions, guide learners in crafting effective responses, and provide iterative feedback with greater ease. This process not only builds student confidence and adaptability but also gives educators hands-on experience with AI-powered dialogue, supporting both instructional goals and professional growth.

Learning Goals

This experiment aligns with the following learning objectives.

- Understand the fundamentals of successful interviews and their importance in various contexts.
- Develop skills in using AI tools to practice interview responses and strategies.
- Learn to use the PROMPT Recipe for effective AI interaction during interviews.
- Apply the CHECK AI Framework to review and refine AI-generated interview feedback.
- Identify and address biases in AI-generated content using the BIAS Identification Framework.
- Enhance critical thinking, communication, and self-presentation skills through AI-assisted interview practice.

Focus Skills

Critical Thinking	Interviewing	Communication
Reflective Thinking	Problem Solving	Digital Literacy
Analytical Thinking	Ethical Reasoning	Self-Management

Experiment Protocol

Use the following steps to engage with this experiment.

1. If necessary, model how to use the generative AI tool as well as the PROMPT Recipe, CHECK AI, and BIAS Identification frameworks.
2. Discuss the importance of interview skills in personal and professional contexts, highlighting key principles and common formats like the STAR method.
3. Have learners work independently or in small groups (for example, two to four participants) based on their needs and the available resources, ensuring each participant or group has access to the generative AI tool of your choice.
4. Explain how you will evaluate learners. Share the evaluation criteria (for example, clarity, alignment with goals, creativity) and clarify whether feedback will come from peers, the educator, or both.
5. Remind learners to apply the PROMPT Recipe to ensure their prompt inputs are comprehensive and clear. Direct them to apply the generative AI tool to areas or scenarios for interview practice (for example, job interviews, college admissions, scholarship applications).
6. If needed, provide sample prompts, such as the following, to use with the AI tool to initiate interview scenarios.

   > Engage in a simulated interview with me regarding [job position or interview type]. I will use the [interview format] format. You (the AI) will play the role of the interviewer. The interview will include the following elements, with each side taking turns to respond: You (the AI) will start by asking a question, then I will answer that question. You will then provide feedback or follow-up questions. I will respond with further details, emphasizing [key justification or examples]. You will then ask about potential challenges or concerns. I will propose solutions to address those challenges. You will mention any relevant requirements or expectations. I will suggest how my skills and experiences meet those expectations. Finally, you will conclude by summarizing the discussion and providing next steps. Please wait for my response after each of your points before proceeding to the next one. Let's begin the interview.

   The learner may also create their own prompt to increase the cognitive challenge.
7. Encourage learners to apply the CHECK AI and BIAS Identification frameworks as part of their iterative refinement process to ensure clarity, accuracy, and ethical considerations in their outputs.

8. Have learners document their interview strategies, AI-generated feedback, and improvements made based on the feedback.
9. Facilitate discussions on the effectiveness of AI in interview preparation, addressing any challenges or improvements.

Experiment Customization AI Prompt

Customize the following prompt to collaborate with AI.

> How can I customize an AI-driven interview preparation learning experiment for my [grade] [subject] class focused on [specific interview scenario]? The learning experiment involves learners working individually or in groups with access to a generative AI tool to practice interview skills using the STAR method. They will engage in interview scenarios, receive and respond to feedback, and evaluate the AI-generated content for accuracy and relevance. Adapt the learning objectives, activities, and assessments to fit my classroom context. Consider intrapersonal and interpersonal skill development along with cultural uniqueness.

Experiment Differentiation AI Prompt

Customize the following prompt to collaboratively differentiate with AI.

> How can I adjust an AI-driven interview preparation activity for [grade] [content] learners who [specific needs] and need [specific support]? The current activity entails learners working individually or in groups with access to a generative AI tool to practice interview skills. They will engage in interview scenarios, receive and respond to feedback, and evaluate the AI-generated content for accuracy and relevance.

Integration Examples

Explore integration examples across various learning contexts.

- **Academic counseling:** Learners use AI to simulate college admissions interviews, engaging with varied question types. They practice narrative techniques to craft compelling responses while enhancing communication, critical thinking, and reflective skills for real-world applications.
- **Social studies:** Learners prepare for AI-simulated interviews as historical figures, defending significant decisions or policies. This activity develops their understanding of historical contexts while enhancing argumentation, empathy, and perspective-taking skills.
- **Business:** Learners engage in AI-simulated interviews for entrepreneurial ventures or internships, presenting business plans or strategies. They strengthen communication, strategic thinking, and problem-solving skills while learning to convey complex ideas effectively.

- **Science:** Learners engage in AI-driven mock interviews for internships in scientific fields, focusing on explaining complex research and experiments. They practice tailoring their responses to specific audiences while improving their problem-solving and analytical thinking skills.
- **Professional learning:** Educators use AI to practice interview scenarios for teaching roles, focusing on articulating their teaching philosophy and classroom management strategies. They analyze AI feedback to refine their answers and address potential gaps.

EXPERIMENT

Tutoring for High-Stakes Exams

AI is transforming how learners prepare for high-stakes exams like the SAT, ACT, GRE, MCAT, or AP assessments. In this experiment, learners engage with generative AI tools to strengthen their understanding of key content areas, practice problem solving, and receive real-time feedback customized to their individual needs. This hands-on approach empowers learners to focus on their strengths, address weaknesses, and develop effective test-taking strategies.

For educators, this experiment provides an opportunity to integrate AI as a supplemental tool for personalized tutoring and differentiated instruction. Teachers can use AI tools to generate tailored practice materials, simulate exam conditions, and track learners' progress. By leveraging AI's capabilities, educators can support learners in mastering test content, refining their skills, and building confidence for various standardized assessments.

Learning Goals

This experiment aligns with the following learning objectives.

- Understand the role and capabilities of generative AI in assessment preparation.
- Develop skills in using AI tools for targeted practice and feedback.
- Learn to use the PROMPT Recipe for effective AI interaction in exam preparation.
- Apply the CHECK AI Framework to ensure the accuracy and relevance of AI-generated practice materials.
- Identify and address biases in AI-generated content using the BIAS Identification Framework.
- Enhance problem solving, critical thinking, and test-taking skills through AI-assisted tutoring.

Focus Skills

Critical Thinking	Problem Solving	Self-Directed Learning
Reflective Thinking	Adaptability	Digital Literacy
Analytical Thinking	Strategic Planning	Information Literacy

Experiment Protocol

Use the following steps to engage with this experiment.

1. If necessary, model how to use the generative AI tool as well as the PROMPT Recipe, CHECK AI, and BIAS Identification frameworks.
2. Discuss the importance of targeted practice and personalized feedback in assessment preparation. Highlight the role of targeted practice, effective study strategies, and personalized feedback in preparing for assessments. Share examples of successful preparation techniques tailored to different standardized tests.
3. Have learners work independently or in small groups (for example, two to four participants) based on their needs and the available resources, ensuring each participant or group has access to the generative AI tool of your choice.
4. Explain how you will evaluate learners. Share the evaluation criteria (for example, clarity, alignment with goals, creativity) and clarify whether feedback will come from peers, the educator, or both.
5. Remind learners to apply the PROMPT Recipe to ensure their prompt inputs are comprehensive and clear. Direct them to use the generative AI tool to identify the specific assessments they are preparing for and their areas of strength and weakness. Instruct them to document the resulting outputs effectively.
6. If needed, provide sample prompts, such as the following, to use with the AI tool to initiate tutoring sessions.

    > Engage in a simulated practice session with me regarding [specific topic] for the [specific assessment]. I will play the role of the learner and you (the AI) will act as the instructor. Please provide me with one practice question related to [specific topic] at a time and give me feedback on my responses. Please vary the question types to accommodate all the formats (for example, multiple-choice, short-form, and long-form responses) on the examination. Let's begin with a few questions to test my understanding.

    The learner may create their own prompt to increase the cognitive challenge.

7. Encourage learners to apply the CHECK AI and BIAS Identification frameworks as part of their iterative refinement process to ensure clarity, accuracy, and ethical considerations in their outputs.
8. Have learners document their initial performance, AI-generated feedback, and progress made based on the feedback.
9. Facilitate discussions on the effectiveness of AI in assessment preparation, addressing challenges and potential improvements.

Experiment Customization AI Prompt

Customize the following prompt to collaborate with AI.

> How can I customize an AI-driven assessment tutoring learning experiment for my [grade] [subject] class focused on [specific assessment]? The learning experiment involves learners working individually with access to a generative AI tool to receive personalized tutoring and practice materials. They will identify their specific assessments and areas for improvement, interact with the AI tool, and evaluate the AI-generated content for accuracy and relevance. Adapt the learning objectives, activities, and assessments to fit my classroom context. Consider intrapersonal and interpersonal skill development along with cultural uniqueness.

Experiment Differentiation AI Prompt

Customize the following prompt to collaboratively differentiate with AI.

> How can I adjust an AI-driven assessment tutoring activity for [grade] [content] learners who [specific needs] and need [specific support]? The current activity entails learners working individually with access to a generative AI tool to receive personalized tutoring and practice materials. They will identify their specific assessments and areas for improvement, interact with the AI tool, and evaluate the AI-generated content for accuracy and relevance.

Integration Examples

Explore integration examples across various learning contexts.

- **Mathematics:** Learners prepare for standardized mathematics assessments like the SAT or AP Calculus by solving AI-generated practice problems on algebra, geometry, or calculus. They analyze their mistakes with AI feedback to refine problem-solving strategies and logical reasoning.
- **English:** Learners practice reading comprehension and writing skills with AI tools, preparing for tests like the SAT or AP English Literature. They analyze text passages, respond to essay prompts, and refine their arguments based on AI-provided feedback.

- **World languages:** Learners practice language-specific assessments like AP Spanish or French with AI simulating oral and written exercises. They improve grammar, vocabulary, and fluency by receiving personalized feedback on their linguistic accuracy.
- **History:** Students prepare for AP History exams by practicing document-based questions with AI tools, crafting essays that synthesize historical evidence and address multiple perspectives. They receive AI feedback on thesis strength and source integration.
- **Professional learning:** Educators explore AI tools to generate practice materials tailored to diverse learners, ensuring alignment with exam formats and addressing individual challenges. This fosters differentiated instruction and supports learner-specific needs.

This following discussion, "AI—The Double-Edged Sword of Human Advancement," challenges learners to weigh both the promises and the potential dangers of AI as it shapes many aspects of human life. While the previous experiment highlights the benefits of AI in personalized learning and test preparation, this discussion serves as a counterbalance—inviting learners to critically examine the ethical, societal, and developmental risks that come with increased AI dependency, especially in high-stakes educational contexts.

Discussion: AI—
The Double-Edged Sword of Human Advancement

Instructions: Use this protocol to plan and adapt a discussion that fits your audience, setting, and goals by reviewing the guidance and prompts prior to facilitating the discussion. This protocol serves as a flexible planning tool designed to help you frame the conversation, customize the experience, and support meaningful participation.

Big Question

How can AI help or hurt humanity in various aspects of life, such as employment, ethics, privacy, and social interactions?

Learning Goals

- Understand the potential benefits of AI in improving quality of life, healthcare, and efficiency.
- Analyze the ethical implications of AI, including biases, privacy concerns, and decision making.
- Evaluate the impact of AI on employment and the future job market.
- Investigate how AI can influence social interactions and human relationships.
- Examine the role of AI in security and surveillance.
- Discuss the potential risks of AI, including dependency and misuse.
- Investigate the importance of empathy and emotional intelligence in AI design.
- Develop strategies for using AI to support emotional well-being in educational and personal settings.
- Develop critical thinking regarding the regulation and control of AI technologies.
- Promote awareness of the skills necessary to thrive in an AI-augmented world.

Focus Skills

Critical Thinking	Ethical Reasoning	Evaluation and Synthesis
Technological Literacy	Information Literacy	Decision Making
Communication	Strategic Thinking	Problem Solving

Discussion Customization AI Prompt

How can I customize a discussion for my [grade] [subject] class focused on the benefits and risks of AI?

For example:

How can I customize a discussion for fifth-grade science learners exploring AI advancements and how they apply to different scientific fields?

Discussion Differentiation AI Prompt

How can I adjust a discussion for [grade] [content] learners who [specific needs] and need [specific support] to understand the benefits and risks of AI?

For example:

How can I adjust a discussion for ninth-grade learners who need culturally relevant examples to explore the benefits and risks of AI based on representation in its outputs?

Discussion Extension AI Prompt

How can I extend a discussion to challenge advanced [grade] [content] learners and deepen their understanding of the benefits and risks of AI?

For example:

How can I extend a discussion for tenth-grade social studies learners with strong research skills to explore the benefits and risks of AI?

EXPERIMENT

Data Creation, Preparation, and Comparative Analysis

Data lies at the heart of meaningful analysis and decision making. In this experiment, learners will explore how generative AI tools can create synthetic datasets or upload existing datasets, clean and format the data, and analyze similarities and differences between data sources. *Cleaning* or *preparing data* refers to the process of identifying and correcting errors, inconsistencies, duplicates, and missing values to ensure that datasets are accurate, reliable, and ready for analysis. This hands-on activity empowers learners to critically examine information while leveraging AI for data-driven storytelling, decision making, and problem solving.

For educators, this experiment offers a dynamic approach to teaching data analysis and visualization in a way that resonates with learners. Teachers can demonstrate how AI tools simplify the process of generating or extracting insights from raw data, equipping learners with essential analytical and data management skills. Educators also gain valuable experience in integrating AI into classroom instruction, enhancing their capacity to model effective data practices and engage learners in technology-enhanced learning.

Learning Goals

This experiment aligns with the following learning objectives.

- Understand the role and capabilities of generative AI in creating, uploading, and comparing datasets.
- Develop skills in preparing, uploading, generating, cleaning, and formatting data for AI analysis.
- Learn to use the PROMPT Recipe for effective AI interaction in data creation and comparison.
- Apply the CHECK AI Framework to review and refine AI-generated and analyzed data.
- Identify and address biases in AI-generated content using the BIAS Identification Framework.
- Enhance analytical thinking, digital literacy, and data visualization skills through AI-assisted data preparation and comparison.

Focus Skills

Critical Thinking	Reflective Thinking	Data Management
Ethical Reasoning	Problem Solving	Digital Literacy
Analytical Thinking	Strategic Planning	Technical Proficiency

Experiment Protocol

Use the following steps to engage with this experiment.

1. If necessary, model how to use the generative AI tool as well as the PROMPT Recipe, CHECK AI, and BIAS Identification frameworks. Note that not all generative AI tools support both data generation and analysis functions. Learners may need to make adjustments, and results may vary depending on the capabilities of the AI tool the learner uses.
2. Discuss the importance of accurate, well-structured data for creation, comparison, and visualization. Highlight examples of effective datasets and common issues that may require cleaning, such as missing values or inconsistent formatting. Guide learners in identifying the specific type of data they need for their projects. Learners may either upload existing data files, such as CSV files—a comma-separated values file is a common format for structured data that can be easily imported into many tools for analysis—Word documents, or images, or generate synthetic practice datasets with the AI tool if real-world data is not available. Remind learners that AI-generated data is fictitious and intended for practice purposes.
3. Have learners work independently or in small groups (for example, two to four participants) based on their needs and the available resources, ensuring each participant or group has access to the generative AI tool of your choice.
4. Explain how you will evaluate learners. Share the evaluation criteria (for example, clarity, alignment with goals, creativity, and data accuracy) and clarify whether feedback will come from peers, the educator, or both.
5. Remind learners to apply the PROMPT Recipe to ensure their prompt inputs are comprehensive and clear. Direct them to use the generative AI tool to either upload existing datasets or generate synthetic datasets based on a specific project, scenario, or topic (for example, demographic information, scientific measurements, survey responses). Instruct learners to document the resulting outputs effectively. Remind them never to use confidential or identifying information when working with real data.
6. If needed, provide sample prompts to use with the AI tool to initiate the data preparation or cleaning process. For example, use the following for uploading and comparison.

    Please compare the variables [field 1] and [field 2]. Analyze the dataset, ensuring the data is accurate, relevant, labeled, and formatted correctly for analysis. Begin by uploading the dataset and displaying the first few rows for an initial review. Clean the data by identifying and correcting any errors, inconsistencies, duplicates, or missing

> values, and display summary statistics to identify potential outliers or anomalies. Visualize the data by creating a [chart type] to illustrate the relationship between [field 1] and [field 2], differentiating data points based on [field 33] (for example, gender) if applicable. Label the x-axis and y-axis appropriately and provide a clear title for the chart. Save the cleaned dataset in a CSV format and provide a download link. Finally, display both the cleaned dataset and the chart within the chat thread.

For data generation, use the following example.

> Create a synthetic dataset for [specific project or class] that includes [number] rows. The dataset should contain [specific type of data], with variables such as [list of variables]. Ensure the data is accurate, relevant, labeled, and formatted correctly for analysis. Once generated, clean the data by identifying and correcting any errors, inconsistencies, duplicates, or missing values. Show the cleaned dataset in the chat thread, save it as a CSV file, and provide a download link for the user.

The learner may also create their own prompt to increase the cognitive challenge.

7. Encourage learners to apply the CHECK AI and BIAS Identification frameworks as part of their iterative refinement process to ensure clarity, accuracy, and ethical considerations in their outputs.
8. Support learners through the process of cleaning and formatting their data based on AI feedback, making adjustments and improvements as needed. Learners should document their initial data (whether uploaded or AI-generated), AI-generated comparisons or outputs, visualizations, and all steps taken to clean and format their data.
9. Facilitate a discussion on the effectiveness of AI in creating, uploading, cleaning, and comparing datasets, addressing challenges, ethical considerations, and potential improvements.

Experiment Customization AI Prompt

Customize the following prompt to collaborate with AI.

> How can I customize an AI-driven data preparation and comparison learning experiment for my [grade] [subject] class focused on [specific topic]? The learning experiment involves learners working individually or in groups with access to a generative AI tool to create synthetic datasets or upload existing datasets. Learners will clean, format, analyze, and compare data, and evaluate the AI-generated content for accuracy and relevance. Adapt the learning objectives, activities, and assessments to

fit my classroom context. Consider intrapersonal and intrapersonal skill development along with cultural uniqueness.

Experiment Differentiation AI Prompt

Customize the following prompt to collaboratively differentiate with AI.

How can I adjust an AI-driven data preparation and comparison activity for my [grade] [content] learners who [specific needs] and need [specific support]? The current activity entails learners working individually or in groups with access to a generative AI tool to create synthetic datasets or upload existing datasets. Learners will clean, format, analyze, and compare data, and evaluate the AI-generated content for accuracy and relevance.

Integration Examples

Explore integration examples across various learning contexts.

- **Physics:** Learners compare experimental data from two motion experiments, such as free-falling objects under different conditions. AI tools assist in identifying trends and anomalies, creating visualizations, and refining their analysis, enhancing analytical thinking and technical proficiency.
- **World history:** Learners compare historical data, such as population growth and urbanization rates during the Industrial Revolution across countries. Before analysis, learners use AI to clean and format inconsistent or incomplete historical datasets. AI tools then help identify correlations, uncovering insights into how industrialization shaped societal changes, building critical thinking and research skills.
- **Economics:** Learners compare gross domestic product (GDP) data from different countries or regions, examining economic trends and factors affecting growth. AI tools assist in cleaning and visualizing data, enabling learners to identify disparities and propose solutions, enhancing problem-solving and analytical skills.
- **Music:** Learners generate synthetic datasets on streaming metrics or performance trends of hypothetical musical genres or artists. AI tools enable them to identify patterns, visualize popularity trends, and propose strategies for emerging artists, building creativity and data literacy.
- **Professional learning:** Educators collaborate on data-driven projects, such as comparing community needs or anonymous feedback from parents and learners. AI tools streamline the process, allowing for actionable insights that enhance engagement and school initiatives.

EXPERIMENT

Data Visualization and Forecasting

Data visualization plays a central role in analyzing patterns, identifying trends, and making informed predictions. In this experiment, learners will explore multiple methods for visualizing data relationships, including scatterplots, line graphs, and dual-axis line graphs. Learners will upload or generate datasets, clean and format data, and create visualizations that reveal correlations, trends, and forecasts. *Cleaning* or *preparing data* refers to the process of identifying and correcting errors, inconsistencies, duplicates, and missing values to ensure datasets are accurate, reliable, and ready for analysis. This hands-on activity empowers learners to interpret data, draw conclusions, and communicate findings through clear, meaningful visuals.

For educators, this experiment provides a comprehensive approach to teaching data visualization and forecasting skills. Teachers can model effective data practices by demonstrating how different visualization methods help analyze relationships, predict trends, and present insights. Instructors can also apply these techniques to classroom or institutional data to inform decision making, planning, and instructional design.

Learning Goals

This experiment aligns with the following learning objectives.

- Understand how to use data visualization techniques (scatterplots, line graphs, dual-axis line graphs) to analyze trends and relationships between variables.
- Develop skills in preparing, uploading, generating, cleaning, and formatting data for visualization and forecasting.
- Learn to use the PROMPT Recipe for effective interaction in data visualization and forecasting tasks.
- Apply the CHECK AI Framework to review and refine data visualizations and forecasts.
- Identify and address biases in AI-generated content using the BIAS Identification Framework.
- Enhance analytical thinking, digital literacy, and data storytelling skills through visualization and forecasting.

Focus Skills

Critical Thinking
Ethical Reasoning
Analytical Thinking
Creativity
Problem Solving
Data Storytelling
Data Management
Digital Literacy
Technical Proficiency

Experiment Protocol

Use the following steps to engage with this experiment.

1. If necessary, model how to use the generative AI tool as well as the PROMPT Recipe, CHECK AI, and BIAS Identification frameworks. Note that not all generative AI tools support data analysis, visualization, or forecasting. Learners may need to adjust and may receive varied results.
2. Discuss the importance of accurate and well-structured data for analysis, visualization, and forecasting. Highlight examples of effective data visualizations, such as scatterplots, line graphs, and dual-axis line graphs, along with forecasting models. Guide learners in identifying the specific data and variables to analyze, visualize, and forecast within datasets. The data created by the AI may be fictitious and is intended for practice purposes only when other data is not available.
3. Have learners work independently or in small groups (for example, two to four participants) based on their needs and the available resources, ensuring each participant or group has access to the generative AI tool of your choice.
4. Explain how you will evaluate learners. Share the evaluation criteria (for example, clarity, alignment with goals, creativity) and clarify whether feedback will come from peers, the educator, or both.
5. Remind learners to apply the PROMPT Recipe to ensure their prompt inputs are comprehensive and clear. Direct them to use the generative AI tool to upload an existing dataset or generate a synthetic dataset for analysis, visualization, and forecasting. Learners may select appropriate visualization types—such as scatterplots, line graphs, or dual-axis line graphs—based on their data and objectives. Instruct them to document the resulting outputs effectively. Remind them never to use confidential or identifying information.
6. If needed, provide sample prompts, such as the following, to use with the AI tool to simulate the data forecasting and visualization process.

    Please analyze the dataset to ensure it is accurate, relevant, labeled, and formatted correctly for analysis. Begin by uploading the dataset and displaying the first few rows for an initial look. Proceed to clean the data by identifying and correcting any errors or inconsistencies and display summary statistics to identify potential outliers or anomalies. Visualize trends by creating an appropriate chart based on the dataset, such as a scatterplot, line graph, or dual-axis line graph. Use the cleaned dataset to generate a forecast for [specific variable] over the next [time period]. Provide several talking points at a [grade or reading level] comprehension level to explain the visualization and forecast. Save the cleaned dataset and any forecasts in a CSV format

> and provide a download link for it. Finally, display both the cleaned dataset, the selected visualization(s), and any forecasts within the chat thread. Conclude the analysis with a reflection on the results. Compare the visualization and forecast to expectations by evaluating whether the trends align with typical patterns for each category. Identify anomalies by highlighting any unusual findings, such as unexpectedly high or low values for certain categories, and suggest potential reasons or the need for further review. Propose next steps by recommending actions for further investigation or data validation to ensure the dataset's accuracy and reliability.

The learner may also create their own prompt to increase the cognitive challenge.

7. Encourage learners to apply the CHECK AI and BIAS Identification frameworks as part of their iterative refinement process to ensure clarity, accuracy, and ethical considerations in their visualizations and forecasts.
8. Support learners through the process of cleaning and formatting their data based on AI feedback, making adjustments and improvements. Learners should document their initial data, AI-generated visualizations, forecasts, and the steps taken to clean and format their data.
9. Facilitate a discussion on the effectiveness of AI in data analysis, visualization, and forecasting, addressing challenges and potential improvements.

Experiment Customization AI Prompt

Customize the following prompt to collaborate with AI.

> How can I customize a generative AI-driven data visualization and forecasting learning experiment for my [grade] [subject] class focused on [specific topic]? The learning experiment involves learners working individually or in groups with access to a generative AI tool to analyze, visualize, and forecast data trends. They will upload an existing dataset or generate a synthetic dataset, interact with the AI tool, and evaluate the AI-generated content for accuracy and relevance. Adapt the learning objectives, activities, and assessments to fit my classroom context. Consider intrapersonal and intrapersonal skill development along with cultural uniqueness.

Experiment Differentiation AI Prompt

Customize the following prompt to collaboratively differentiate with AI.

> How can I adjust a generative AI-driven data visualization and forecasting activity for my [grade] [content] learners who [specific needs] and need [specific support]? The current activity entails learners working individually or in groups with access to a generative AI tool to analyze, visualize, and forecast data trends. They will upload an existing dataset or generate a synthetic dataset, interact with the AI tool, and evaluate the AI-generated content for accuracy and relevance.

Integration Examples

Explore integration examples across various learning contexts.

- **Economics:** Learners analyze historical data on GDP and inflation rates. AI tools assist in cleaning datasets, creating dual-axis line graphs to compare variables, and forecasting future trends, strengthening analytical thinking and data literacy.
- **Environmental science:** Learners upload or generate climate data to explore temperature and precipitation patterns. AI assists with cleaning, visualizing trends through line graphs, and forecasting climate shifts, building problem-solving and environmental reasoning.
- **Mathematics:** Learners generate or upload datasets to explore variable relationships using scatterplots, line graphs, and dual-axis line graphs. AI supports cleaning, visualization, and forecasting, reinforcing quantitative reasoning and technical proficiency.
- **Health science:** Learners examine public health datasets on vaccination rates and disease prevalence. AI helps clean the data, create scatterplots and dual-axis line graphs, and forecast healthcare needs, enhancing analytical and evidence-based reasoning.
- **Professional learning:** Educators analyze anonymous institutional data such as enrollment trends and staffing needs. AI supports cleaning data, generating visualizations, and forecasting future resource needs, supporting strategic planning and decision making.

EXPERIMENT

Developing Games

Coding and game development are valuable skills for today's digital world, offering learners a creative and interactive way to engage with technology. In this experiment, learners leverage generative AI tools to build their own Guess the Number game using HTML, CSS, and JavaScript. Through AI-guided step-by-step instructions, they will explore the basics of web development while cultivating an understanding of coding logic and functionality.

For educators, this experiment provides a framework to introduce coding concepts in a structured and accessible way. Teachers can use AI tools to support learners as they build coding confidence, debug errors, and test functionality. Additionally, educators can model creative problem solving by using AI tools to create their own coding projects, enhancing their technical proficiency and demonstrating real-world applications of coding in education.

Learning Goals

This experiment aligns with the following learning objectives.

- Understand the role of generative AI in supporting coding and game development.
- Develop skills in using HTML, CSS, and JavaScript to create a functional web-based game.
- Apply the PROMPT Recipe for effective AI interaction in coding.
- Identify and address biases in AI-generated data using the BIAS Identification Framework.
- Enhance problem solving, critical thinking, and digital literacy skills through AI-assisted coding.

Focus Skills

Critical Thinking	Coding Proficiency	Data Management
Ethical Reasoning	Problem Solving	Digital Literacy
Analytical Thinking	Strategic Planning	Technical Proficiency

Experiment Protocol

Use the following steps to engage with this experiment.

1. If necessary, model how to use the generative AI tool as well as the PROMPT Recipe, CHECK AI, and BIAS Identification frameworks. Note that not all generative AI tools support coding and data analysis. Learners may need to adjust, and results may vary.
2. Discuss the importance of coding and game development skills. Highlight examples of simple web-based games and their educational benefits. Guide learners in setting up their project folders and creating the necessary files for their coding project.
3. Have learners work independently or in small groups (for example, two to four participants) based on their needs and the available resources, ensuring each participant or group has access to the generative AI tool of your choice.
4. Explain how you will evaluate learners. Share the evaluation criteria (for example, clarity, alignment with goals, creativity) and clarify whether feedback will come from peers, the educator, or both.
5. Remind learners to apply the PROMPT Recipe to ensure their prompt inputs are comprehensive and clear. Direct them to interact with the generative AI tool to create coding instructions, build the necessary files, and write or run the code for their game. Instruct them to document the resulting outputs effectively.

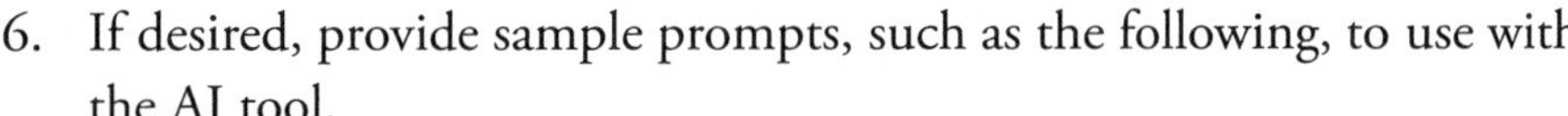

6. If desired, provide sample prompts, such as the following, to use with the AI tool.

   > Guide me through creating a Guess the Number game using HTML, CSS, and JavaScript. Provide step-by-step instructions for setting up the project folder and creating the necessary files (index.html, styles.css, and script.js). Include detailed code snippets and directions for running the game in a web browser.

   The learner may also create their own prompt to increase the cognitive challenge.
7. Encourage learners to apply the CHECK AI and BIAS Identification frameworks as part of their iterative refinement process to ensure clarity, accuracy, and ethical considerations in their outputs.
8. Support learners through the process of critically evaluating the AI-generated code and checking for functionality, relevance, and potential errors. Encourage testing and debugging as part of the learning process. Learners should document their AI-generated code, outcomes, and steps taken to clean and correct potential errors.
9. Facilitate a discussion on the effectiveness of AI in coding support, addressing challenges and potential improvements.

Experiment Customization AI Prompt

Customize the following prompt to collaborate with AI.

> How can I customize an AI-driven coding experiment for my [grade] [subject] class focused on creating a Guess the Number game? The learning experiment involves learners working individually or in groups with access to a generative AI tool to create a simple web-based game. They will set up their project folders, create the necessary files, and write the code for the game using HTML, CSS, and JavaScript. Adapt the learning objectives, activities, and assessments to fit my classroom context. Consider intrapersonal and intrapersonal skill development along with cultural uniqueness.

Experiment Differentiation AI Prompt

Customize the following prompt to collaboratively differentiate with AI.

> How can I adjust an AI-driven coding activity for [grade] [content] learners who [specific needs] and need [specific support]? The current activity entails learners working individually or in groups with access to a generative AI tool to create a simple web-based game. They will set up their project folders, create the necessary files, and write the code for the game using HTML, CSS, and JavaScript.

Integration Examples

Explore integration examples across various learning contexts.

- **Computer science:** Learners develop the Guess the Number game, learning foundational web-development concepts such as HTML structure, CSS styling, and JavaScript functionality. AI assists in debugging and optimizing code, enhancing problem-solving and technical skills.
- **Mathematics:** Learners incorporate probability and number theory into their game by customizing the range of numbers or the scoring system. AI supports coding adjustments, helping learners link mathematical principles to interactive applications.
- **English:** Learners design branding and marketing strategies for their game, including creating a logo, promotional text, and target audience analysis. AI aids in generating design ideas and refining marketing copy, integrating creativity with strategic thinking.
- **Social studies:** Learners modify the game to feature historical trivia or geographic challenges, combining coding with content knowledge. AI supports by generating questions, feedback, and layout adjustments, linking game design with interdisciplinary learning.
- **Professional learning:** Educators design cross-disciplinary projects that incorporate coding and game development, supported by AI-generated lesson plans. This fosters hands-on engagement and provides a replicable framework for integrating coding across the curriculum.

The following discussion, "Innovation and Regulation in AI," invites learners to examine how governments and organizations are approaching the complex challenge of regulating AI development and innovation.

Discussion: Innovation and Regulation in AI

Instructions: Use this protocol to plan and adapt a discussion that fits your audience, setting, and goals by reviewing the guidance and prompts prior to facilitating the discussion. This protocol serves as a flexible planning tool designed to help you frame the conversation, customize the experience, and support meaningful participation.

Big Question

What are the current policies and regulatory approaches to AI development at local, national, and international levels, and what are the implications for the future of AI technology?

Learning Goals

- Understand the various regulatory frameworks and policies governing AI development globally.
- Explore the ethical, social, and legal considerations involved in AI regulation.
- Analyze the differences and similarities in AI regulation across different regions.
- Evaluate the impact of these regulations on innovation, privacy, and security.
- Investigate current events illustrating the implementation and effects of AI regulations.
- Develop critical thinking about the balance between innovation and regulation in AI development.

Focus Skills

Critical Thinking	Ethical Reasoning	Policy Analysis
Technological Literacy	Information Literacy	Evaluation and Synthesis
Communication	Strategic Thinking	Decision Making

Discussion Customization AI Prompt

> How can I customize a discussion for my [grade] [subject] class focused on the regulation of AI development?

For example:

> How can I customize a discussion for seventh-grade social science learners using case studies to explore the ethical considerations of regulating AI?

Discussion Differentiation AI Prompt

> How can I adjust a discussion for [grade] [content] learners who [specific needs] and need [specific support] to understand the regulation of AI development?

For example:

> How can I adjust a discussion for ninth-grade civics learners with learning disabilities who need simplified summaries and visual supports to understand AI regulation?

Discussion Extension AI Prompt

> How can I extend a discussion to challenge advanced [grade] [content] learners and deepen their understanding of AI regulation?

For example:

> How can I extend a discussion for tenth-grade global studies learners with strong analysis skills to compare international AI regulations and suggest improvements?

Reflecting and Taking Action

At this stage, you have moved beyond experimentation: You are shaping AI's role in leadership, innovation, and strategic decision making. The experiments in this chapter challenged you to go beyond using AI as a tool and begin directing it as a collaborator, refining its potential in business planning, negotiation, coaching, and interactive learning.

You also engaged with AI's role in data analysis, forecasting, and coding, pushing the boundaries of what AI can achieve when guided with precision. These experiences reinforced a critical shift: AI is no longer just a tool to use—it is a force to cocreate with, refine, and direct strategically. The experiments in this chapter challenged you to think like a designer, innovator, and leader, ensuring AI enhances human expertise rather than replaces it.

Now, as you reflect on this journey, consider how to apply these insights moving forward, ensuring that your AI fluency continues to evolve with both purpose and responsibility.

1. Equip yourself with AI-driven leadership and innovation skills.
    a. Revisit the AI-supported business planning, negotiation, and coaching techniques explored in this chapter.
    b. Identify how to use AI in decision making and strategic forecasting, testing its ability to support long-term planning and professional leadership.
    c. Explore ways to customize AI tools to fit your unique needs, refining your advanced prompting, workflow automation, and data analysis techniques.
2. Engage in ethical and strategic AI integration.
    a. Facilitate discussions on how AI-driven automation and analytics impact industries, education, and leadership roles.
    b. Compare AI-generated predictions and insights with human intuition, evaluating where AI enhances accuracy and where critical human oversight remains essential.
    c. Reflect on the role of ethical decision making in AI integration. How can AI-driven data analysis and forecasting be used responsibly and equitably?
3. Experiment with purpose.
    a. Apply AI-assisted data visualization, trend forecasting, and predictive modeling to real-world problems, testing AI's potential in your professional or educational settings.
    b. Use AI to develop interactive content, such as custom simulations, coaching tools, or educational games, exploring how AI can shape adaptive learning and engagement.

   c. Experiment with AI-driven workflow automation, evaluating how it can improve efficiency, organization, and collaboration while maintaining ethical oversight.
4. Pursue continued learning and AI mastery.
   a. Stay informed on emerging AI applications in business, education, and data-driven decision making, ensuring that your AI strategies remain relevant and impactful.
   b. Explore how AI is evolving in high-level leadership roles, entrepreneurship, and policymaking, identifying new ways to adapt and integrate AI effectively.
   c. Encourage colleagues and learners to think beyond AI as a simple tool, fostering AI literacy that prioritizes critical engagement, ethical reflection, and long-term adaptability.
5. Reflect on your role as a leader and innovator.
   a. Consider how you can shape AI's role in your industry or educational space, moving from passive adoption to active leadership in AI integration.
   b. Reflect on how AI-driven tools can enhance innovation, strategy, and complex reasoning rather than simply improving efficiency.
   c. Commit to leading with strategic foresight and ethical responsibility, ensuring that AI is developed and used with intentionality, adaptability, and human-centered purpose.

Consider the following questions to guide your thinking.

- How can AI be used strategically and ethically in leadership, planning, and problem solving?
- In what ways can AI enhance innovation and design, and where does human oversight remain critical?
- How can you move from AI adoption to AI mastery, ensuring that you are shaping its future use in meaningful ways?

As AI continues to evolve, the way we engage with it will define not just our professional roles but the trajectory of society itself. The final discussions will challenge you to consider your place in this transformation, ensuring that as AI grows in capability, we grow in wisdom, adaptability, and ethical responsibility alongside it.

Let's take this final step together, toward a future where AI is not just used, but understood, guided, and integrated with purpose.

EPILOGUE

The journey through AI experimentation has been one of discovery, challenge, and growth. When you first began this book, AI may have seemed like an emerging tool on the periphery of education and professional practice. Now, after engaging with hands-on experiments, critical discussions, and ethical considerations, you have explored AI's capabilities and learned how to direct and refine them with purpose.

Like any transformative learning experience, mastering AI is not a destination but an ongoing process. The skills and insights gained here are not just about using AI tools but about developing a mindset that embraces curiosity, adaptability, and ethical reflection. Whether you have used AI to enhance creativity, streamline workflows, or support critical decision making, your engagement with these technologies has positioned you as an active participant in shaping AI's role in education, work, and society.

Yet, with every step forward, new questions arise. What does responsible AI integration look like in the years ahead? How will AI continue to evolve, and what role should humans play in guiding its development? These questions are at the heart of the next phase of this journey.

The Evolving Relationship Between Humans and AI

Throughout history, technological advancements have transformed industries, reshaped education, and redefined how we interact with the world. AI is no different—it is an accelerant, amplifying human potential in ways that were once unimaginable. But as we integrate AI into daily life, we must shift our focus from what AI *can* do to what AI *should* do. This shift requires critical reflection on how we harness AI's strengths while preserving the uniquely human qualities that define innovation, creativity, and ethical decision making.

AI is not just about automation; it is about augmentation—enhancing human capabilities rather than replacing them. The experiments in this book demonstrate that AI can assist in research, writing, problem solving, and strategic planning, but they also highlight the necessity of human oversight, adaptability, and ethical reasoning. As AI becomes more advanced, the responsibility to use it intentionally and critically falls on those who engage with it. The question is no longer *whether* AI will be a part of our professional and educational landscapes but rather *how* we will shape its integration to ensure it strengthens, rather than diminishes, human intelligence.

This leads us to a critical reflection: What kind of relationship do we want with AI? Should AI remain a tool that supports human thinking, or should it become a deeply integrated collaborator? What are the risks and benefits of deeper human-AI interaction?

As AI becomes an integral part of education, work, and creative processes, we must consider not just whether we use AI but *how* we use it. Some approach AI cautiously, treating it as an occasional tool for efficiency, while others embrace deeper collaboration, integrating AI into their thinking and workflow. These different approaches shape how we learn, create, and solve problems. Are we using AI as a powerful assistant, or are we evolving into cocreators alongside it?

As I alluded to in the introduction (page 7), researchers identify two primary models of human-AI interaction: (1) centaur behavior and (2) cyborg behavior (Dell'Acqua et al., 2023). The centaur model, named after the half-human, half-horse creature from mythology, represents a partnership where humans and AI divide tasks based on their respective strengths. In this approach, individuals consciously decide when to rely on AI and when to take direct control of a task, using AI as an assistant rather than a cocreator. For example, an educator might use AI to generate lesson plans or summarize research articles but will take full responsibility for adapting the content to their learners' needs. This task-based division of labor allows for greater control over AI outputs while still benefiting from AI's efficiency.

In contrast, cyborg behavior describes a much deeper integration between human and AI capabilities, where the two work interchangeably at a sub-task level. Rather than simply delegating work, cyborg users continuously interact with AI throughout a process, such as refining AI-generated writing in real time, codeveloping code, or using AI-driven simulations to explore complex problems. This approach mirrors cocreation, where AI is not just an assistant but an active, iterative collaborator. In education, a cyborg approach might involve learners working alongside AI to draft essays, analyze historical events, or generate creative projects, constantly refining and questioning AI-generated content rather than simply using it as a tool for efficiency.

Both models offer valuable perspectives on AI integration. Centaur behavior provides structured control, ensuring human oversight at key decision points, while cyborg behavior embraces fluid collaboration, allowing for deeper experimentation and innovation. Neither model is inherently superior, but each requires intentionality. Educators and learners must consider how they engage with AI to maximize benefits while maintaining ethical and intellectual rigor.

Now that we have explored these two models of AI collaboration, it is important to reflect on how they apply to education, professional development, and the evolving role of AI in society. Do educators and learners function more like centaurs, strategically assigning tasks to AI while maintaining clear human oversight? Or do they operate as cyborgs, fully integrating AI into their creative and analytical processes?

The following discussion, "AI Cyborgs and Centaurs—Which Are You?" (page 244) invites you to consider these questions through the lens of productivity, knowledge work, and ethical decision making. By analyzing the implications of each approach, you will have the opportunity to reflect on your own AI use style and how it influences learning, teaching, and professional growth.

Discussion: AI Cyborgs and Centaurs—Which Are You?

Instructions: Use this protocol to plan and adapt a discussion that fits your audience, setting, and goals by reviewing the guidance and prompts prior to facilitating the discussion. This protocol serves as a flexible planning tool designed to help you frame the conversation, customize the experience, and support meaningful participation.

Big Question

How do the concepts of AI cyborgs and centaurs reflect different styles of interacting with generative AI, and what are the implications for productivity and quality in knowledge work?

Introduction

The terms *cyborg* and *centaur* have roots in culture and mythology, offering powerful analogies for understanding how humans interact with generative AI. A *cyborg*, blending human and machine, represents complete integration where human and AI work seamlessly together. Meanwhile, a *centaur*, half human and half horse, signifies a partnership where tasks are divided between human and AI based on their strengths. In their study, researcher Fabrizio Dell'Acqua and colleagues (2023) use these metaphors to describe two distinct approaches to using generative AI in knowledge work:

> One set of consultants acted as "Centaurs," like the mythical half-horse/half-human creature, dividing and delegating their solution-creation activities to the AI or to themselves. Another set of consultants acted more like "Cyborgs," completely integrating their task flow with the AI and continually interacting with the technology. (Dell'Acqua et al., 2023)

These metaphors illustrate different styles of interacting with AI, each with unique implications for productivity and quality.

Learning Goals

- Understand the concepts of AI cyborgs and centaurs.
- Explore how these metaphors relate to different styles of interacting with generative AI.
- Analyze the productivity and quality implications of each approach.
- Evaluate the ethical and practical considerations of integrating AI into workflows.
- Investigate the role of policy and regulation in governing AI surveillance.
- Develop strategies for effectively leveraging AI in various professional contexts.

Focus Skills

Critical Thinking	Information Literacy	Evaluation and Synthesis
Technological Literacy	Decision Making	Ethical Reasoning
Communication	Strategic Thinking	Problem Solving

Discussion Customization AI Prompt

> How can I customize a discussion for my [grade] [subject] class focused on understanding the concepts of AI cyborgs and centaurs regarding AI use styles and their implications for productivity and quality?

For example:

> How can I customize a discussion for middle school career exploration learners using the cyborg and centaur analogy to reflect on AI use styles and productivity?

Discussion Differentiation AI Prompt

How can I adjust a discussion for [grade] [content] learners who [specific needs] and need [specific support] to understand the concepts of AI cyborgs and centaurs regarding AI use styles and their implications for productivity and quality?

For example:

How can I adjust a discussion for tenth-grade study skills learners with diverse processing needs using cyborgs and centaurs to reflect on personal tech use habits?

Discussion Extension AI Prompt

How can I extend a discussion to challenge advanced [grade] [content] learners and deepen their understanding of AI cyborgs and centaurs regarding AI use styles and their implications for productivity and quality?

For example:

How can I extend a discussion for eleventh-grade business learners who enjoy problem solving and need a challenge to evaluate how AI cyborgs and centaurs influence productivity in the workplace?

Reference

Dell'Acqua, F., McFowland, E., III, Mollick, E., Lifshitz-Assaf, H., Kellogg, K. C., Rajendran, S., et al. (2023). *Navigating the jagged technological frontier: Field experimental evidence of the effects of AI on knowledge worker productivity and quality* (Working paper no. 24-013). Harvard Business School. Accessed at www.hbs.edu/ris/Publication%20Files/24-013_d9b45b68-9e74-42d6-a1c6-c72fb70c7282.pdf on April 20, 2024.

Watching the Watchers: AI, Surveillance, and Ethics

As we continue integrating AI into education, professional settings, and daily life, the question is no longer just how we use AI but how AI is shaping us in return. The cyborg and centaur models offer two perspectives on collaboration with AI, yet neither addresses one of the most complex and controversial aspects of AI's role in society: surveillance.

I was speaking at an education conference in California, held at a casino, when I encountered a striking example of AI in action. As I walked through the lobby, I noticed an R2-D2-like robot surveying the space, its cameras scanning, sensors processing, and algorithms analyzing its surroundings in real time. Was it ensuring security, monitoring for suspicious activity, or simply gathering data? At that moment, I couldn't help but wonder: How much did it already know about me?

This experience was a stark reminder of the growing presence of AI-driven surveillance in both public and private spaces. In education, AI-powered monitoring tools are being implemented to enhance security, proctor exams, and track learner engagement. But with these advancements come critical ethical questions: Where is the line between safety and intrusion? Who decides how AI surveillance is used, and how do we prevent bias from influencing its decisions?

Research shows that AI-powered recognition systems struggle with accuracy, particularly for individuals with darker skin tones and women (Buolamwini & Gebru, 2018). When AI misidentifies a learner in a school hallway or flags an innocent individual as a security threat, what are the consequences? How do we ensure AI surveillance serves communities equitably rather than reinforcing systemic biases?

As we close this chapter of AI experimentation, we turn to one of the most urgent discussions in AI ethics: surveillance. The following discussion, "AI Surveillance—What Is Too Far?" invites you to critically examine AI's role in monitoring, security, and data collection. What is too far when it comes to AI-driven surveillance, and what policies should be in place to ensure that its use remains fair, transparent, and accountable?

Discussion: AI Surveillance—What Is Too Far?

Instructions: Use this protocol to plan and adapt a discussion that fits your audience, setting, and goals by reviewing the guidance and prompts prior to facilitating the discussion. This protocol serves as a flexible planning tool designed to help you frame the conversation, customize the experience, and support meaningful participation.

Big Question

What are the ethical, social, and legal implications of AI surveillance, and how far is too far in its use?

Learning Goals

- Understand the capabilities and applications of AI surveillance technologies.
- Explore the ethical concerns related to privacy, consent, and autonomy in AI surveillance.
- Analyze the impact of AI surveillance on different communities and public spaces.
- Evaluate the balance between security benefits and privacy rights.
- Investigate the role of policy and regulation in governing AI surveillance.
- Discuss strategies for responsible and ethical deployment of AI surveillance.
- Examine the impact of algorithmic bias and the lack of diverse training data on AI surveillance outcomes.
- Develop critical thinking about the long-term societal implications of widespread AI surveillance.
- Promote awareness of the importance of ethical AI development and inclusive practices.

Focus Skills

Critical Thinking	Information Literacy	Evaluation and Synthesis
Technological Literacy	Decision Making	Ethical Reasoning
Communication	Strategic Thinking	Problem Solving

Discussion Customization AI Prompt

> How can I customize a discussion for my [grade] [subject] class focused on AI surveillance, its ethical limits, and the impact of algorithmic bias?

For example:

> How can I customize a discussion for eleventh-grade Latinx studies learners using case studies to explore ethical questions around AI surveillance and algorithmic bias?

Discussion Differentiation AI Prompt

> How can I adjust a discussion for [grade] [content] learners who [specific needs] and need [specific support] to understand AI surveillance, its ethical limits, and the impact of algorithmic bias?

For example:

> How can I adjust a discussion for fifth-grade social studies learners with dyslexia by using audio texts and visual supports to understand AI surveillance and algorithmic bias?

Discussion Extension AI Prompt

> How can I extend a discussion to challenge advanced [grade] [content] learners and deepen their understanding of AI surveillance, its ethical limits, and the impact of algorithmic bias?

For example:

> How can I extend a discussion for twelfth-grade civics learners who enjoy policy analysis to design a mock framework addressing AI surveillance and bias?

Moving Beyond the Experiment: Shaping the Future With AI

As we conclude this book, it is clear that AI is not just a tool: It is a force actively shaping the way we learn, create, and interact with the world. The discussions in this book have highlighted AI's potential to enhance education, streamline workflows, and expand creative possibilities. At the same time, we have explored the risks of bias, ethical concerns, and the need for responsible oversight. AI is neither inherently good nor bad—it is what we make of it. The responsibility lies with us, as educators and leaders, to ensure that AI is used with purpose, integrity, and intentionality.

The discussion on AI surveillance underscores a critical truth: AI will reflect the priorities of those who design and implement it. If we allow AI to be used primarily for control and monitoring, it will reinforce systems of surveillance. If we harness AI as a tool for exploration, equity, and empowerment, it can become a force for good. This is the choice before us—not just as users of AI but as shapers of its future.

But this is not the end of the journey; it is only the beginning. Every time you refine a prompt, evaluate an AI-generated response, or introduce an AI-driven lesson, you are shaping the evolving relationship between humans and AI. You are conducting a living experiment that demands ongoing curiosity, adaptability, and ethical reflection.

Like any hero's journey, this transformation has been about more than just acquiring new tools—it has been about learning how to use them with purpose, wisdom, and integrity. The world of AI will continue to expand, and the real challenge is leading AI's evolution with intentionality.

Every experiment begins with a question. The real power of AI lies not just in the answers it generates but in the curiosity it sparks and the ideas it helps bring to life. As you continue experimenting, refining, and leading, you are pioneering the future of human-AI collaboration.

So, what will you create next?

REFERENCES AND RESOURCES

AASA, ASCD, ISTE, NAESP, & NASSP. (2023). *Bringing AI to school: Tips for school leaders*. Authors. Accessed at https://cdn.iste.org/www-root/2023-07/Bringing_AI_to_School-2023_07.pdf on February 27, 2025.

AI4K12. (n.d.). *5 big ideas in AI*. Accessed at https://ai4k12.org on July 8, 2025.

Anyoha, R. (2017, August 28). *The history of artificial intelligence*. Accessed at https://sites.harvard.edu/sitn/2017/08/28/history-artificial-intelligence on February 26, 2025.

Arizona Institute for Education and the Economy. (2024). *Generative artificial intelligence in K–12 education: Guidance for Arizona schools and school systems—A balanced perspective*. Northern Arizona University. Accessed at https://nau.edu/wp-content/uploads/sites/222/2024/05/NAU.GAIGuide.pdf on February 27, 2025.

Asimov, I. (1950). Runaround. In *I, robot*. Doubleday.

Auburn University. (n.d.). Isaac Asimov's "Three laws of robotics." Accessed at https://webhome.auburn.edu/~vestmon/robotics.html on August 1, 2025.

Baidoo-Anu, D., & Ansah, L. O. (2023). Education in the era of generative artificial intelligence (AI): Understanding the potential benefits of ChatGPT in promoting teaching and learning. *Journal of AI*, *7*(1), 52–62. http://dx.doi.org/10.2139/ssrn.4337484

Bajwa, J., Munir, U., Nori, A., & Williams, B. (2021). Artificial intelligence in healthcare: Transforming the practice of medicine. *Future Healthcare Journal*, *8*(2), e188–e194. https://doi.org/10.7861/fhj.2021-0095

Brown, S. (2021, April 21). *Machine learning, explained*. MIT Sloan School of Management. Accessed at https://mitsloan.mit.edu/ideas-made-to-matter/machine-learning-explained on February 26, 2025.

Buolamwini, J., & Gebru, T. (2018). Gender shades: Intersectional accuracy disparities in commercial gender classification. In S. A. Friedler & C. Wilson (Eds.), *Proceedings of the 2018 Conference on Fairness, Accountability, and Transparency (FAT), Proceedings of Machine Learning Research* (Vol. 81, pp. 1–15). PMLR. http://proceedings.mlr.press/v81/buolamwini18a/buolamwini18a.pdf

California Department of Education. (2024). *Artificial intelligence: Learning with AI, learning about AI—Resource kit*. Author. Accessed at www.cde.ca.gov/ci/pl/documents/cdeairesourcekit.pdf on February 27, 2025.

California Department of Education. (2025, February 11). *Learning with AI, learning about AI*. Author. Accessed at www.cde.ca.gov/ci/pl/aiincalifornia.asp on February 27, 2025.

Campbell, J. (2004). *The hero with a thousand faces*. Princeton University Press. Accessed at www.eriesd.org/site/handlers/filedownload.ashx?moduleinstanceid=35845&dataid=53662&FileName=The%20Hero%20with%20a%20Thousand%20Faces.pdf on August 1, 2025.

Canadian Centre for Cyber Security. (2023, July 14). *Generative artificial intelligence (AI)—ITSAP.00.041*. Accessed at www.cyber.gc.ca/en/guidance/generative-artificial-intelligence-ai-itsap00041 on February 27, 2025.

Carson, R. (1962). *Silent spring*. Houghton Mifflin.

Darwin, C. (1859). *On the origin of species by means of natural selection*, or, *The preservation of favoured races in the struggle for life*. John Murray.

Dell'Acqua, F., McFowland, E., III, Mollick, E., Lifshitz-Assaf, H., Kellogg, K. C., Rajendran, S., et al. (2023). *Navigating the jagged technological frontier: Field experimental evidence of the effects of AI on knowledge worker productivity and quality* (Working paper no. 24-013). Harvard Business School. Accessed at https://www.hbs.edu/ris/Publication%20Files/24-013_d9b45b68-9e74-42d6-a1c6-c72fb70c7282.pdf on July 18, 2025.

Development Dimensions International. (n.d.). *STAR method: Behavioral interviewing*. Accessed at www.ddiworld.com/solutions/behavioral-interviewing/star-method on June 13, 2025.

Dickerson, A., Rossi, G., Bocock, L., Hillary, J., & Simcock, D. (2023, May 25). *The Skills Imperative 2035: An analysis of the demand for skills in the labour market in 2035*. Accessed at www.nfer.ac.uk/publications/the-skills-imperative-2035-an-analysis-of-the-demand-for-skills-in-the-labour-market-in-2035/ on February 27, 2025.

Digital Economy and Remote Work Applications Office. (2023). *100 practical applications and use cases of generative AI*. Accessed at https://ai.gov.ae/wp-content/uploads/2023/04/406.-Generative-AI-Guide_ver1-EN.pdf on February 26, 2025.

Dweck, C. S. (2016). *Mindset: The new psychology of success* (Updated ed.). Ballantine.

EDSAFE AI Alliance. (2023). *S.A.F.E. benchmarks*. Accessed at www.edsafeai.org/safe on February 27, 2025.

Exec. Order No. 14110, 88 F. R. 75191 (2023, October 30). Accessed at www.govinfo.gov/app/details/FR-2023-11-01/2023-24283 on February 27, 2025.

Family Educational Rights and Privacy Act, 34 C. F. R. § Part 99 (2023). Accessed at https://studentprivacy.ed.gov/ferpa on February 27, 2025.

Federal Communications Commission. (2019). *Children's Internet Protection Act (CIPA)*. Accessed at www.fcc.gov/consumers/guides/childrens-internet-protection-act on February 27, 2025.

Federal Trade Commission. (n.d.). §6501. Definitions. Accessed at https://uscode.house.gov/view.xhtml;jsessionid=73AE96CA0AB6CAD6BE49A2B8EE082DA9?path=&req=%28title%3A15+section%3A6501+edition%3Aprelim%29+OR+%28granuleid%3AUSC-prelim-title15-section6501%29&f=treesort&fq=&num=0&hl=false&edition=prelim#sourcecredit on July 8, 2025.

Federal Trade Commission. (2025). *Children's Online Privacy Protection Rule*, 16 C. F. R. § 312. Accessed at https://www.ftc.gov/system/files/ftc_gov/pdf/coppa_sbp_1.16_0.pdf on June 13, 2025.

Fry, R., Kennedy, B., & Funk, C. (2021, April 1). *STEM jobs see uneven progress in increasing gender, racial and ethnic diversity: Higher education pipeline suggests long path ahead for increasing diversity, especially in fields like computing and engineering*. Pew Research Center. Accessed at https://www.pewresearch.org/science/2021/04/01/stem-jobs-see-uneven-progress-in-increasing-gender-racial-and-ethnic-diversity/ on July 8, 2025.

Google. (n.d.). *Our AI journey*. Accessed at https://ai.google/our-ai-journey/?section=intro on July 3, 2025.

Groh, M. (n.d.). *Detect deepfakes: How to counteract misinformation created by AI*. MIT Media Lab. Accessed at www.media.mit.edu/projects/detect-fakes/overview/ on February 27, 2025.

Groh, M., Sankaranarayanan, A., Singh, N., Kim, D. Y., Lippman, A., & Picard, R. (2024). Human detection of political speech deepfakes across transcripts, audio, and video. *Nature Communications*, *15*, Article 7629. https://doi.org/10.1038/s41467-024-51998-z

Hugo, V. (1862). *Les misérables*. Pagnerre.

IBM. (2023, November 2). *What are large language models (LLMs)?* Accessed at www.ibm.com/topics/large-language-models on February 27, 2025.

IESE Business School, University of Navarra. (2020, March 12). *Keys to beat volatility, uncertainty, complexity and ambiguity*. Accessed at www.iese.edu/insight/articles/volatility-uncertainty-complexity-ambiguity/ on May 10, 2023.

Individuals With Disabilities Education Act, 20 U. S. C. § 1400 *et seq.* (2004). Accessed at https://sites.ed.gov/idea/statute-chapter-33/subchapter-i/1400 on July 3, 2025.

Kaggle. (n.d.). *Datasets.* Accessed at www.kaggle.com/datasets on February 27, 2025.

Kohnová, L., & Salajová, N. (2019). Industrial revolutions and their impact on managerial practice: Learning from the past. *Problems and Perspectives in Management, 17*(2), 462–478. https://doi.org/10.21511/ppm.17(2).2019.36

Lange, O., & Perez, L. (2020, September 3). *Traffic prediction with advanced Graph Neural Networks.* Accessed at https://deepmind.google/discover/blog/traffic-prediction-with-advanced-graph-neural-networks/ on February 27, 2025.

Lansing-Stoeffler, K., & Daley, N. (2022). *Cross-cutting capabilities: Transferable skills for the 21st century.* ACT. Accessed at www.act.org/content/dam/act/unsecured/documents/2022/Cross-Cutting-Capabilities-21st-Century-07-2022.pdf on February 27, 2025.

Lee, H. (1960). *To kill a mockingbird.* J. B. Lippincott & Co.

Liang, W., Yuksekgonul, M., Mao, Y., Wu, E., & Zou, J. (2023). GPT detectors are biased against non-native English writers. *Patterns, 4*(7), Article 100779. Accessed at https://arxiv.org/pdf/2304.02819 on July 18, 2022.

Licklider, J. C. R. (1960). Man-computer symbiosis. *IRE Transactions on Human Factors in Electronics, 1*(1), 4–11.

Lin, C. Y., & Lobo Marques, J. A. (2024). Stock market prediction using artificial intelligence: A systematic review of systematic reviews. *Social Sciences & Humanities Open, 9*, Article 100864. Accessed at www.sciencedirect.com/science/article/pii/S2590291124000615 on February 27, 2025.

Los Angeles County Office of Education. (2024). *Generative artificial intelligence in TK–12 education guidelines.* Author. Accessed at https://lacoe.edu/content/dam/lacoeedu/documents/technologyservices/tlss/LACOEGenAIGuidelines.pdf on February 27, 2025.

Machajewski, S. (2024, November 15). The AI revolution in chess and its impact on education. *EdTech Digest.* Accessed at www.edtechdigest.com/2024/11/15/the-ai-revolution-in-chess-and-its-impact-on-education on June 16, 2025.

Maslej, N., Fattorini, L., Brynjolfsson, E., Etchemendy, J., Ligett, K., Lyons, T., et al. (2023). *The AI Index 2023 annual report.* Stanford University, Institute for Human-Centered AI. Accessed at https://aiindex.stanford.edu/wp-content/uploads/2023/04/HAI_AI-Index-Report_2023.pdf on February 27, 2025.

McKinsey & Company. (2024, April 2). *What is generative AI?* Accessed at www.mckinsey.com/featured-insights/mckinsey-explainers/what-is-generative-ai on February 27, 2025.

Mednick, S. A. (1968). The remote associates test. *Journal of Creative Behavior, 2*(3), 213–214. https://doi.org/10.1002/j.2162-6057.1968.tb00104.x

Mollick, E. (2024). *Co-intelligence: Living and working with AI.* Portfolio.

Moor, J. (2006). The Dartmouth College Artificial Intelligence Conference: The next fifty years. *AI Magazine, 27*(4), 87–89.

National Center for Science and Engineering Statistics. (2023). *Diversity and STEM: Women, minorities, and persons with disabilities 2023* (Report No. NSF 23-315). U. S. National Science Foundation. Accessed at www.nsf.gov/reports/statistics/diversity-stem-women-minorities-persons-disabilities-2023 on February 27, 2025.

Neethirajan, S. (2023). Artificial intelligence and sensor technologies in dairy livestock export: Charting a digital transformation. *Sensors, 23*(16), Article 7045.

Nguyen, A., Hong, Y., Dang, B., & Huang, X. (2024). Human-AI collaboration patterns in AI-assisted academic writing. *Studies in Higher Education, 49*(5), 847–864. https://doi.org/10.1080/03075079.2024.2323593

North Carolina Department of Public Instruction. (2024). *North Carolina generative AI implementation recommendations and considerations for PK–13 public schools.* Accessed at https://go.ncdpi.gov/AI_Guidelines on February 27, 2025.

Office of Educational Technology. (2023). *Artificial intelligence and the future of teaching and learning: Insights and recommendations.* U. S. Department of Education. Accessed at https://www.ed.gov/sites/ed/files/documents/ai-report/ai-report.pdf on February 27, 2025.

Office of Educational Technology. (2024). *National education technology plan.* U. S. Department of Education. Accessed at https://drive.google.com/file/d/1hiz0ZYZRi2hxncbvf6ksk4E11rEwFH3r/view on February 27, 2025.

Office of Science and Technology Policy. (2022, October). *Blueprint for an AI Bill of Rights: Making automated systems work for the American people.* The White House. Accessed at https://bidenwhitehouse.archives.gov/ostp/ai-bill-of-rights on February 27, 2025.

Oregon Department of Education. (2023). *Developing policy and protocols for the use of generative AI in K–12 classrooms.* Author. Accessed at www.oregon.gov/ode/educator-resources/teachingcontent/Documents/ODE_Developing_Policy_and_Protocols_for_the_use_of_Generative_AI_in_K-12_Classrooms_2023.pdf on February 27, 2025.

Orwell, G. (1949). *1984.* Secker & Warburg.

Piaget, J. (1954). *The construction of reality in the child* (M. Cook, Trans.). Basic Books.

Plato. (2013). *Phaedrus* (B. Jowett, Trans.). Accessed at www.gutenberg.org/files/1636/1636-h/1636-h.htm on July 21, 2025. (original work 370 BC)

Power, R. (2024, May 12). Next-level ecommerce: AI's secret weapon for personalized experiences. *Forbes.* Accessed at www.forbes.com/sites/rhettpower/2024/05/12/next-level-ecommerce-ais-secret-weapon-for-personalized-experiences on February 27, 2025.

Sahota, N. (2024, March 18). Streaming into the future: How AI is reshaping entertainment. *Forbes.* Accessed at www.forbes.com/sites/neilsahota/2024/03/18/streaming-into-the-future-how-ai-is-reshaping-entertainment on February 27, 2025.

Sarker, I. H. (2021). Machine learning: Algorithms, real-world applications and research directions. *SN Computer Science, 2,* Article 160.

Shashkevich, A. (2019, February 28). Stanford researcher examines earliest concepts of artificial intelligence, robots in ancient myths. *Stanford Report.* Accessed at https://news.stanford.edu/stories/2019/02/ancient-myths-reveal-early-fantasies-artificial-life on February 27, 2025.

Taylor, A., Nelson, J., O'Donnell, S., Davies, E., & Hillary, J. (2022, March 3). *The Skills Imperative 2035: What does the literature tell us about essential skills most needed for work?* Accessed at www.nfer.ac.uk/publications/the-skills-imperative-2035-what-does-the-literature-tell-us-about-essential-skills-most-needed-for-work/ on February 27, 2025.

University of Illinois Chicago. (2024, May 7). *What is (AI) artificial intelligence?* Accessed at https://meng.uic.edu/news-stories/ai-artificial-intelligence-what-is-the-definition-of-ai-and-how-does-ai-work/ on February 27, 2025.

U. S. Equal Employment Opportunity Commission. (2019). *Special topics annual report: Women in STEM.* Accessed at www.eeoc.gov/special-topics-annual-report-women-stem on February 27, 2025.

Vanderbilt University Center for Teaching. (n.d.). *Bloom's taxonomy.* Accessed at https://cft.vanderbilt.edu/wp-content/uploads/sites/59/Blooms-Taxonomy.pdf on February 27, 2025.

Virginia Department of Education. (2024). *Guidelines for AI integration throughout education in the Commonwealth of Virginia.* Author. Accessed at www.education.virginia.gov/media/governorvirginiagov/secretary-of-education/pdf/AI-Education-Guidelines.pdf on February 27, 2025.

Vygotsky, L. S. (1978). *Mind in society: The development of higher psychological processes* (M. Cole, V. John-Steiner, S. Scribner, & E. Souberman, Eds.). Harvard University Press.

Washington Office of Superintendent of Public Instruction. (2024). *Human-centered AI: Guidance for K–12 public schools*. Author. Accessed at https://ospi.k12.wa.us/sites/default/files/2024-01/human-centered-ai-guidance-k-12-public-schools.pdf on February 27, 2025.

World Economic Forum. (2024). *Global risks report 2024*. Accessed at www.weforum.org/publications/global-risks-report-2024 on February 27, 2025.

Xie, B., Sarin, P., Wolf, J., Garcia, R. C. C., Delaney, V., Sieh, I., et al. (2024). Co-designing AI education curriculum with cross-disciplinary high school teachers. *Proceedings of the AAAI Conference on Artificial Intelligence, 38*(21), 23146–23154. https://doi.org/10.1609/aaai.v38i21.30360

Xu, Y., Liu, X., Cao, X., Huang, C., Liu, E., Qian, S., et al. (2021). Artificial intelligence: A powerful paradigm for scientific research. *The Innovation, 2*(4), 100179. Accessed at https://www.researchgate.net/publication/355738811_Artificial_Intelligence_A_Powerful_Paradigm_for_Scientific_Research on July 21, 2025.

Yu, P., Xu, H., Hu, X., & Deng, C. (2023). Leveraging generative AI and large language models: A comprehensive roadmap for healthcare integration. *Healthcare, 11*(20), Article 2776. https://doi.org/10.3390/healthcare11202776

Zhu, R. (2024, March 4). *A sky full of data: Weather forecasting in the age of AI*. Accessed at https://sites.harvard.edu/sitn/2024/03/04/ai_weather_forecasting on February 27, 2025.

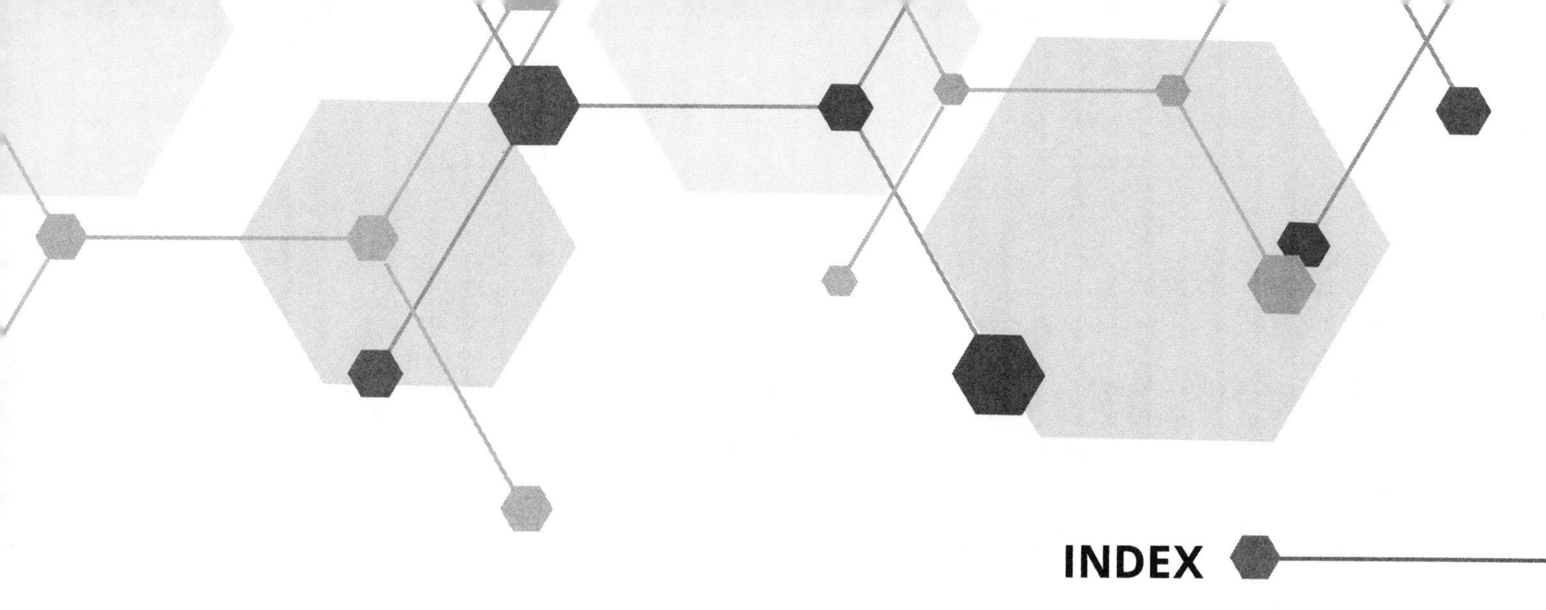

INDEX

50 AI Prompts for Teachers
Paul J. Cancellieri
Through this book's ideas and guided prompts for generating lessons using AI chatbots, teachers will increase their opportunities to do what they do best: connect with their students on an individual and personal level to help them reach their greatest potential.
BKG217

Teaching Writing in the Age of AI
Troy Hicks and Kristen Hawley Turner
AI quite literally changes how students write. Authors Troy Hicks and Kristen Hawley Turner explore how to use AI ethically to enhance creativity, nurture student thinking, support academic honesty, and encourage student writers in an AI-driven world.
BKG203

The Digital Projects Playbook
John Arthur
Students in today's classrooms live in a digital world. Tap into the unique opportunities this offers with author John Arthur's collection of resource-packed projects designed to leverage students' digital skills and support their academic, cognitive, and creative development.
BKG171

Making the Move With Ed Tech
Troy Hicks, Jennifer Parker, and Kate Grunow
In this book, the authors help educators wade through ed-tech jargon and frameworks to learn how to employ technology tools strategically. Explore moves, or instructional strategies, both familiar and new, that facilitate student inquiry, dialogue, critical thinking, and creativity.
BKG101

Co-Teaching Evolved
Matthew Rhoads and Belinda Dunnick Karge
The authors offer a revived approach to co-teaching that accounts for pressing topics in today's classroom. PreK–12 teachers will learn to create collaborative co-teaching partnerships and navigate key co-teaching components—such as lesson design, conflict resolution, and communication with stakeholders—with research-backed tools and strategies.
BKG202

Solution Tree | Press 

Visit SolutionTree.com or call 800.733.6786 to order.